Vote 4 Loyalty

Vote 4 Loyalty

Kandice Green

© 2017 Kandice Green
All rights reserved.

ISBN-13: 9780692889343
ISBN-10: 0692889345

Table of Contents

To My Readers · vii
Acknowledgements · ix
In Loving Memory · xiii
Preface · xv
Intro · xix

Chapter 1   "A Rough Start" · 1
Chapter 2   "Hood Adjustments" · 6
Chapter 3   "Get In Where You Fit In" · · · · · · · · · · · · · · · · · 12
Chapter 4   "Young Love" · 20
Chapter 5   "Hello High School" · 28
Chapter 6   "Love vs Drugs" · 34
Chapter 7   "You Will Respect Me" · · · · · · · · · · · · · · · · · · · 45
Chapter 8   "Hurricane Hell" · 53
Chapter 9   "New Company" · 64
Chapter 10   "Ride The Wave" · 77
Chapter 11   "Just Be Loyal" · 90
Chapter 12   "Wife on Duty" · 106
Chapter 13   "Welcome Home" · 128
Chapter 14   "Roll With The Punches" · · · · · · · · · · · · · · · · · 144
Chapter 15   "Starting Over" · 165

Chapter 16 "Expect the Unexpected" · · · · · · · · · · · · · · · · · · · 181
Chapter 17 "Beginning of The End" · · · · · · · · · · · · · · · · · · · 192
Chapter 18 "The Cost of Trust" · 205
Chapter 19 "Living With Reality" · 214
Chapter 20 "The Mustard Seed" · 226
Chapter 21 "Crazy Love" · 232
Chapter 22 "More Lessons" · 240
Chapter 23 "Dream Chaser" · 247
Chapter 24 "Life is but A Dream" · 253
Chapter 25 "Epilogue" · 256

    Forgive Me for A Day · 261
    Post Face · 263

To My Readers

THANK YOU ALL FOR JOINING me, as I walk you through a brief look into a world that replays through my mind. Nothing is guaranteed, but opportunity is always around for you to step out on faith and see what God has planned for you. Forgive and release people who mean you no good and pray for those who wronged you. If you let a persons actions towards you change your character, then you wouldn't be any different from a hypocrite. I truly believe I am a living testimony. I can only move forward in my life with wisdom, no longer being who I was. I'm trying my best to avoid the same mistakes and never stay captured by the same life. God set my standards so high that even I couldn't keep up. Yet, He kept me going!

I'm here to witness His greatness and give him the glory from my story! I was told to seek the kingdom of God first and everything else would fall in place. Unfortunately, I began doing the opposite, then God rearranged my life before my very own eyes. Here is when I began to seek the Kingdom of God they spoke of. I started to see things as a blessing and I battled with either I was going crazy or I was someone that was chosen to be great. God has already ordered our steps, you just have to keep walking by faith! If it wasn't for people hurting me, I wouldn't know how it feels to allow God to heal me.

Plenty of times I had for sure hit rock bottom but it made me appreciate His grace that allowed me to reach for the top.

I pray that every weak bone in your body gains strength. I pray every ache in your soul finds healing. I pray every hole in your heart finds comfort. Nothing will save you but the Word of God.

DON'T GIVE UP!

Acknowledgements

I DON'T BELIEVE THERE ARE any words that can express how thankful I am to have been favored by God. Allowing me to walk in the path that had already been decided for me. I thank His son Jesus for His mercy and grace. For opening my heart and granting me knowledge to understand his word. Giving me wisdom and courage to move forward in such a way that others may be inspired by the blessings he has reigned upon my life. For giving me strength when there were so many times I wanted to give up. God knew what he placed on my heart would not allow me to hang my head in defeat but raise my hands in praise. Thank You Lord, Thank You! You are my everything!

I give thanks to my parents Debra and RJ Baltimore, who raised me beyond a child. Because even as an adult, I still learn from you both. My mother is the hardest working, strongest woman I know who will take care of others even if her health didn't allow. God made you with an iron fist. Although we didn't have the best of everything, you made sure we had everything we needed. My dad is the funniest man I'm proud to call my father. I can't count how many times I've needed you and you made a way for me to keep pushing. I won't apologize for being the bad apple out of the bunch. In fact, I thank you both for understanding that I've always been misunderstood. I love You

To my Siblings, Tomeka, Katrina, Keisha, Kimberly, and Rodney, I thank you for all the things siblings are supposed to do. (Whatever that means lol) I pray God leads you all, the way he has shifted my life. One day you'll be proud to know your little sister never gave up, despite everything.

To my in-laws, Judy Green and Michael Brown, I couldn't picture raising my kids without you. My heart truly goes out to you both everyday for the children you have lost and the heartache you both have endured. God definitely picks his toughest soldiers. Life feels like a war sometimes but the battle is not yours. Boobie and Jacobby are forever in my prayers. May Punch and Gator live on through us all. They will never be forgotten! I love you both.

To my children, Journei, Jream and Klover… you girls took away the meaning of peace and quiet. Three different personalities and three different looks, you're all completely a breed of your own and I couldn't have asked for such greater blessings. I want my mistakes to be your lessons and my success to be your blueprint. Through Christ, All things are possible. I can't protect you from everything, only God can do that. I'm here to help you conquer anything that captures your heart. Be great!

To my friends, who saw the best and always pointed out the worst in me. Thank you for understanding the change in me throughout the years. With your criticism and tough love, I wouldn't know how to heal from hurt without grudge. I wouldn't know the meaning of sacrifice, because I've definitely had to endure some things and realize that all company, isn't good company. Everyone you love as a friend, you may have to outgrow as an adult. Although there's no love lost, there's nothing more to gain. So we become detached and we move on. I was voted Most Popular my senior year and I couldn't believe that so many people would even cast a vote for me! I mean I was no goody two shoes but I realized even then, just being yourself is all the recognition you needed. I'm not really sure about the term *friend*, so let me just say I love my day ones.

Thanks to my people who were there through periods of my life where the lesson and help was needed for my growth. Latisha F., Danacia V., J'zmene H., Alissa J., Ashley H., Katrina A., Donielle P., Monique D., and Vanecia 'Shell' Chargois.

To Mrs. Darlene Guidry, thank you for my very first Bible. I still have it! My heart goes out to you for the loss of your son. He will never be forgotten. Rest In Peace, Dwight 'Baby Boy' Guidry.

To CP Palmer, I remember when we wanted to be rappers! Crazy idea that everyone had as a hobby but I had a little more to say. I just didn't know a real story would be the outcome. So here it is. Thanks for always believing in me.

To Remi Umanah, you have played such a huge role in the start of my success and the paths that I've crossed. I want to thank you unconditionally for all your help and support.

To Larry Sainz, thanks for your honesty and encouragement. You are definitely a witness from the very first night I put my ideas into action. When it was just a memoir and here I am still a dreamer, "… see you on Oprah" (wink) Thanks for Everything!

To Robert Thomas, I remember in my interview, you had such a beautiful spirit. You've been a straightforward, non-judgmental friend and I thank you for being there when I got the worst news ever. Oh, please tell Chris William, I am NOT CRAZY!

Best for last, I couldn't have done so much without God blessing me with a person who holds such a large heart. Jakobi Holland, I can't thank you enough for everything you've done in my life and loving my girls as your own. You are a challenge to deal with but I believe God led you to me, so we can be led back to Him. Thank you for putting up with me through it all. Staying by my side through the hardest trial I've ever endured… You have my vote! I love You baby

In Loving Memory

To my late husband, thank you for the life I once lived that allowed me to become who I am. I've learned to regret nothing and embrace everything. I raise our girls with every piece of strength I have left. Never in my life have I experienced the kind of pain your absence has introduced me too. I forgive you for every mistake and love you for every lesson. I will forever miss you Jerome.

Preface

I was told that I dream too much, like I always keep my head stuck in the clouds. I use to sit and think about what does dreaming too much really mean. Like, isn't that what you're supposed to do? At some point your thoughts become louder and you can't help but let imagination capture the moment. One day, I decided to become what I was thinking and chase what was right in front of me. I realized there's nothing stopping me from being the greater form of myself I envisioned. I was my only downfall and had to learn that doubt will kill your dreams before failure even has a chance. I can't dispute whether your situation is wrong or right but whatever you're involved in, be loyal to it. Period!

I love the very famous Poem "*Foot Prints*" because I feel it relates to my life and many of us who get discouraged during our hardest times. When the person noticed only one set of footprints, he became worried thinking God had left. Instead, he was being carried. Throughout my life, I have seen many dirt roads and high hills. I'm most certain I quit on myself but God didn't quit on me. He held me. There is definitely a table he has prepared in the presence of your enemy.

One night I was up reading the bible and this scripture will always stick with me. Job 42:10 "Job prayed for his friends, the Lord restored his fortunes and gave twice as much as he had before".

Even when you are going through a storm, don't forget that it may be raining on someone else's head too. Be mindful and don't get caught up in your own struggle that you ignore someone else's needs. Try not to let your pride or anger strip away the humanity in you. For survival, we must trust cautiously and pray for wisdom to lead the misguided. I've made so many mistakes and I believe it's why I speak of my wrongs so much. I want someone to do what's right and know that you will only live life one time. I've personally watched someone battle a spiritual attack with themselves. The devil will come to steal, kill and destroy. Do not let him win! Jesus will come so that you may have life and have it more abundantly. The devil knows scriptures too; don't forget he once was an angel and is a magician with his disguises.

So after the hardest thing I've endured, brought about the best change in myself. I actually cried at least once a day for 365 days, until slowly things began to become more bearable. Someone once told me, that they've noticed how numb I've become. I couldn't believe someone who wasn't so close to me could see my reality. I thought I had been sheltering the anger and nonchalant attitude that grew in me. Some things won't affect you so greatly after you've been dealt the hardest hand you've played in life. I became addicted to dreaming about success and the more it crossed my mind, the more anxious I became. My thoughts would scare me because it started to seem possible but this time I was willing to bet everything I had to pursue my wildest dreams. I accepted responsibility for my life and owned up to my mistakes. I encourage you to conquer the most impossible thing you never thought you could do. It feels Amazing!

The pain made me but the hurt grew me! My strength has defined me and the time has definitely changed me. I realized there is so much I can handle without folding. Sometimes we lose focus but we must never lose sight of what we're after. Timing is everything and the worst thing about that is we don't actually know how much time God is giving us. If happiness comes with struggle, I pray we all have strength to endure each trial. Find something that inspires you and gives you a reason to reach the highest form of yourself. Motivate yourself to get started. Find a reason to remain consistent, because habit is what keeps you going.

I call myself a survivor, because I'm still here. Look at me, I'm doing it but I cannot take all the credit. So, I'm here to give God the glory! I feel like my life has been worth living, so it's definitely worth reading. I want people like me, to know that we can be heard even if we didn't speak. Actions mean everything. There's no rewind button and life is not a game. I can't chase yesterday. I'm just walking into tomorrow like the past didn't faze me. Nothing means more when you're living, than what you will be held accountable for when you die. Make your future brighter, do something adventurous and live a little. You must outgrow your normal! Go after your destiny, because that's what makes you an achiever. Take the initiative to be beyond good and become great.

Please be advised, that some of what you read here is based on real life events. I mean no harm by expressing my thoughts. They say the truth hurts, which explains my life of pain. So I write down the words and give my secrets to the pages. May the lessons of myself and those involved, mean you more good than the troubles I've seen.

Intro

A RED LIGHT CAN REALLY be the longest two minutes of your life, especially when you've already lost patience before the signal even switched to yellow. One foot held down on the brake pedal and her head faced down on the horn with both arms hugging the steering wheel. Life suddenly became a movie replaying in her mind, as her imagination took a stroll down memory lane. It was all so bittersweet, from as far back to what her memory recollected. It was like an invisible rain cloud followed above her head. Even if it seemed all good, she still carried the bad around like dead weights. For so many reasons, she pitied herself for everything unfolding the way it did. No matter what happened, all ten fingers pointed at the reflection of her very own that she began to hate.

"What is the point?" She shouted. "I can't go through any more, I'm telling you… I've had it."

Her foot was starting to give in to the thoughts of releasing the brake and allowing her truck to roll into traffic. Thinking of dying is one thing but to actually take your own life is something most people are actually too coward to do. Yet, her tears began to roll faster while she was releasing such a silent cry. Her soul ached from the pain her heart kept enduring. Then her body suddenly felt numb to any more emotion or feeling of being afraid to just *do it*.

"Here it goes." She thought.

She picked her head up to watch the movement of the busy intersection near Highway 145 in Houston, Texas. Assuming traffic was heavy enough to crash her car fatally, she prayed no one else would get hurt in what she hoped would be a successful attempt to take her life. She licked her lips out of habit and closed her eyes while she began to ease her foot off the brake. Just at the second her foot inched for the accelerator, her phone rang and an unfamiliar number grabbed her attention. Startled, yet with hesitation, she sofly answered. "Hello"

"Hi, sister Dawkins?"

"Yea, this is me. What is it?" Instantly annoyed from the approach, she knew it was related to church, yet the voice was so familiar.

"Well, sorry to bother you but I was just calling to see how you were doing, maybe pray for you and the family. Possibly invite you to church?" The male rambled off through the phone.

Loyalty couldn't believe it but she could then place his voice with the words, it was the Pastor. What made him call at this particular moment and interrupt her perfect date with death? The tears began to flow even harder as she tried to reply.

"Everything is just so messed up. I mean, if you don't mind, I do have so many questions… and I sure could use me some God right now."

Green Light.

CHAPTER 1

"A Rough Start"

Sometimes reality is more like a nightmare, when you have images that can't be erased. You start to believe that the life you live is just a new normal. With each new passing day she just wanted to run. She wanted to break free and escape the life that was tying her to unhappiness. Yet being so young, where would she go, what would she do, how would she survive? Instead of trying to find the answers, she stopped questioning herself and just let it be.

"You can go ahead, I'll be out here." The man stated, who always stood in the shadows, waiting.

Being so young and innocent, she was unsure of what was always happening. She felt that it was not right but just didn't know who to tell or would they even believe her. When she came out of the bathroom, she slowly walked over to the bed. Being use to his disgusting routine, she began to lie down and let the man clean her, as he would say.

"We don't use toilet paper, the best way to clean yourself is to let an adult do it." He began licking at her skin in an area that she knew was not to be touched. She just did not know how to say stop. She couldn't tell a grown up to leave her alone. She knew in her mind what he was doing was wrong but he taught her to believe that he was an adult taking care of children.

"I want to go outside and play." Her voice was shaky but she spoke loud enough to where he could hear her. He stood up and wiped his mouth, then dried her bottom with the sheets that were lying on the bed. As he walked out of the room, he made sure to give her his closing command.

"Go outside and play Loyalty but remember, I take care of you. While your mom is at work, I'm the one responsible. Don't go too far and make sure not to ever tell anyone how good I take care of y'all. Ok?"

As she looked at the tall man who was a disgustingly six-foot tall, she wanted so badly to spit in his face. Yet, with manners and a little bit of uncertainty, she just softly replied, "OK."

Sitting on the steps not too far from the apartment door, she just watched all the other kids play and run around like they had no worries. She wished so badly that she had a watch or some sort of clock that told her when her mom would be coming. There was an old lady sitting on her porch that always came out with a rocking chair or some sort of stool. Her name was Ms. Pat and she watched over the projects all day.

She called out to Loyalty, "Hey pretty girl, get your little self out there and run around like kids supposed to do."

Not in the mood for small talk, Loyalty just looked at her and shook her head from side to side, saying no. Her thoughts were everywhere as she looked down at her shoes and just played with the laces. Looking at the pavement, she saw a shadow coming and noticed that Ms. Pat had gotten up from her stool. Now she stood blocking the sun in her old raggedy slippers.

"What's wrong with you child? You sitting over here like you got a bunch of bills with no money. All kids need is a quarter for a cool cup to keep them happy. I know the projects may be a little rough but don't let nothing or nobody scare you. You hear me? The world is too big to be afraid. By the things I've seen sitting on this little ol' chair, you better get up off your butt and go do something. Cause trouble going to find you anyway. Instead of sitting down waiting on it, you better get up and chase something outside these fences. Now run along."

Just like that, Ms. Pat walked off without even getting a response from Loyalty. Her words would forever stick with the girl and for some reason she believed they were meant just for her. She started kicking up rocks until she heard her sister, Londyn yell "Come on Loyalty, mama coming through the front gate."

When she saw her mom's brown Oldsmobile Delta 88 come around the corner, relief filled her body and she knew it was really time to go home.

Her mother, Daphne, worked two jobs with four kids and was currently pregnant with her last child. She was a phlebotomist during the day and a part-time cashier in the evening. Childcare was just more convenient leaving her two younger kids with a friend of hers. Loyalty stared at her mom from the backseat in silence. She thought of all the ways she could just come out and say what was really happening when her friend left that strange man alone with them. Not wanting to put any more stress and sadness on her mother, she just sat back on the dirty old cloth seats and let her young mind wonder.

They pulled into the driveway of their three-bedroom house. It was located in a decent neighborhood, considering the circumstances of having four children with just enough money to get by. She went inside to greet her other two siblings with a bag of burgers their mother had just purchased from the ShortStop burger stand. Liberty was the oldest of the four, being in high school she was just about as busy as a bee making honey. Lucky, the second born, actually shared the same birthday as Loyalty. She was currently in middle school, while Londyn and Loyalty attended elementary. Being that they were so close in age; they fought more than a WWF match every day.

The next day when they awoke, their dad Ralph, was finally home from his weekly job duties. He was a truck driver who stayed on the road, so the girls would talk his head off the moment he hit the door. This time, instead of having exciting things to say, Daphne came out of the room and said their grandmother had died. There was disbelief in everyone's face. Not sure of what death really meant, Loyalty was in a state of confusion and anger.

The following weekend, the family all went out to the country, in Silsbee, to pay their last respects and see their grandmother one last time. It was the most horrible thing she had ever seen, unsure of why her grandmother was in a casket, laying cold and still while everyone cried for her. As they walked down the aisle along with family that was proceeding behind the casket, her heart was filled with more and more anger. She watched her parents hug each other as the casket was no longer in view. With every tear that fell, she angrily pushed each one off her cheek, breathing heavily, she knew life was much harder than she expected.

Once they returned home and things seemed to be back to normal. Daphne began having stomach pains followed by contractions, which led up to the birth of their new baby brother, Rome. When she first laid eyes on him, she smiled and was filled with a little joy knowing that her mom finally got a baby boy. Daphne was released from the hospital and allowed time off from her jobs, to heal and bond with her new addition to the Brown family.

It's funny how they say, "the same thing that makes you laugh will make you cry" because all the joy from having a new brother began turning into aggravation. Loyalty's behavior began to change in school, making her less pleasant to the teachers and labeled her a problem child. She was punished for her behaviors at home but that only made the hateful side of her grow.

She was so sick of Rome's presence, she took it upon herself to try and shut him up for good. He was in his crib crying when she walked into her parent's room and grabbed a pillow off of their bed and climbed on the stool. Looking down into the crib, she placed the pillow above his moving body and lowered it right above his head. Just as she was about to cover his mouth with the plush pillow, she heard her mother's voice.

"If you put that over my baby's face, I'm going to beat you." Daphne stated.

Looking over her shoulder, Loyalty jumped down and hesitantly walked past her mother. Neither of them said another word.

About a year later, Loyalty and Londyn were getting off of the school bus when they noticed a U-Haul truck in the driveway. Walking up to the home, they noticed their things were packed on the back, while Liberty and Lucky were hugging their dad tightly.

"Where are we moving?" She asked, knowing that she wasn't ready for the response.

Ralph replied, "Come here baby girl, daddy has made some bad choices and now you have to move away. I promise I will come and see you girls a lot. Y'all be good for Mama, okay."

Loyalty stared at the grass, with tears filling her eyes. She didn't understand why the family was splitting up. She wasn't ready to give up her old home to start living a new life. Sure, things weren't perfect as she knew they could never be but she didn't want them to go out and search for something that was impossible to find. Not really having much to say and not really sure on just how to feel, she could only hug her daddy in return, as she accepted their departure.

CHAPTER 2

"Hood Adjustments"

Relocating to another part of town was quite a challenge for the family, because it was a new neighborhood and a different environment. Once they got settled into the four-bedroom apartment, the girls all sat outside and just watched, quietly. There were a few kids playing marbles by the playground, some were even shooting basketball with only a rim nailed to a wooden phone pole. The section 8 apartment community was so much different than the comfortable home they all were accustomed to. Without trying to stick out like a sore thumb, Loyalty took a deep breath and just figured she would make the best of it, before the entire situation got the best of her.

Suddenly, something sounded familiar, which was the attractive tune blaring from the speakers of an ice cream truck. Liberty and Lucky turned their noses up, and headed back in the house, deciding they would rather spend time indoors. Loyalty wanted that tasty bombstick from the ice cream truck and she knew the only way to get it was to make Londyn go inside to ask for two dollars.

"I know you want some candy, so why don't you go inside and ask mama for two dollars. I been in trouble so I know she won't give it to me. Just tell her you want candy and ice cream off the truck you hear coming." Loyalty knew the answer would be N to the O, if she went inside and pleaded for the 2 bucks.

Still staring at the kids running around the playground, Londyn responded. "Why don't you go. You're the one who want the stupid thing."

"Look, just do it. I'll give you the change from my bomb stick so you could buy more candy. I won't even ask for none, just hurry up." Loyalty stated with aggravation, as she rolled her eyes.

"Whatever Loyalty and you better not ask for none either." She replied.

As the two hurried away, they tried to catch the ice cream truck that sounded just as far as it did when they first heard it. Once they reached the end of the sidewalk, they noticed it was at the front gate just sitting there, waving for the crowd to come closer.

"What kind of ice cream man is this? Don't he want to get paid." Loyalty sarcastically stated.

"Well, what y'all waiting for, Christmas? If you want something, you better hurry up because he won't sit there long. Trust me." A young girl stated, as she walked past them with a handful of change.

"Come on, don't just stand here and look like the new girl. Let's go." Loyalty demanded.

"Where are you going? You think you could just follow every little hood rat around you meet? Mama said don't go too far and that gate looks mighty far to me." Londyn ruled.

"What are you, a good listener now? We will be back before she even peeps her head out of the door. You keep moving this slow, then you for sure will get us caught." Loyalty said with irritation.

They both walked towards the gate following closely behind the young girl. Once they reached the front of the line, Loyalty purchased her bombstick popsicle that to her surprise, was only 50 cents. Londyn proceeded to buy just about every candy on the truck. With the help of two extra quarters from Loyalty, she walked away happily with a brown sack full of Lemonheads, Now and Later's, gumballs, and Air Heads.

Walking back up the sidewalk, they approached a set of stairs where the young girl and her sisters were sitting.

"Glad y'all made it back alive. Poor things must've been scared to walk to the gate." They all chuckled at the girls comments.

Even Loyalty thought it was funny, so she laughed a little herself but then noticed Londyn didn't see any humor in it. Usually the more serious one, she knew she had to tell her to relax.

"She's not serious Londyn, she's just saying." Loyalty convinced.

"She's just saying what? She don't know us like that." Londyn barked.

"Girl chill out. We only playing with your scary tail." They all laughed again. "What school y'all go to? I hope y'all don't be waiting on the bus like you were waiting on that ice cream truck. The buses don't run this way. Unless y'all a car rider, you might want to get up early and walk with the rest of us." She informed them.

"I'm not sure what school it is but I think its right around the corner. So I guess that means we will be walking too. Our mama goes to work too early to drop us off." Loyalty stated, devouring her bomb stick. Londyn stood there in silence as they talked, while she unwrapped and ate just about every candy she had.

"Ok cool, my name is Joy and these are my two sisters, Robin and Arielle. Looks like we'll see you girls bright and early. Just don't bring any goofy sack lunches with you. The school has pretty good food. Besides, we don't want to get chased by a dog behind a stupid ham sandwich." Joy finished her last statement.

They got up from the staircase and headed for their front door, then said their goodbyes in unity. "Holla Back."

Loyalty shrugged, looking over at her sister, she didn't know how to say it but this was going to be a long school year.

For the next few years, school was great but she was finally happy that she reached fifth grade. They switched schools so much, she rarely got a chance to make any genuine friends. By the time she got to know someone, her mother was already packing up to move them once again. She had a few fights and to say she was only in elementary, this was just the beginning. One fight in particular, she was being picked on by a girl that was twice her size, named Angela. Every day she came to class, Angela would find something to throw at her or just have some ugly words to say. Being that she already had warnings from the principal that if she fought again, they were going to send her off to pathways. Her mother reminded her every day to complete all her work and she had better not get a call about her behavior.

Tired of Angela picking with her every day, she was ready to just get the fight over with. When Angela walked into class, Loyalty just began staring at her to get a reaction.

"You want a problem little girl?" Angela challenged, when she noticed the stares.

Loyalty just chuckled; she figured that laughing it off would annoy Angela and make her become more aggressive. All she wanted her to do was to touch her first and she would do the rest. Just as she expected, Angela was now standing in front of her desk, waving her hand across Loyalty's face.

Looking up at the bully with every inch of seriousness, she stated "You better have a seat and get your hand out of my face."

"Who is gonna make…" Before Angela could finish her sentence, Loyalty had her against the chalkboard teaching her a lesson of her own. All she remembered mama saying was, 'if somebody hits you, you have every right to hit them back'. That was going to be her only argument once her mother found out. Angela had only pushed Loyalty's forehead with her index finger and before she knew it the fight was over.

When Mrs. Daphne came to pick Loyalty up, she fussed the whole way home. Loyalty just sat in silence as she listened to her mother preach on and on about her behavior. She couldn't help but notice that the radio was playing Tupac nonstop. After about the 5th song in a row, it announced that he was dead and immediately followed by another classic. For a moment, she wanted to tell her mother to just chill out so she could be alone with her thoughts. She was very much into music. To hear that one of her favorite rappers had been shot, only reminded her that the world was far crueler than it seemed. She could only shake her head while looking out the window as she turned up the volume to enjoy the lyrics of one of the greatest.

When she got home and bathed for bed, she gathered her favorite Cabbage Patch dolls and snuggled in her twin size comforter. Looking over at Londyn, she wondered just how many people were fortunate enough to have a mattress and cover to sleep on. Sometimes her mind went beyond the average thinking but she also remembered her daddy saying, "If you think more than you speak, you might be better off." Just the thought of him saddened her little heart.

She used the hallway light to guide her to the bathroom as she made her way through the quiet house. When she returned back to her room, her heart skipped a beat when she noticed the man that once waited.

"I told you. We do not use toilet paper." The tall, dark skinned man stated.

"I'm clean. I just want to go to sleep." Loyalty couldn't figure out how he got into their home. She thought they lost contact with his girlfriend years ago and it took everything inside of her not to scream. He motioned for her to come inside her room, where he was already standing next to her bed. As she laid down with tears pouring down her face, the hate for him became more intense. When he leaned over to lick her, she kicked him right in the nose. Startled by her reaction, he grabbed her by the neck and began choking her until she could barely breathe.

Loyalty then woke up in the same pajamas she dressed in for bed and looked around the room. She was relieved to realize that it was only a nightmare. She kicked the Cabbage Patch off of her mattress and was no longer interested in fake or make-believe things. Aggravated with the thoughts running through her mind, she began to silently pray that one day those horrible nightmares will no longer exist in her sleep.

CHAPTER 3

"Get In Where You Fit In"

Now that she was in junior high school, she knew it was time to become serious about something. If her conduct allowed her to make it through one day, she definitely had the intelligence to pass her classes. She wasn't quite the average girl who fantasized about dresses and jewelry but she knew she had the looks to pull off whatever personality she wanted.

When it was time for choir tryout, she went inside the classroom and was immediately turned off just by the vibe of the other girls. Music was the only thing that seemed to interest her the most, so she figured she would try out to play an instrument. Once she was on her way to the band department, she was stopped in her tracks by one of her elementary friends.

"Loyalty, is that you? What's up girl, I'm so glad to see you. How you been?" It was Niecy, her close friend from fourth grade. Although it was a sudden surprise, she was ecstatic just to have a familiar face around.

"Hey girl, what's up? I have been trying to figure out what kind of sport or activity I'm going to be in. I'm not sure yet though. I would like to take something other than P.E. because that course is so typical. Besides, I hate dressing out in some stupid school uniform doing jumping jacks for a grade." Loyalty explained, as they continued to walk.

"Why don't you come with me to cheerleading tryouts? I'm sure you will like it, we even have the privilege to wear those cute little skirts every Friday and cheer on the cutest football players. Here, take this paper. It's a copy of the cheer chant that we have to learn by Friday." Niecy handed her the cheer to memorize but she still wasn't convinced it was a good idea.

"I don't know man, what if they don't even pick me. I mean, you know! I'm not into all that cheesy smiling for no reason and yelling at the crowd to cheer on a bunch of losers. This team probably haven't won a football game since the Jeffersons moved on up to the East side but whatever!" As they made their way to the gym, a paper was hanging on the door filled with a list of girls' names that had already signed up, Loyalty hesitantly scribbled her name.

Patting her long-lost friend on the back, Niecy chuckled, "Cheer up Loyalty, gosh, don't look like you just signed your life over to the devil. It's only a tryout, if we don't make it; we have nothing but time to choose something else. Here's my number so we can stay in touch, see you later."

Tryouts came as quick as she knew they would and it was finally time to stand in front of the crowded bleachers in the auditorium. With her hands on her hips and a forced smile, she nervously ran across the floor and began yelling and chanting just as she had practiced.

"Go team. Let's win tonight. Let's show them that we're dynamite. We've got the spirit, let's go let's run. Let's show them that we are number one." She did a few jumps, kicks and hoorays, then ended it as quickly as it started.

Relieved that her time was over, she watched her friend go up next and to her surprise, Niecy actually seemed like she was enjoying it. When she approached Loyalty behind the curtains, they both started questioning each other about their performance. It was now time to see the results, so they went outside and checked the list to see if they made it.

"Do you see your name? Do you see mine?" Niecy asked.

"Nope." Loyalty nonchalantly responded.

"Man I really tried, that sucks. I wonder why they didn't pick us? Oh well forget it, I'm going to sign up for choir. What about you?" Niecy questioned.

"I'm going with my first mind. My sister played the clarinet and said that it was easy, besides I love music anyway. So, I guess I'm going to join the band. I'll catch you later." Loyalty felt her heart a bit broken by the rejection.

She noticed that many girls walked off from the building crying and disputing the fact that they were not chosen. Tears won't change anything, so she saw no reason to start with the dramatics. Yet the experience on its own, taught her that failure was only a step towards what's meant for you.

The end of the school year was near and Loyalty was surely glad to have made it through both semesters without a fight. However, as she and her sister sat on the school bus waiting for their bus stop, a young boy kept picking with her. The only thing that intimidated her was the absolute fact that he was probably stronger and tougher, being that he was a dude. It appeared that he was upset because she always sat in his seat. Although he never asked politely and even if he did, she was not about to move.

"What did you do to him Loyalty? Why does he keep talking smack about you? You think he would really hit a girl?" Londyn stated, confused about the whole situation.

"I don't know but just hold my backpack in case he tries. I didn't do anything, we sat here first! There are no assigned seats Londyn, he just wants to tell us what to do." Loyalty whispered, bracing herself for the altercation she knew was about to happen.

"I know she hear me talking to her. Little dumb ass girl always want to sit in my seat. She must think she's somebody but I will pull those nappy braids out of her head." The young boy continued, loudly ranting off to the other students.

Although she knew it wouldn't be a fair fight because he was a boy, she was not about to let that stop her from speaking up.

"Who are you talking too? You must be dumb if you think somebody scared of you. I wish you would." Her heart rate picked up speed but she was trying to keep calm.

"What are you doing? He could knock you out. You better not forget about mama. You can't get into any more trouble and you know it." Londyn tried to plead with her sister but it was no use.

"Just shut up. You hear him talking to me don't you? I didn't start anything. I don't even know him and this is not my fault. I can't help it if -----." In the middle of Loyalty's sentence, the young boy had walked by and pulled her hair as he was getting off at his bus stop.

Her only reaction was to catch him before it was too late and he was out of reach. She did the only thing she could do and leaped off of the bus steps to tackle him. Landing on top, she began hitting him in his face repeatedly, trying to connect every punch. As the fight continued, she could hear onlookers outside cheering her on and rooting for her to win. An adult hanging near the corner store broke it up and forced Loyalty to get back on the school bus. Her clothes were so filthy from the scuffle as she straightened her shirt and walked down the aisle to her seat. She could only look down in embarrassment as everyone quietly watched her sit down. Nonetheless, she was so proud of herself for actually surviving a fight with a boy, that she smirked to herself in achievement.

Londyn nudged her sister and jokingly whispered, "I'm proud of you girl, you really showed him. That was too funny but all jokes aside, how are you going to tell Mama that you got kicked off the school bus now."

"WHAT!!" Loyalty couldn't believe her ears as her sister explained to her that while she was outside fighting, the bus driver instructed her to relay the message.

"You heard me, I just hope mama understands. Now, looks like you're gonna need a ride to school homegirl." Londyn just shook her head as they both sat quietly until their destination.

Once Mrs. Daphne learned of the incident, she reported it to the principal about the young boys' bully attacks. To no avail, Loyalty was still suspended from school transportation. For a few days, her mother had to drop her off to school before she rushed off to work. It didn't last long and luckily for Loyalty she found another way, because she hated putting too much on her mother's plate.

Walking out of detention one day, she bumped into her Aunt outside, who was there picking up her cousin from tutorials. It was a sigh of relief because she was just about to walk home to avoid having to call her mom and tell her about detention.

"Hey Ms. Thing. Where you headed to?" Aunt Mary yelled out.

"I just had some after school stuff to do but now I'm headed home. Can you bring me?" Loyalty replied.

"Yeah, of course child, hop in." Aunt Mary answered, as she opened the passenger door.

They talked for just a few moments before her cousin, Nyla, came walking out of the building and hopped into the backseat. She started discussing her current bus situation, then they explained to her that Nyla is actually dropped off to school every morning. So, it would work out perfect for them to pass by and pick her up also. In fact, it was a good thing that she had this opportunity to hang out more with her cousin.

"Thanks for the ride. I'll be up and ready in the morning. See ya later." Loyalty waved, as she headed inside.

The next following weeks of Loyalty and Nyla hanging around each other more, they became more like sisters instead of cousins. Mrs. Daphne and Aunt Mary even allowed them to sleep over at each others houses during the school week from time to time. They were hanging out at the mall, school dances and just living a normal childhood life in a ghetto neighborhood.

"Hey mama, can we go and pick up Nyla? She wants to stay over tonight. I promise we will go to bed on time. We just want to hang out, that's it." Loyalty asked, as her mother was preparing dinner for the family.

"Yes, that's fine, we can pick her up once the food is ready." Mrs. Daphne replied.

When they arrived to pick Nyla up, she was completely packed with her sleeping bag and school books. The girls both sat in the backseat, laughing and catching up as if they weren't just together less than 24 hours ago. When they got inside, they went into the room that Loyalty and Londyn shared. Pulling out magazines and looking at television, that night in particular, they discussed everything they would want to be when they grew up.

Morning came and the girls were all up getting prepared for school. As they clowned around for breakfast, Mrs. Daphne immediately reminded them that they had no time to waste and school was about to take in. They grabbed their bags and were off, trying to get in every word possible.

Loyalty was in third period English class, when she heard an announcement over the loudspeakers that changed everything.

"Attention faculty and students, if you have been in contact with Nyla Brown any time today, can you please report to the cafeteria." The principal instructed.

Loyalty immediately jumped up along with a few other students and rushed towards the cafeteria. Approaching the lunchroom doors, she noticed Londyn standing by the vending machine talking to a few teachers. They were questioning students about Nyla's morning behavior.

"It appears that she may have been on some type of medication? Does she have seizures? Is she diabetic? Was she fine when you last spoke with her?" The counselor continued with her questions towards the group of students.

"What's going on? Where is Nyla? What happened and why are we here?" Loyalty began to shake, feeling that something wasn't right.

Londyn pulled her sister to the closest table to began explaining to her what the nurse and teachers were saying.

"What did y'all do last night? Did you eat the same thing? Did she complain about anything hurting? Did she seem ill? Was anything weird about her?" Londyn rambled off, question after question.

"No. No, she was fine. She was even fine this morning. She didn't eat last night because she said her stomach felt funny but that was it. Where is she? Londyn. Where is she?" Loyalty began to tear up.

"Can I have your attention please, we will need everyone to remain calm and stay seated. We have paramedics in the hallway and we need everyone to stay inside these doors." The counselor yelled out.

"What? Paramedics for who? Is Nyla okay?" Loyalty jumped up and headed for the doors but was only able to make it to the nurse's window in the front office.

Looking inside, she spotted Nyla sitting in a chair while rocking back and forth with a look of pain on her face. When they locked eyes with each other, before any words could be spoken, a teacher pulled

Loyalty away from the window as they shut the blinds. Everything went numb and she could no longer hear the questions the faculty was bombarding her with. When they opened the nurse's doors, the paramedics had Nyla on a stretcher, wheeling her away. Covered in a sheet, the last she saw of her cousin was a pair of light blue socks that she had on her feet.

Church never seemed so sad for Loyalty, until this very day where she was old enough to understand death a little bit more. It's like they had become so close, just to be torn apart within the blink of an eye. Apparently, they were informed that the cause of her death, was a rare and sudden case of Wolf Parkinson White Syndrome. Even if someone explained it to her, she knew that her heart would never accept how it all played out. How could Nyla not tell her something was wrong, or did she even know? So many questions began going through her young mind. She felt that if she could have done something different, then just maybe, Nyla would be alive.

She stood at the entrance of the funeral, unable to bring herself to walk down the aisle and view a casket that was the final resting place for someone she loved. She knew that tears wouldn't change anything but the fact that she wanted to cry only upset her more. She placed one hand on the glass that separated her from the family and sanctuary, as she watched from a distance. Silently crying, she walked away from the ceremony.

"Goodbye Nyla." She whispered.

CHAPTER 4

"Young Love"

It seemed that so much was happening in her life, that she was starting to go in search of something that could fix it. Being that it was her second year in junior high, she pretty much was involved in every sport she thought would occupy her time. From volleyball, basketball, tennis and then her very favorite, track and field. During her afterschool practices, she noticed that there was this one boy, named Justice, who was exceptionally sweet to her. She was unsure of whether he was just being nice, or trying to get her attention to show he was interested. Every day after practice when they hopped on the track bus, it was routine that he sat with her and showed the most charming side of himself.

One morning, she noticed him standing with a group of guys by her locker. While she was turning the knob entering her combination, she could see in her peripheral that he was standing next to her, just watching. Nervously, she must have entered the wrong code a few times before she finally got it to unlock.

"Dang girl, I was starting to think you were at the wrong locker." Justice joked.

"I'm starting to think you're in the wrong grade. Why are you in the seventh graders hallway? You failed your last report card or something?" She slammed her locker shut, after grabbing her jacket and a few books out.

"Ha Ha Ha, that's cold. I actually lost something but now I found it." He smirked, charmingly staring at her with his tongue poking his right cheek.

She sighed. "What do you want Justice?"

"Girl stop being all mean, fronting like you don't like me or something." He replied.

Her back was positioned on the lockers, while her arms folded across her chest. She looked up towards the ceiling and replied. "You know what, I actually don't."

Justice burst into laughter and put his arm around her neck as they walked off. "Man, you are a piece of work Loyalty. Come on, I'll walk you to class before you have us both late and stuck in detention. I know you're use to trouble, unlike me. I'm a good guy. No worries, you'll learn that once you get use to being my girlfriend."

She could only roll her eyes and shake her head at his charm once again, because in actuality, she liked him. He never seemed to amaze her, by waiting for her in the mornings, after classes and of course after practice. He would give her a few dollars to eat the cafeteria snack line, instead of always eating her average free tray lunch. He definitely made her feel loved and placed her on a pedestal like she was an intelligent and gorgeous young girl.

Hanging with a few new friends that she met along the way, she started picking up a bad habit of stealing. With a new boyfriend that was paying her a little bit more attention than what she was used to, she started trying to keep up with her jewelry and wardrobe. So almost every weekend she went to the mall with a friend of hers, named Casey, who had an older cousin that worked in Dillard's. At first, she was scared to go in but once she saw how easy Casey made it out, she figured it was worth the amount of clothes they would get. The girls had been going into the store for over a month and figured this was an easy way to keep up their looks. There was no way Mrs. Daphne was going to buy Loyalty the type of things she desired and she was too young to work, so she knew that taking it was her only option.

"Now remember, we're going to be in and out like any other time. My cousin said that security is gone for the night and no one is here to watch the cameras. So same routine, you push the stroller inside and just pretend that you are attending to a baby. I'm gonna walk around and gather all the stuff we like and then once you come over, I'll dump everything in. When we place the baby blanket on top, my cousin will signal for us to walk out the door. My big sister is already waiting for us in the parking lot, so we have to be quick. Now let's go!" Casey instructed.

The girls maneuvered their way through the store and walked between each rack of clothing, gathering the outfits and accessories of their choice. Loyalty would occasionally sit down on a bench nearby and pretend to rock the stroller that was housing the imaginary baby. Once she noticed that Casey was finished gathering everything, she casually strolled over between the racks and they hurriedly stuffed everything inside. Placing the baby blanket on top of everything as usual, they proceeded to walk towards the exit doors. Noticing that her cousin was waving at them saying 'have a good night', signified that everything went okay and according to plan.

However, Casey accidentally grabbed a few things that had a buzzer on them, so the store alarm rang out.

"Ding. Attention store shopper, please step back and return to the cashier's desk to check your merchandise. Ding." The alarm repeatedly sounded.

Frightened by the sudden attention, the girls immediately took off running with the merchandise inside the stroller. Casey's big sister parked at least 20 feet away, so by the time they reached her car, there were a few workers from the store that began to chase after them.

They were only able to unload the merchandise and throw it into the backseat before they jumped inside, leaving the stroller behind. When they looked out the back window, they noticed the workers had made it to the stroller with their hands resting on their knees. Exhausted, one of the workers kicked the stroller over in frustration, knowing that the girls had once again gotten away.

"You have got to be kidding me. That has never happened before and now we don't have the stroller anymore. Looks like the gig is over until we find a better way of getting what we want." Casey shouted out.

Loyalty could only shake her head in agreement as she sat back in her seat, just thankful they did not get caught. She couldn't even picture the type of punishment she would have gotten if Mrs. Daphne knew she was out stealing. All she could do was stare up at the stars and let her mind wonder, as she listened to Casey joke about the whole incident.

One day Loyalty was lying across the bed with her headphones on and her tablet out, writing a little music of her own. Londyn, who was sitting on her own bed across the room watching television, had thrown a pillow to get her attention. Someone was knocking on the window, which was usually none other than Justice. She hopped up and threw on some jeans, a T-shirt and some tennis shoes. She passed by her mother's room to let her know she was going outside to play, then went on the back porch to grab her bike. They usually met up sometimes after school or on the weekends to just ride bikes and hang out. When he stopped by to ask if she wanted to grab some snow cones, it was no surprise to her.

Her mom said that it was okay if she went swimming with a few friends. So she changed into one of the swimsuits she picked up from the mall and met back up with Justice so they could attend the pool together. After nearly everyone was leaving, she figured that it was time for her to go inside before it got dark. Justice rode with her to the stop sign of her street and watched her make it to her driveway. Once she was inside, she realized she had left her backpack at the pool with her clothes that she changed out of earlier that day. When she peeked back outside, she could look down the street and see that Justice was still there talking to a few guys from school. She rushed back inside to grab her sandals, so she could tell him to go back and get her backpack. Once she got closer and tried to get his attention, she could tell that he was occupied with one of the known fast girls in their neighborhood. Wanting to make her appearance known, she continued to walk closer as her heart began to break more and more. She couldn't believe that her boyfriend was in the middle of the street, touching all over another half-naked girl. One of his friends noticed her coming and tapped Justice on the back so that he could see her approaching. Once he noticed his girlfriend with a look of confusion on her face, he immediately walked off from the hoochie and proceeded to meet Loyalty.

"What's up baby girl, you coming back out?" He asked nervously, knowing she had just seen his actions.

"Who is she Justice? Your baby girl too?" She asked, tears forming in her eyes.

"Come on baby, don't do that. Everyone at school knows who my girl is. She's just somebody begging for attention." He argued.

"Well, it looks like you're giving her what she wants. Go ahead, continue what you were just doing. It's over." She cried out.

Attempting to walk away, Justice jumped in front of her path and placed his hands into a praying position in front of his face. He paused and closed his eyes for just a second to gather his words, before he began to speak.

"Look, you got my heart, I promise. I have always liked you Loyalty and I am proud to have you as my girl. Honestly, I'm already sexually active. I've had sex before, plus I'm older than you. My relationship is different with you, I just waste time with other chics. I'm not trying to force you into anything just because I'm doing it. I respect you because you're on a special level. Don't move too fast, I like that kind of girl more." He leaned in and smacked her on the lips for the first time.

He grabbed her by the hand and walked her back down to her home. Before she went inside, he just reminded her that she was worth more than being hurt by anyone. She let him know she appreciated his honesty as they agreed to keep their friendship solid, rather than a commitment that he wasn't ready for. He apologized over and over until he had her smiling once again. Yet, until he left for high school, he treated her just the same as if she was still his girl.

Now that it was her time to be an eighth grader, she became more popular and definitely much more of a problem child. Still focused on her studies, she was no stranger to weekly detention and being suspended for her disruptive behavior. Her mom was called to the school several times and after so many counseling sessions, she just admitted to the teachers that her daughter had a problem being understood.

Excelling in sports, she was on the A-Team in volleyball and although basketball was not her sport of choice, she managed. She won a few medals and awards in track and field when it came to the 100-meter hurdles. Following in her sisters footsteps, band was a piece of cake once she mastered how to play the clarinet. She was so proud of herself and her accomplishments that she was finally able to see the finish line and kiss middle school goodbye.

Meeting someone new, she had the pleasure to become the girlfriend of another popular guy at school, named Ali. They started dating at the beginning of the school year, which gave them more than enough time to have feelings. What she loved about him most was his sense of humor that made them more like best friends instead of a couple. She considered him to be the funniest guy she had ever met. By the things she had been through, she truly believed that laughter soothed the soul.

This time, she was going to be the one leaving her boyfriend behind. She intended to do so, in the honest manner as Justice had done to her. Communication is always the key; however honesty leaves no room for confusion. She dreaded that very day she would have to break the news to him. Their relationship was so cool, she knew he would have the perfect understanding and respect her decision. On the last day of school, she mentally prepared herself to cut off their relationship without leaving any bad blood. She approached him sitting with his friends after school and once she came around, he got up so they could take a walk around the field.

"Hey babe, what's up? You passed all your finals or what?" Ali asked.

"Yep, you know your girl did her thang." She stated, sticking her tongue out in a joking manner.

"You still going to Central High? Leaving me all alone. You know I'm going to miss you, right?" Ali stated, as if he knew what was about to happen.

"Yeah, I'm still going there. Hopefully I adjust to it really quick, because I hate being the new girl." She continued.

"Well, what's on your mind? You know I can tell you have something to say. Just tell me. Go ahead and break my heart." He playfully bumped their shoulders together.

As much as she hated to call it quits, she knew there was no way they could keep a relationship together while attending two different schools. She definitely did not want to lead him on into thinking that she would not date anyone in high school. So she stopped in their tracks and grabbed both of his hands, looking up at him face-to-face.

"I really enjoyed your company this year Ali. You are such a great person and I love your sense of humor, so don't lose that. You know that we can't see each other every day or talk as much as we do now. So as much as I'm going to miss you too, I guess this is where we say farewell." As she was speaking to him, she felt horrible inside because she didn't know how he was truly taking her words.

"I guess it hurts because you're not just my girl, you are so much like my homie too. I plan on going to Central as well, so I'll see you in a year. Hey, who knows!? If high school is as hard as they say, maybe you will fail so we can be in the same grade when I get there." He replied, as they joined in laughter at his joke.

"Boy please. I might be your tutor when you arrive. Take care babe." She stated, as she began to walk off.

"Wait. Wait. Wait. Dang, you can't even give your new ex-boyfriend a hug. Chill baby! You acting brand-new already, it's only high school, not College." He continued to laugh.

"Shut up, Ali. You hating already, with your eight grade ass." She playfully shoved him, as they embraced.

Sharing their last hug, they realized that it was really the last day of school. They stood with their arms around each other for another two minutes and held on a little tighter.

CHAPTER 5

"Hello High School"

CENTRAL HIGH WAS A BIG change from the childish environment where she had just spent the last three years of middle school. The old, brick modeled high school consisted of three floors, two gyms, a fieldhouse with its own track, a field for their marching band, and parking lots that divided the teachers and students. Some of the students who attended looked so far in age, she was most certain that she shared a few classes with adults. She was grateful to have her sister Londyn, who was now a sophomore, show her around to get the hang of things.

"Here you go sis, homeroom. Would you look at that. It's a room full of freshmen's, just like you!" Londyn laughed at her own joke, accompanied by a few upperclassmen.

"Yes girl, I remember those days. I'm glad we are no longer fresh meat." One of Londyn's friends joined in.

"The only thing fresh about me are these Force 1s on my feet. Now go run along with your nerdy friends. Thanks for the tour but I can take it from here." Loyalty stated as she rolled her eyes at the group of bragging sophomores.

When she walked into class, it was no surprise that no one looked familiar. The homeroom teacher began to give a list of rules and regulations that were necessary to welcome them. Once the teacher finished giving the school's policies, they sat in class for every bit of three hours until the bell rang for first period. Gathering their things, there was a petite light skinned girl who helped pick up Loyalty's papers that had fallen on the floor.

"Appreciate it! I like your rings. Nice outfit too. What school you come from?" Loyalty asked.

"Thanks boo, I love your hair. I came from King. I'm so glad this class is over; they say the first day of school is always the longest. What's your name? I'm Kali." The girl introduced herself as they walked through the halls to their next class.

"Alright then Kali, I'm Loyalty. Maybe I'll see you later." She replied.

"Loyalty? I like it, with a name like that, you better be a good person." They both laughed and went their separate ways.

Once lunch time came, she couldn't help but look around the huge cafeteria that favored a hip-hop restaurant. There were students sitting on tables and rapping by the vending machines. The food lines were ridiculously long, there was no way possible she could eat lunch in 30 minutes without being late to class. So she decided to stick with chips and a soda, while she continued observing. Within a few minutes of walking, someone bumped her shoulder so hard that she had to turn around and see what the problem was. She couldn't help but smile once she saw him, because he knew that gesture would grab her attention.

"Are you crazy? I almost smacked you. I could have spilled my soda genius." She rhetorically stated.

"Girl relax, there are a hundred more sodas in this place in case you haven't noticed. There is only one me! Aren't you glad to see me?" Justice smirked.

"I mean, I guess you look a little different. Let me find out that high school made a man out of you." She chuckled at her own comment.

"You always with the jokes. I been a man, that's why you always baby girl. I'll check you later though, my boys waiting for me outside. We always leave after lunch." He stated, then rushed off through the exit door.

The end of the day was near and she was quite thrilled to finally be in high school. Heading to marching band practice, she passed a group of girls and noticed that a few of them looked familiar.

"What's up, Loyalty? You look, exactly the same." Arielle stated. "Remember us?"

"Mannnnn." She laughed. "Yeah I remember y'all. Hey Joy. What's up, Robin?"

"It looks like you are on a mission so we'll let you go. We're just chilling, waiting on our mom to pick us up. Walking to school is a little played out when you get older." Joy joined in, as she joked about their past.

"I feel you on that, well holla at me later." Loyalty replied, proceeding to practice.

Entering the band hall, it looked like one big family reunion. Everyone was laughing and joking, appearing to be having the best time of their life. She was happy to see one of her close childhood friends, Alexi, who had joined the band as well. The more she walked around, the more faces she continued to recognize and her perception of the organization was correct. She reunited with so many old friends, it felt like she was right at home. Another friend of hers, Cherish, mentioned that between band practices and school, she overheard that you only had to be 15 years old to work at Sonic Drive-in. That was more music to her ears than the instruments that sounded off through the building. Cherish continued informing them, so that once they became 15 years of age, they would by law be considered hirable.

While the girls continued to talk about employment, Loyalty's attention was captured by a boy who had chocolate skin, with an adorable smile and perfect white teeth. She couldn't help but to keep glancing at him, as he then noticed and returned the favor by matching her stares. Trying her hardest not to look his way again, she was shocked when he came over and sat next to her.

"You sitting over here looking real new. Freshman, right? I'm Dylan. What's your name?" He stared.

"Yes, a freshman. Seems like that's the first thing people call you by instead of your name but I'm Loyalty. What grade are you in?" She admired.

"For you, baby I'll be a freshman too." He laughed. "I'm just a sophomore with freshman year still on my breath. I'm single too, in case you were wondering. I mean, I'm absolutely free until I notice a pretty freshman that I connect eyes with waiting for me to approach her. This is a total coincidence though, ya know." He sarcastically grinned.

"You trying to be funny but I wasn't staring at you. For one, you are banging on the loudest instrument in the room. Besides, your goofy and obnoxious laugh caught my attention, then I peeped that you are just a little cute." She said in defense.

"Just a little?" He smirked.

"Boy, don't flatter yourself. You came all the way over here to ask if I was fresh meat? Okay, point made. Anything else, Mr. Drummer boy?" She stared.

"Owee girl, I like you! No, I came over here because I'm glad you noticed me. I saw you come in. Because you are so beautiful, I'm going to just write down my number, smack dead on the front of your tablet. If you don't call me, I'm going to write my number down again, every day on this same tablet until you call." He announced, then got up and headed back towards his drums.

For the next three weeks, she would see Dylan during school and they would walk the hallways as if they had known each other forever. He seemed to be a pretty cool guy but she had never done the whole phone conversation thing with a boy, so she really didn't know what to say. Doing just as he promised, her tablet was filled with his number on the front so many times, that it looked like her math folder.

One day, she found herself wanting to hear his voice outside of school, so she decided to pull out her tablet covered in digits. When she dialed the number, her heart rate began to speed up because she didn't know what to say, besides *Hello*.

Ring. Ring. Ring.

"Domino's Pizza, what can I get you?" The voice answered.

"I'm sorry, I have the wrong num…" She was interrupted.

"Wait. Loyalty? Is this Loyalty? This is me, Mr. Lover man, Shabba! What's up girl, I thought you'd never call. Y'all must didn't have a phone or something." He chuckled.

"Ha Ha, very funny. Yes, as a matter of fact, we had a phone the very first day you gave me your number. I just had better things to do." She bluntly stated.

"Oh yea, like what? Call Domino's." He joked, bursting into laughter.

"You are so stupid, why would you do that. Now you want to be a pizza boy too?" She laughed.

"Nah, it's just something I do in case it's a bill collector for my mama or something." He replied, as they fell into laughter and held a conversation for hours about everything. It was then that she knew, he was the one.

The more she began to hang out with Dylan, the less she became interested in band and her mind started to focus on goals. She became real close with a guy named Caesar, who she saw a lot of due to band

and the fact that he was a friend of Dylan's. She noticed that he drove to school and asked him a few questions about how he obtained his driver's license so young. Getting all the information that she needed to enroll into Drivers Ed, she called and asked her father to pay for the course. At first he refused but after a few tears and pleading, he eventually gave in and funded what she needed.

Being 15 years old with a driver's permit, Loyalty knew that her next step was to find some type of employment that put a little change in her pocket. Finally, it was time to do the application at Sonic Drive-in, which she managed to get hired on as a car hop. It was only enough to have lunch money and to enjoy a few things during the weekends. She was at least happy to be receiving the paycheck, so she started saving her money to keep from going broke. One thing she hated was going in and out of the doors at night because she was not a fan of bugs at all. Trying to accommodate her fears of any insect that flies or bug with wings, she continued to work at the drive-in until she got another job.

A few months later, she was hired on at McDonald's and was content with working the drive-thru because she was safely indoors without having to dodge grasshoppers. One thing she believed in, was to say you at least tried to get what you want, instead of accepting failure at first sight. There was a constant battle of conflict between getting enough sleep for school and getting enough hours from work. Mrs. Daphne always warned her that if her grades dropped, then she would have to quit working to concentrate on what was important. By watching her mom struggle, she figured that the only important thing was to get money. True, you need to educate yourself but there is also a lesson in the struggle. You must remember how you got there, so you won't ever go back.

CHAPTER 6

"Love vs Drugs"

SHE WOULD OFTEN CALL INTO the radio and give her quickest raps through a hip-hop challenge called, *High School Holla*. She would make her mom rush her home from school so she could write down a few lines. She would have to call the radio station, only to get a busy line at least ten times in a row. To hear her voice, they were thrilled it was her calling back to compete again.

The joy with being on the radio, her friends would call just to say, "We heard you on the radio girl, you were tight." At school, she use to pass through the halls and some of the upperclassmen noticed her by being Londyn's little sister. She soon developed a name for herself because of the trouble she couldn't stay out of mostly, yet she was easygoing and free-spirited. Still working her job at McDonald's when she left band practice, she would always make time for her most favorite hobby, poetry. Feeling refreshed from her bath and full from dinner, she decided to take out her tablet and write down her thoughts.

Where are you when I need you
when my eyes are filled with tears
my soul is tired of pain
I hate the way I feel.
Where are you when I need you

you said you'd hold me tight
but your promises get broken
my sunny days, become cold nights.
Where are you when I need you
to comfort me with words
to pray and say the kindest things
my ears have never heard.
Where are you when I need you
my body shakes with fear
I would close my eyes and wish
to be anywhere, but here.
Where are you when I need you
if only humans could fly
one day I will be an Angel
and live beyond the sky.
Where are you when I need you
do you even know what's love?
If you cannot answer my question
don't love me just because.

She was now a junior and the eleventh grade seemed to have come around so quickly that she could only think about being an adult. She had been dating Dylan for two years now and their relationship was the best thing that she loved about school. She knew that love was only a word, backed up by emotions that were proven through actions. She had agreed to a relationship with Dylan in the ninth grade. By him being a sophomore, his experience and popularity only gave her more pull when it was needed. Although she was no pushover and didn't take crap from anyone, her genuine personality made her pleasant to be cool with. He warned her many times that he was becoming more jealous of the way she was so friendly and approachable.

"Why are you helping this grown man with homework, Loyalty? You owe him or something? He is not your responsibility, yet you seem to care whether he passes or fails." Dylan began to argue. Although she understood him, she could only come to her own defense.

"Dylan, be real, you act like I don't give you every ounce of love I have. If I give another guy a second of my attention, I'm not flirting or pretending to care about their needs. I'm just giving him the answers, because he doesn't know them and I do. That's it." She stated.

"Look, let him find his own girl that's smart enough to love and help educate him at the same time. I'm not going to sit here and allow him to find that in my girlfriend." He replied.

"Why are you being so mean about this? Not to mention, you're making it a bigger deal than it is. What do you want me to do, just start frowning at every guy that asks for help? It's not like I'm leading anyone on to believe that I'm single, when the whole school knows I'm very much taken." She stated, as she began to pull him close for a hug.

Not in the mood for love, he pushed her back. "Look, life is about decisions. If you keep making all the wrong choices to do the things I asked you not to do, then we're both going to have to decide what's more important. You're not a tutor, so stop acting like it. You're my girlfriend, so start acting like that." He walked off, leaving her standing in the hallway.

She couldn't understand for the life of her, why his emotional rage was starting to become a daily discussion of their relationship. She didn't know how to fix their problem, because even if she stopped helping guys with their homework or even giving them the answers. At the end of the day, she wasn't sure if that would be the answer to solve Dylan's problems. Walking off to her next class, she decided to find the solution he was looking for. How could she choose the friendship of others, over the relationship she adored? Sacrificing is one thing but to not even know the point in the sacrifice was the mind boggling moment she couldn't snap out of.

She did the only thing she could do, be honest. She saw her upperclassmen homies who were innocently, always speaking to her and made it known. Her boyfriend felt she was being too friendly, so she pushed back from their daily conversations. She could no longer stand outside the gym after school with her friends, because he hated other guys showing her attention. It wasn't that she was isolating herself from the opposite sex. She just had to place some sort of distance in between their friendship that would respect Dylan's wishes.

Weeks later, instead of always hanging out at the movies or chilling with friends, they decided to spend time alone. She decided to stay indoors and asked Mrs. Daphne if he could come over so they could watch movies while she cooked. Her mom always said it was okay, only if she was home while he was there.

That Sunday after church, Dylan decided that instead of going to their parents' houses, they would stop and eat at *Cheddars*. He then mentioned to Loyalty that he had enough to buy them a hotel room.

"How did you get enough for that and still be able to pay for the food? I bought so much stuff with my last check that I only have enough for lunch money until I get paid again. Of course I don't mind going, so it's whatever you want to do. It is Sunday, so we can't stay out late because school is tomorrow." She stated.

"Well, duh. If you think I don't know the days of the week, then maybe you should've been tutoring your own man instead of the football team." He joked. "I'm not broke, I'm just not rich. Let's eat so we can take a nap before your curfew. You had me on the phone all night talking my head off."

Leaving the restaurant with a to-go bag of food, he drove over to the Holiday Inn and went inside to purchase their room. She leaned her passenger seat back to relax as she closed her eyes and waited for him to return.

When he came back with the hotel key, he moved his car towards the back of the parking lot, as they usually would to keep from being seen. His car was very noticeable, being red, with dark tinted windows that had Dayton rims poking out, like the car Jody fixed up for Evette in, *"Baby Boy."*

Walking into the hotel, she sat her things down and turned on the television. Dylan began to take off his clothes, then jumped in bed with his boxers and socks on. Instantly climbing under the sheets, he wasted no time falling asleep. Taking off her dress, she put on his muscle shirt and kept on her boy shorts. She sat next to him on the bed, eating the extra food they had left, while watching lifetime network. He had never made her feel uncomfortable before or out of place when they laid together. Once she was finished with the food, she got underneath the covers and fell securely in his arms, drifting off into a nap of her own.

Someone started knocking at the door and she called out for Dylan to get up and answer it. When she didn't feel his arms around her, she looked over and noticed he was gone. Figuring he must of went to the vending machine because she ate all of his leftover food, he must had left his hotel key to get back in. Smirking, she got up to get the door but the happy feeling was quickly replaced with fear when she saw the dark six-foot man standing in the doorway. He stood there scratching his head with one hand on the door frame.

"Well, are you going to let me clean you?" He asked.

She jumped up in panic, breathing heavily, as she startled a sleeping Dylan. He could tell that she was frightened, so he grabbed her tightly.

"What is wrong with you Loyalty? Chill out, I got you. You see a bug or something?" Knowing how scared she was of even the smallest ladybug, he figured she must've seen an insect.

"Nothing, a bad dream I guess. Just go back to sleep, I'll wake you when it's time to leave." She stated, irritated.

"Didn't I tell you only dreams can be good. If something scares you, then it's a nightmare. You are too old and tough to fear the boogie man. Besides, don't be scared when you're with me. You make me feel like I can't protect you." He softly replied and kissed the back of her neck while holding her around the waist.

"My head is so filled with crap and my heart is so perfectly shattered. I'm not even sure how you love me sometimes. I just appreciate that you accept my flaws and beyond a boyfriend, you are always such a good friend to me." She spoke.

"I love you, so much more." He responded, while planting soft kisses along her back, neck and arms. Although she felt safe with him, she was starting to feel uncomfortable but couldn't let him know it.

"Are you ready?" He whispered.

She closed her eyes and couldn't even respond because it felt like her soul had jumped out of her body. She could assume that what he meant, was ready to leave the hotel. Although by the size growing in his boxers, she knew that he was speaking of her virginity. She could feel his manhood make a drastic change as he continued to hold her. He paused a moment, then asked again.

"Loyalty? Can I make love to you? Whatever you want, I'll do it. I promise I won't hurt you. Are you ready to take it there? Only if you want me to, I will make you feel good." He stated, while his hands roamed her small frame.

"Only because I love you so much Dylan but you already know what to do. Just don't laugh at me." She nudged his arm with her shoulder.

Knowing that he was no virgin, she felt inexperienced, so she allowed him to be in control. As he moved to position his body on top of her, she could tell that he was trying to look in her eyes, so she shyly closed them shut. Feeling his movements, she knew he was taking his boxers off and could only take a deep breath as she didn't know what to expect. Taking her underwear off, he never came back up and she could then feel his head between her legs. She tried to just relax but the old memories from her childhood started to play a part in what was currently happening. She was stuck between enjoying the moment from the pleasure and fighting back the unwanted memory from her past.

Kissing her thighs and then making his way up to her stomach, he removed the muscle shirt from her, while still kissing in every spot he thought he may have missed.

"Open your eyes. Look at me and only me. You are so beautiful and I've never been with anyone more gorgeous." He whispered, as he began to kiss her lips. With each passing second, he began to push inside of her more and more, taking away the very gift, she was scared to give away.

When she woke up, she noticed it was nine o'clock and she had to hurry to beat her curfew by ten. She went into the bathroom and took a shower, hoping to wash away whatever she thought Mrs. Daphne might notice different about her. She then woke up Dylan, by hitting him on the back at least six times until he finally decided to hop up and drive them home. When they got to his car, she couldn't bring herself to look at him in his face anymore and he noticed it.

"What's wrong with you baby, why are you acting different?" Stopping in their tracks, he grabbed her by the hand.

"Hello, because something is a little different now Dylan. Did you wake up with amnesia? Do you know what we've just done? I even feel different." She pouted.

"Come on babe, please don't do that. Don't act like we're guilty of something, because we're not. Nothing is going to change! I'm not going to break up with you and you damn sure are not going to break up with me. Amnesia? Ha! Oh, I remember very well what we just done. I won't ever forget it! I love you for trusting me. Don't feel bad like you just sinned on a Sunday, because it's no different from any other sin on a Thursday. God knows how much we love each other, so He will forgive us." He tried to convince.

"Ok, I'm sorry for overreacting. I just have a lot to think about and what just happened only made me feel more attatched to you." She pouted.

He chuckled. "You are such a baby Loyalty and I love it. Now let's go, I own you now girl. Chop. Chop." He joked, clapping his hands together.

Rolling her eyes at his humor, they drove away with the radio blasting. She could tell by his demeanor that he was in pure bliss about their evening. Although she enjoyed what happened and she was perfectly fine with her decision, sometimes the reality of your actions will replay through your mind until you accept it.

It was towards the end of the school year and things between them were still the same. They had their moments of disagreement and breakups but they were absolutely, unbreakable. Their bond was like no other and it seemed as after their first sexual encounter, they made it happen every chance they got. Hanging around Dylan more, she continued to be close friends with one of their mutual buddies, Caesar. They spent so much time at the studio because just like Loyalty, rapping was also a hobby of Dylan's. They had been there all day when she finally decided to tell him that it was time to get something to eat.

"Come on babe. I'm hungry, we can come right back." She whined.

"Not right now baby, I'm busy. Tell Buzz to take you. Your homegirl Cherish is with him, so you can go. You just better come right back. Here, get me something too." He demanded.

Smacking her lips, she stated. "Whatever Dylan."

"Cherish, can you and your boy take me to Taco Bell? Dylan is not going to let me drive his car, he says I don't know how to drive that good. So let's go, tell him." She nudged Cherish.

Now Buzz, who was a senior that hang around with Caesar and Dylan, had gotten his nickname from his favorite hobby, smoking marijuana. He would stay so high and reeked of the smell so much, that even if you got a whiff of his clothes, you would get a buzz. Once Cherish convinced him to bring her to get something to eat, he said that it was cool but he had to stop by and grab some weed first.

When they grabbed his marijuana, he pulled over to the corner store and purchased a pack of Swisher sweets. He handed the Swishers to Cherish and made her split it open. Then he reached in the backseat and handed Loyalty a tray that had a bag of marijuana on it.

"What am I supposed to do with this? I don't smoke." She stated.

"What else would you do with it smart girl, eat it? Just break it down for me. You know, pull it apart and bust the buds down into small pieces so Cherish can roll it for me. I'm driving and you getting a free ride, so help a brother out." He instructed.

She just shrugged her shoulders and did as she was told, then handed the tray to Cherish. Her homegirl however, was apparently no amateur when it came to rolling the swisher. She even grabbed a lighter from the ash tray and lit it up for him. Loyalty looked back and forth, observing their every move. They came to a red light and she couldn't help but cough from the contact, just by sitting in the car that was now covered in smoke.

"How does it make you feel? Is it like a cigarette? Or crack? Or like, would you turn into a dope fiend?" Loyalty continued to question. Knowing that she hated the smell of cigarette smoke, she could never be a cigarette smoker. Seeing the side effects from crack, she knew that she would never want to try such a drug. Weed was the most common drug at school and judging by her peers, they seemed to be perfectly fine.

Buzz laughed. "What are you, the police? You got a badge or wired with snitch tape? No, you won't be a dope fiend, you'll just be a weed smoker. It's not like crack but you will be hooked, if you like the feeling of being on another planet." He explained.

Cherish could only laugh at his explanation, as he tried to break down the aftermath of smoking.

"Let me see it. I just want to try it one time." Loyalty stated.

Buzz turned around and looked at her to see how serious she was, then handed her the Swisher, attempting to coach her on how she should inhale it. After taking at least two puffs, she began to feel a little different as they continued to ride. Since she joined the rotation, they said she couldn't just drop out. Those were the rules. By the time they reached Taco Bell, her appetite had grown tremendously and she began to simply order everything that looked good on the menu.

When they pulled back up to Caesars studio, Buzz warned her to chill and act as normal as possible, because Dylan would notice just by looking at her that she smoked. That's when she began to freak out and worry about him being upset with her actions. Before getting out the car, she put on some lip gloss and rubbed lotion in her hands, then grabbed their bag of food. It took no time for the scene to start, because both guys smelled it immediately.

Caesar, jokingly shouted to Buzz. "Man y'all smell good, you must've hit the perfect skunk. Let me inhale it."

"It took long enough. I thought y'all ran to the border just for tacos." Dylan laughed, looking through the bag of food.

When he looked at her, she couldn't even look him into the eyes without grinning. He could tell she was up to something, so he started to stare at her suspiciously. He finally put his finger on it, then set his food down and began to walk closer before he called judgment.

"Why can't you look at me? You guilty? I don't know, are you high maybe?" He grilled her.

"What?" She looked shocked, as if he was wrong.

"You heard me. High! Something that happens after you smoke weed? You want to be cool now? You want to be a follower? Because I sure thought you were a leader!" He raised his voice.

"I'm not a follower. Besides, you smoke. I just tried it, that's it. I'm sorry." She replied, with sadness.

"Look, I don't want you out here doing what everybody else does, or even what I do for that matter. Just be you and don't lose sight of that hanging with someone else. If you ever pick up another drug habit, I'll smack you. If you wanted to smoke, you could've been asked me. I'm your man, so I would've made that call. I don't want you doing any kind of drug with someone else because they could take advantage of you. I'm not trying to hurt your feelings but you have to be smarter than that." Dylan was now sitting on the chair in front of her, trying to explain himself.

"Come on man, you know me better than that. Don't ever think I'll let something happen to your girl. Plus, Cherish was with us and you know she going to look out for her friend. Relax." Buzz jumped in.

"I understand what you're saying bro but she's not your responsibility. She needs to understand where I'm coming from. It's not about who you're friends with. It's about who you can trust in any situation and sometimes that's a tough call to make." He replied.

Dylan began scratching his head and sighed, then pushed his chair back to the table where he was making a beat for their new song. She couldn't help but agree with him more, because she understood his argument and concern. Listening to him work, she just leaned back on the couch and enjoyed her new high. Respecting his wishes, she kept him informed about her new habit and only smoked when he knew of her whereabouts.

CHAPTER 7

"You Will Respect Me"

NOW THAT HIGH SCHOOL WAS over, it was time for something she had always dreamt of, college. Not planning on taking a break, she wanted to jump right back into her studies while she still felt like a student. There were plenty of valuable lessons she had learned during her four years at Central high. She gained a few friends yet also left more behind than she could recall. She was a popular girl in school, even though it couldn't get her free groceries at a store, it served its purpose when needed.

Her plans were initially to attend Southern University in Louisiana to join Dylan, who had gotten a scholarship with the band. She managed to become drum major when she tried out senior year but now that it was time to make that final call, band was just not one of her dreams. Dylan was already a freshman at the college and he would tell her how awesome the experience was every day. They continued their long-distance relationship, although it was a rocky road, the two still seemed inseparable.

Deciding to stay close to home, she enrolled into Lamar University so that she could continue living with her mother while she figured out her future. Telling Dylan of her plans, she was ecstatic to hear that he was also returning home to Texas for his sophomore year.

Loyalty had quit working at McDonald's when she began employment at Target, which was an upgrade because she was tired of working fast food. It was a pretty cool job because they worked around her college hours and even allowed her to pick up extra shifts on the weekends. Her only focus was to save up for a car and be able to purchase a new set of rims as well.

Still hanging tight with one of her close high school friends, Kashmere, she also remained close with Robin and Arielle. The girls were like a magnet for trouble, even though all they wanted to do was party, get a little money and live. It seems as if no matter what you're chasing, trouble will hunt you down anyway.

Waiting on her ride home from work, she saw Kashmere's 2002 silver Honda Accord with a nice set of rims, come around the corner and stop in front of her. She could tell by the thick smoke creeping out the cracked window, that her friends had come to pick her up with a blunt already lit.

"Girl, guess what. I saw this nice car for sale, it was parked right around the corner from here. A boujee neighborhood, so you know it's legit. Plus, she only wants four stacks for it. Do you have it?" Kashmere questioned, as she passed Loyalty the Swisher.

"No, not all of it. Just take me by there anyway so I can see it." She replied.

When they pulled up to the yard, Loyalty could tell that she was already sold and planned on buying this car. It wasn't much but it only had 30,000 miles on it, clean interior and seemed to be in good condition for a white, 1999 Ford Escort.

"Kash, take me home right quick. I have two grand in my radio at home, so I'm going to see if she will let me come back with the rest." She thought.

"Okay, put the blunt out though. I'm not pulling up with dro smoke coming out of the car if Mrs. Daphne is home." Kash replied.

Once the girls returned with the two grand, Loyalty approached the door and explained her situation to the elderly lady. She had a way with words, so she had high hopes that she could finesse her way into the car. It seemed to flatter the lady, once Loyalty explained that she was in college just trying to get back and forth from school while trying to help her mom with bills at the same time. Agreeing to leave the car parked inside the woman's garage, Loyalty faithfully showed up every two weeks with her paycheck until the car was paid off. She believed in working for what you wanted and no matter how you got it, no one can say they did it for you.

About a month later, she had worked enough hours and was now able to buy her first set of rims. Caesar helped her find the perfect set of 17-inch Stiletto rims and tires, that put the finishing touches on her very own whip.

Right after Loyalty accomplished her first goal, she was at work when she noticed one of the many girls that claimed to be dealing with Dylan, named Stacy. Kash, who also worked at Target, noticed Stacy come into the store and she immediately got eye contact with her friend. Stacy was more than likely up to no good, walking inside the store talking extremely loud and noticeable, so it wasn't hard to peep game.

Together, they both just watched her. "I hope she don't think she cute. I don't care how pretty her dress is, there is nothing cute about being a hoe. Trust me girl, she doesn't bother me." Loyalty stated.

"Well, she bothers me. She only walking in here to be seen and I'm sure they don't have money to buy nothing out of this store but a piece of gum. She just better not make the mistake and check out at either one of these registers. Because it will go down, uniform and all." Kash smirked.

When Stacy and her group of friends walked past the registers, they made a few remarks about Loyalty and Kash. Knowing exactly where the group of girls hung out, they planned on paying them a visit as soon as their shift ended.

Wanting to be in a different car, the girls called Alexi and explained to her the situation so that she could give them a ride. Trying to be low key and unseen, the three of them parked on the side of the house where Stacy and her friends were hanging out that night. Knowing that the girls had to eventually come outside, they just sat in Alexi's car as if it were a stakeout.

Within twenty minutes, the front door opened and out walked four girls, one of them being Stacy. Loyalty hopped out of the car, accompanied by her two friends, as she approached Stacy with immediate confrontation.

"So you came to my job to be seen, like I wouldn't see you in the streets. You couldn't have Dylan if I gave him to you. Now look where being a hoe got you." Loyalty grilled.

"Girl, I am not worried about you and I do not like Dylan either. I'm not trying to fight…" Stacy tried to reply but was interrupted by a punch to her face.

Knowing that she was only trying to talk her way out of confrontation, Loyalty was not trying to hear her plea full of lies. She had already warned Stacy before about the rumors she had heard but only gave Dylan the benefit of doubt. She couldn't put it past him of his dealings with the girl but she was also not about to keep dealing with the drama. In her eyes, the fight was inevitable and it was very well asked for.

Weeks later, Loyalty and her friends had attended a college party that ended in a fight, which apparently had her accidentally connected to. Maybe she looked like one of the girls who fought or maybe looked like an easy target. Either way, Sade, a girl from the other end of town approached her after the party and told her she wanted to fight.

Confused on the reason behind it, Loyalty frowned her face at the girls' statement but did not back down from the challenge. During the midst of chaos, she mentioned to her friends who attended the college party with her, that Sade wanted to fight. With everyone on the same page, they all left the party to meet up at the closest park to avoid any arrests by campus police.

"So, what did you do? How does she even know us? Why did she say she wants to fight? She must think you scared but it's cool, just don't stop swinging once it starts." Kash eagerly stated.

"I don't know, she just came up and looked right at me saying that she wanted to fight. I started to explain that I'm not who she must think that I am but on the other hand, she approached me all wrong. So, it's whatever." She shrugged.

Being that the college was on the opposite side of town of where they were from, Kash called her family to meet them in the South, in case they were outnumbered. When she dialed her grandmother's number, she spoke with her cousin Paris, who relayed the message. She told everyone there that the girls had gotten into some trouble on the other end of town. By the time the girls pulled up to the park, they noticed there were about thirty people from the South just waiting for them to get out.

"Man look at this, did they really have to get this many people for little ol' me." They all laughed at Loyalty's statement.

With it only being five of them, they knew for sure if they had gotten out the car, it would have been thirty against five. You did not have to be a wiz in math to know that wasn't fair. As soon as the girls tied up their hair, they noticed headlights from about six cars pull into the open parking lot. Paris came right on time and had quickly gathered up the right amount of people who came for some action. Once the cars parked, everyone got out to greet each other and catch up on what just transpired.

"What's the problem? We got here fast, huh? Is that them over there? What are we standing over here for?" Paris stated, accompanied by her best friend Arin, cousin Vicki and a few other family members, including guys.

"They said she wants to fight me because I'm from the North. She is supposed to be one of the toughest from the other side, so let's find out." Loyalty informed, as they all walked across the pavement.

Robin, Arielle, Alexi, and Kash each joined the crowd as everyone from both sides gathered in a huge circle to surround the girls. Curiosity filled everyone as they anticipated watching the fight that was about to take place. Once the girls were in arms reach, they wasted no time connecting fists. Everyone gathered around in the open circle and gave the two just enough space to have a brawl that was asked for. You could hear both sides chanting and coaching for their friend to win when things took a turn for the worst.

Once Sade was tired of swinging, she grabbed Loyalty by the hair and tried to wrestle her down. The crowd began moving in closer, in fact too close, that it escalated into something the South had enough people for but not enough fighters. Vicki threw the first punch at Sade to stop her from wrestling Loyalty to the ground. That was the only lick everyone needed to see before a few other fights broke off into their own corner. Once Loyalty was free from the scuffle, she noticed one of Sade's friends who had a lot to say earlier that night. She directed a few words to the girl as she slowly walked to approach her for an altercation. Before she could even reach her, some of Kash's cousins that were not already fighting, jumped all over the girl when they noticed Loyalty had a new problem. She did the only thing she was supposed to do at that time, which was started throwing a few punches of her own. Everyone heard sirens and they knew someone had called the police, so the crowd began to disburse. Trying to make it back to their cars, they had to break up a few of the guys who had started fighting as well.

They all met up at the nearest Waffle House and ate breakfast as they sat there laughing the whole night about the fight. Kash was the type of friend that was truly down for whatever, whether she was wrong or right. That was the first time out of many, where they all indulged in a crowd brawl. It seemed as if after that night, they fought nearly every other weekend.

Chilling at Caesar's studio one day with Dylan, they had been arguing for the past few days about some girl named Felicia that constantly came over. He kept trying to explain that she was there for one of his friends but he did admit to her being a little flirtatious with him. Trying to convince his girl that it wasn't what she thought but there is no outsmarting a woman who believes in what she sees.

The couple had gone out to eat and then to a movie, before returning to the studio and recognizing Felicia's truck parked in the driveway when they arrived. She knew that she couldn't control Caesars company but she wasn't there for him because of his relationship with Carli for the past few years. She had every intention on confronting Felicia for her slutty gestures towards Dylan and it was the perfect time.

"I pretty much do everything you ask me too. If you can't tell this slut to respect your girlfriend and her wishes, then I will." She demanded.

"You're overreacting Loyalty, I only speak back to her, to not be rude. You told me to change my number because she had gotten it and was calling unnecessarily, so I did it. Now you want me to tell her to stop sitting on my car when she comes over. I can't do that. What else do you want me to do, vanish?" Dylan argued.

"All right, that's fine, you trying to spare her feelings at the expense of playing with mine. Don't even worry about it." She stormed off.

Walking outside, she was too emotional for confrontation, so she decided that she would just hop in her car and leave. Just as she sat in her drivers seat to close her door, she heard Felicia and her friends' smart remarks. She paused, with her left leg resting on the concrete and her right foot on the floor of her car. She looked at the three girls right in their faces to address them accordingly.

"I'm sorry, it sounds like I heard somebody trying to be funny. What's up?" She asked.

"You wait until you get in your car and start talking trash, bye Loyalty! You a joke." Felicia laughed, not knowing she added fuel to a growing flame.

"Talking? Joke? Well, I'm not in the car anymore. What's up?" Loyalty jumped back out of the car and walked over to Felicia.

She was trying to sit so pretty on the trunk of Dylan's car. Loyalty quickly grabbed her leg that was hanging off and made her fall to the ground. She forgot all about Felicia's two friends that were sitting in the yard as well, who were so tickled by Loyalty's presence. They each just watched their friend get beat up while being pulled by her hair and did nothing. Ceasar, noticed the fight from the camera inside the studio and ran outside to break them up. Loyalty would not let go of Felicia's hair as she kept landing punches repeatedly until Dylan came out. He forcefully grabbed her around the waist and held her three feet from the ground, walking her to her car.

"What are you doing, have you really lost your mind? You out here wilding, acting like a mad woman. Are you crazy?" He shouted.

"Yes, exactly Dylan! As a matter of fact, I am crazy, but I'm not stupid. Move!" She pushed him away, then slammed her car door.

Loyalty smashed on the gas, with her middle finger pointing out of her window. Leaving tire marks in the street, she sped off shouting. "BYE FELICIA".

CHAPTER 8

"Hurricane Hell"

It was the second day of class in fall semester and Loyalty was now a sophomore with more things on her plate than she could handle. Although she knew classes were a bit stressful, she laid in bed that morning with more on her mind than school work. Feeling as if she had came down with the worst cold ever, she had no choice but to visit her family doctor. With a temperature of 103.4, she was advised that she had the flu and strep throat. Due to her unexpected illness, she was forced to miss the next few weeks of her classes.

When she returned to campus, she was advised that she had been dropped from her courses because of her attendance. With proper documentation, she showed admissions her only excuse for missing the previous weeks. Sadly, she was still removed from the courses unless she paid in full because her financial aid was no longer valid. She couldn't believe that although she had a legitimate reason for missing school, she was held accountable for something beyond her control.

Sitting on the stairs in front of the school library, it took everything in her to hold back the tears. With her elbows resting on her knees, both hands gripped together and her chin resting on her thumbs. She could only take a deep breath and close her eyes as she faced reality. Accepting what she could not change, it changed her mood to focus on her next move.

Later that night, she headed home from partying with her friends, trying to take her mind off of things. She had just thrown out the last of her Swisher, when she turned the corner and noticed the flashing lights in her rearview mirror. Unaware of what she did wrong, she smacked her lips and pulled to the side of the street. Agitated, she had her drivers license and insurance ready for the officer when he approached her window.

"Hello Mr. Cop, you mind telling me how I broke the law?" She questioned.

"How you doing ma'am? I noticed you did not use proper signal when you made that left turn. Now that I'm standing here, there is a strong smell of marijuana coming from your vehicle. Do you mind if I search? Unless you want to show me where it is." The officer replied.

"Go ahead, do your job. I don't have any on me because I smoked it all and I'm just trying to go home to get some sleep man." She shrugged, hopping out of the car.

Not finding anything, the officer instructed her to remain standing to the side of the road while he ran her name in for any warrants. She was so happy that she had smoked the last of her weed and didn't have anything illegal on her. Almost certain she was warrant free because she had not been into any trouble, she was becoming impatient waiting for the officer to return.

"Well, Ms. Brown, I'm afraid I'm going to have to take you in because you have an outstanding warrant for assault. By the look on your face I can tell you are not aware but I'm just doing my job." Taking out his handcuffs, he closed them on her wrists.

"Wait. What? Assault on who? What about my car? How much is it to get out? I'm so sleepy and I do not feel like going to jail right now. This has got to be the worst night ever." She stated, as she was placed inside the patrol car.

Arriving to jail for the first time, it was surprisingly an experience she never envisioned for her future. When they allowed her a phone call, she immediately dialed her father. Although he would overreact and preach to her like she was about to serve a life sentence, she knew he would come to bail her out. Learning of the girl who pressed charges against her, she told the cops she had never heard of the girls' name before. They laughed at her statement, saying that she was just like all the others, jailed for being innocent. She honestly stated, that she had so many fights in her past, she couldn't recall most of their names.

When Mr. Ralph picked her up, he talked to her about making better decisions until they reached their destination. She had no comments and could not put up an argument because she was so exhausted from partying. She laid her head on the passenger window and began to think about Nyla. She missed her cousin so much and could only think about where she would be in life if they were still best buds. Feeling that Nyla didn't get the opportunity to graduate high school or even attend the college of her dreams. She began to appreciate even the bad things and be thankful for life itself, because it could be worse.

Since she was no longer in school, they changed her hours so that she could make more money. Noticing that everyone was buying cases of water, bags of ice, coolers and just about the entire store, she couldn't help but ask what was the occasion. Her coworkers informed her that a hurricane was coming their way and the city of Beaumont and surrounding areas were due for a mandatory evacuation. Shocked by hearing the news, she wasn't sure if her mom had heard, so she took a break to give her a call.

"Hey, Ma! Did you know we had to evacuate, why haven't you mentioned that yet? Where are we going? They said it's called hurricane Rita, like a category five that is supposed to hit tomorrow night. I'm about to leave work now so we can get things together." She rambled. This had never happened before so the thought of a deadly hurricane was scary.

"I'm not sure yet, I just heard all of this myself. They just announced the evacuation and we can't go to Liberty's house because Houston must evacuate as well. We may have to go further towards Dallas. We have family there so we will be okay, just hurry home." Mrs. Daphne instructed.

Leaving work, she called her friends to make sure they were aware of what was about to hit their hometown. When she spoke with Dylan, he said him and his mother were not leaving and that they had the necessary things to have a safe stay. She yelled and told him how crazy he sounded because by watching the news, it was definitely not a storm worth taking the chance of waiting out. After hours of convincing Dylan to evacuate, they finally agreed to follow her family to a safe destination out of the storms' path.

After arriving to their safe location at a relative's house in Palestine, they gathered around the television in disbelief as they watched the aftermath of hurricane Rita. Curious to go home and face the wreckage of what the storm left behind, it was now time to return to the normal. Everything seemed unreal when the family drove through their city that was a ghost town. Because there was no power, you could not be seen outside past 7 o'clock or the police would place you in jail for one night. There were empty lots that once stood buildings and cars flipped upside down. Trees laid on top of houses and in the street, so it was like a maze to find your home if it was still standing.

When they came up to their cul-de-sac, Mrs. Daphne could no longer drive because the trees and debris were blocking the rest of the street. The family walked to their home to check out the damage and collect anything that was worth keeping. Water was everywhere inside the home, which damaged a lot of their things. Even allowing a snake inside that rested against the shoes in Londyn's bedroom. Grabbing a few things that were salvageable, they each returned to their cars and headed for the highway. The news had announced that Houston was now allowing the residents back into their homes, so they headed to Liberty's house for shelter. Liberty had a brick two-story home that conveniently housed everyone very comfortably. Even though there was still a power outage, Liberty's husband purchased a generator before evacuating that came in handy. Loyalty wasn't sure what was going on in the world but she could almost guarantee that mother nature called all the shots.

Loyalty's family decided to relocate after hurricane Rita, leaving behind whatever remained in Beaumont, to find employment and a place to stay in Houston. Loyalty on the other hand, was not ready for another long-distance relationship with Dylan. Although their relationship was not perfect and it seemed to be getting worse, she could not just call it quits. She had to explain to Mrs. Daphne, in hopes that she would understand her plans to continue life in their hometown with Dylan. There were so many reasons her mother disagreed with her decision but acknowledging her daughter was of age to make her own choices, she reluctantly let her be.

Caesar allowed Dylan to become his roommate and move in at his three bedroom house. After explaining to him the choice she made to return home, they agreed that she would stay with them as well. Carli, who was Caesar's girlfriend, did not move into the home with them until she graduated high school. Dylan explained to Loyalty that they both needed better jobs with more income, because he was hoping to have their own apartment by the time Carli had her baby. For some reason, Loyalty's luck was wearing thin because that same day she was fired from her job.

She dreaded walking into the house to tell Dylan about her day. When she walked in to prepare for the argument, she overheard him having a conversation of his own. He was speaking in such a low tone that she couldn't make out what he was saying because his voice was nearly a whisper. Knowing that he was being sneaky, she just stood in the doorway until he was done talking. The bathroom door opened and he had the look of guilt across his face.

"Hey babe, you off early. How long you been standing there?" He asked.

"Long enough to hear you barking like the dog that you are." She replied, folding her arms.

"Here you go! I just finished using the bathroom but yes, it was a girl I was talking too. It was my homies' cousin; she's trying to get me hired at the plant so I can stop working at Coca-Cola. We need more money and you know that!" He stated in defense.

"I don't like liars Dylan. You of all people should know that it's not what you do, it's how you go about doing it. I'll be back later." She stated, as she grabbed a few things from their room and left.

Leaving from Caesar's house, she called her home girls to see what they were up to because she needed a deep conversation and someone to vent to. Her family was now residing in Houston and she didn't have anywhere else to go. She started to realize that Dylan was not where she wanted to be. Pulling up to Kash's house, Robin and Arielle, were already sitting underneath the carport smoking a blunt. Knowing that everybody played the fool sometimes, she was ready to tell her friends of her newfound reality.

"What's up y'all? Pass me the Swisher, I got some extra in my purse that you can roll up. Let me tell you about my life in a nutshell. I got fired today. Not to mention, I'm no longer a college student because the flu made me miss too many days. I paid the balance to my lawyer last week, it was only $1000 for him to defend me. Yet, I still end up on probation for assaulting someone I never even heard of. So now, I need a new job and a new place to stay, because I do not want to be with Dylan any longer. He's playing me! I don't know it but I can feel it." She vented.

"Damn girl." Everyone said in union.

"So you mean to tell me, you paid your lawyer to find you guilty? Plus, you were kicked out of school behind some cold symptoms? You're still wearing your uniform from a job that fired you hours ago? After seven years of dating your first love, you're finally ready to move on?" Kash asked in disbelief.

"Thank you for the recap, Kash. You made it sound very delightful. Yes, that's exactly what I'm saying." She sarcastically replied.

"Pass the swisher, because you're doing too much talking and not enough smoking. Besides, it could be worse. All you need is another job that you can start looking for tomorrow. Your dad still stays out here, so why don't you go stay with Mr. Ralph, he seems pretty cool anyway. He's hardly ever home, so it's like you have the place to yourself. Probation is messed up but you can't do anything about it now besides pay your fees and don't get into any more trouble for a year. Dylan? Now that is a problem you must solve on your own. You have to figure out where your heart is, because it will have your mind playing tricks on you." Arielle stated, as a cloud of smoke escaped her mouth.

"I say, let's go change into something cute and see what fun we can bump into tonight. Forget about your problems girl, because they sound so easy to solve." Robin joined in.

The girls agreed and went their separate ways so they could get dressed for a little night of partying. Once they met up that evening, they started off at the towns bowling alley where everyone hung around outside. Afterwards, they went out to eat and had a few drinks then decided to stop by the sports bar to end their night. Before they could make it to hang out at their last destination, Kash noticed Dylan's car was parked on the side of the street in front of an unfamiliar house.

"Wait a minute, is that Dylan's car or am I tripping?" Kash asked, slowing down and turning off her headlights a few houses away.

"Where? Yep, you sure right, that's it. Whose house is this Loyalty? Call him." Arielle stated.

"I know whose house it is, Brenda stays here, Felicia's cousin. The same Felicia you just beat up not that long ago. Let's get out." Robin eagerly replied.

"No. No. No. Let's just wait for him to come out and beat him up. It's four of us, we can take him." Kash convinced.

"What do you want to do Loyalty? While you just sitting here like you don't see what we see." Arielle responded, irritated by the way Loyalty sat in silence.

Gathering her thoughts, there were so many words that she wanted to say all at one time but instead she was speechless. As she always taught herself, crying has never solved anything. Yet for so many reasons, the only thing she could do was sit back and allow the tears to form in her eyes.

"Are you about to cry? That's it, Arielle get in the driver seat. Just be ready to drive in case something bad pops off and I just need to hop in. Robin, you be the lookout, there is nothing that should happen unless you see it first." Kash instructed, as she hopped out of the car and pulled her hooded jacket over her head.

Kash was moving through yards like she was a ninja trying to blend in with the night. Approaching the trunk of Dylan's car, she was just about to reach the back tire, so that she could proceed to put all of them on flat. Just as she pulled her pointed knife from her hoodie, the car cranked up and he drove off. Startled, not wanting him to catch her in mid attempt, Kash dropped to the ground and laid flat until Arielle pulled up alongside of her.

When she hopped into the passenger seat, she couldn't resist the laughter as they drove off and attempted to follow Dylan's car. The whole scenario seemed to change Loyalty's demeanor and she saw humor in the situation even though it was real. Keeping a distance behind his car, she knew by the route he was taking that he was headed back to Caesars. As soon as the girls pulled into the driveway, they allowed Loyalty to go inside and gather her things while they waited.

"What's up babe, looking good! You want to go have some drinks?" Dylan asked.

"No thanks, Dylan. I'm really not feeling this whole relationship thing anymore. You are not faithful, which that's okay because you're young and stupid. Yet for you to be a pretender, I'm not going to sit here and pretend with you. It's over." She firmly stated, walking past him.

Looking puzzled, Dylan was at a loss for words as he watched Loyalty pack up her belongings. Not sure of what to say, he could only react as he began to lose his temper that further escalated the situation.

"What do you mean, over? You must have found somebody else, now you want to join the crowd and be a hoe. Is that it?" He yelled.

"No, I just don't want to be in a relationship with one. You are the only hoe in this room." She shouted back.

By now, Loyalty had gathered all that she was bringing and proceeded to walk outside to place her things inside the trunk. Their argument had become heated and their voices were being raised more than the usual. Caesar and a few guys tried to de-escalate the situation but it was no use as the two continued to yell at each other. Loyalty had never seen Dylan so upset and furthermore, he had never called her out of her name in such a disrespectful manner. She felt that he was hurt but knew that he was a cheater, so he was angry at his own faults that led up to their breakup.

"Go ahead then, leave trick. You been wanting to do that anyway. You think I'm going to cry? Life goes on baby girl but you going to miss me first." He stated, following behind her every step.

"I advise you to stop following me before I turn around and make this physical. I'm glad you acting tough now but remember, the same thing that makes you laugh will make you cry. To say you don't care, you sure are being a little dramatic and making a scene when this could have been peaceful." She smirked.

"Don't get smart and try to show off in front of your little friends. Just make sure you tell them that you can now be the bopper that you are." He laughed, now standing face-to-face.

"Call me one more name and I'm going to smack you." She challenged him.

"I'm not scared of you bit--…" He tried to reply but was cut off by an open hand smack across his face.

When Loyalty slapped him, he grabbed her around the neck and started to choke her. Caesar grabbed him and attempted to pull him back but she charged at him to throw a few punches. He broke the hold Caesar had on his arm and managed to forcefully push her down, sliding her through the dirt. Dylan proceeded to pull her up by her collar, while she laid on her back kicking and swinging. Looking up, she then noticed that Kash was on his back, hitting him with a wire hanger. He threw her off, then tried to grab her but Caesar and the other guys grabbed him again. Pulling him inside the house, they were trying to calm him down and tell him to just let it go.

Driving away from the home, the girls had a brief discussion about how mean and inconsiderate guys are when love is no longer in their favor. Sometimes they do things that they themselves cannot explain and since they can't go back to right their wrongs, they will blame everyone for their own faults. Dylan was the only guy that she had been with, so to end their relationship, she felt like a lost sheep around wolves.

CHAPTER 9

"New Company"

IT HAD BEEN A FEW months since the breakup with Dylan, yet she just couldn't stop the tears from falling every time she heard of him messing with a different chic. She was looking for a job just about every day, filling out application after application but there was just no luck. Luckily, Mr. Ralph still saw her as his baby girl and allowed her to move in and make herself comfortably at home. He had a two bedroom, two bath, townhome located in a nice part of town where she was even able to safely park her car under his shed. Knowing that his daughter had fell on hard times, he paid her insurance and phone bill until she could provide for herself again.

Though it seemed as if all she could do was sit at home and get high. She smoked blunt after blunt until she was numb and unable to feel the heartbreak she was suffering. It seemed crazy that after seven years of dating her high school sweetheart, she felt as if she didn't have a clue of where to even begin a new love-life. What hurt the most was that Dylan appeared to be living happily ever after, enjoying his new life as a bachelor. She wanted nothing more than to get over this phase, so there was something that had to be done to clear her mind.

Unable to find a job, she returned to her old habit of stealing. They would take just about anything that was worth it, as long as it sold. Once boosting became a trend for nearly everyone her age, her clientele wasn't always worth the back and forth trips to the malls.

One day, she was selling a few clothes from her trunk when she spotted Robin's baby's daddy, Polo. He walked over to check out a few of the Levi's she had picked up from the mall that day. She could tell by the way he came over grinning, that he had something smart to say. Always trying to catch a deal, she couldn't help but smirk and roll her eyes as he got closer.

"What up Loyalty? What ya' thieving ass got in that trunk today?" He laughed.

"Something you paying for if you want it! No deals." She barked.

"Man I got you, let your boy get two for 30 bucks." He hustled.

"You must be crazy or stupid high!" She laughed.

"Why you bugging, let's make a deal. Let me get this white and gray pair from ya'. I'll give you this Ziploc of greenery." He stated, then reached in his hoodie and presented a Ziploc bag of weed.

"What I look like, a weed head?" She questioned.

"A little!" He joked. "Look, it's not for you to smoke it all genius. I see you be hustling, so why not make another profit. I'll look out for you since you my baby mama's homegirl and you keep it real. Really, it's some Reggie and I only move dro. Somebody gave it to me because they owed me. I was just smoking out of it but since we can make a trade, this will benefit you more than me."

Hesitantly, she thought about her options, which weren't many. So it didn't take long to accept his offer, then head home to do just as she was told. Trying to avoid her daddy once she got in the house, she had everything inside a shopping bag and walked quickly to her room. He knew that she smoked and was not judgmental to her behavior. To keep her from trouble on the streets, he insisted before that she should only smoke at home to avoid being caught by police while driving.

Pulling out the scale from the shopping bag, she began weighing 7-gram dime sacks in small sandwich bags, then tied a knot into each one. Once she sold them all, she calculated to have an extra two hundred bucks in her pocket. Not bad to say she only sacrificed two pairs of pants to have a bigger fortune.

She pulled up to Kash's house and told her about the Ziploc she had gotten that needed to sell quick. Just as she thought, Kash was ready to assist her in locating all the right smokers.

"We just have to hit the right licks and nine times out of ten, they're just going to pass the word. If we're lucky, we might just bump into a group of weed smokers." Kash laughed.

Surprisingly, it was easier than expected once they rode around and spotted a few friends. Their mission was complete in less than 24 hours. It became easy and not much of a hassle, so she continued to get a Ziploc from Polo every now and then. Looking for a job became a thing of the past, as she became content with her two hustles.

Her mind was less on Dylan, because she was so occupied during the day. Sadly, once night fell, her heart began talking to her and crying out. She continued to go to Caesar's studio, although her relationship with Dylan was over, she remained friends with everyone else. In the midst, of laughter and music, she was startled and taken by surprise when she noticed Dylan walk through the studio door. Apparently, he was bothered by her presence because he really didn't say too much.

Few minutes later, a group of guys walked in to discuss some dog fights. Not interested in the conversation, Loyalty and Kash headed outside and sat on the car to indulge in a daily smoke session. In less than 15 minutes, the crowd gathered outside and she noticed one guy in particular that kept peeping her. The most arrogant one of the bunch, she watched how Dylan interacted with him like this guy was some kind of dog God.

"Come on, let's go get a snack or something. I got the munchies." Kash suggested.

"Cool, me too." Loyalty laughed and slid off the hood.

The girls went to the nearest Dairy Queen for burgers and blizzards as they stood in line with their eyes bloodshot red. Kash paid for her food, then moved aside so Loyalty could take a century to decide on which candy she wanted in her ice cream.

"Is that all for you? Would you like caramel or chocolate?" The cashier asked.

"OMG, Loyalty just pick one. Dang!" Kash rushed.

"Girl hush! Let me see, ummmmmm…" She thought.

"Chocolate!" The voice behind them stated. "Give her chocolate."

When the girls turned around, it was the arrogant guy from Caesar's studio. Noticing that he was quite cute to be a thug, she quickly referred her attention back to the cashier and completed her order.

"Yeah that's fine, just give me chocolate but only a little." She stated, as the guy placed a twenty on the counter for her food.

"What if I want to give you a lot?" He stated, placing his money back into his pocket as if it took a whole bankroll to pay for burgers and blizzards.

He ordered his nachos and soda, then stood next to Loyalty to continue the small talk.

"Thanks, Mr. Stranger but you didn't have to. I'm a big girl." She informed.

"Girl you a baby, stop it. I like light skinned girls, even though you more like a red-bone. Didn't you say you like chocolate?" He asked, licking his lips.

"No, YOU said I liked chocolate." She informed.

"Well, since I'm already making decisions for you, call me later. Better yet, give me your number because you look like the type that act funny." He laughed.

For so many reasons, she was unsure of giving her number because she wasn't ready for a hood dude. Sure, he was cute, dark skinned and had a sense of humor but everything else about him screamed out, thug. From his gold teeth, the big wad of money, the loudspeaker system he had in his car, plus the saggy jeans with the fitted cap was a dead give a way. This wasn't the first time someone had tried to get her number, although this was the only time she could remember that she actually entertained it. Knowing that she had nothing else to lose, she felt wrong in the inside because she still loved Dylan. Yet, because Dylan never thought about her feelings, she smirked as she gave off each digit of her number. Kash was so excited for her once they got back in the car. She couldn't stop talking about how it was time for her friend to finally get over her high school sweetheart.

The very next morning her phone rang, by it being an unfamiliar number, she assumed it was someone who wanted to buy a dime sack.

"Yo, who's this?" She answered.

"What?" He laughed. "That is no way for you to answer your phone little girl. Try, good morning daddy!" He continued to laugh, like it wasn't 8 o'clock in the morning.

"Why are you calling me so early?" Recognizing his voice, she was almost irritated.

"Relax baby, you should be glad you are the first thing I think about when I wake up!" He tried using his charm to disregard the time.

Yawning, she stated, "What do you want?"

"YOU." He bluntly stated. They talked on the phone for the next thirty minutes until her phone died from not being charged the previous night.

When she got out of the shower, she laid back on her bed wrapped in a towel and contemplated what she would do that day. Just when she was about to drift back off into a good sleep, her phone sounded off. Snatching it from the charging cord, she typed in her password and noticed that it was a text notification.

    Incoming : I WANT YOU
    Outgoing : You're not my type
    Incoming : I don't care
    Outgoing : lol that was lame
    Incoming : Let me show you I'm not
    Outgoing : I can't
    Incoming : STOP IT. Can I see you now?
    Outgoing : NO!!!
    Incoming : Meet me at Lucky 7. I'm waiting!
    Incoming : Don't make me come to your daddy house

Reading his last text message, she couldn't help but freak out in an instant. How did he know she stayed with her daddy? She rushed to slip some jeans on and a t-shirt, then slid into some J's. The Lucky 7 was a grocery store in the hood, a very busy store at that, on the corner of Magnolia. She didn't want to be seen in public talking to him, for one, she didn't even know his name yet. As she pulled into the parking lot, she noticed his blue Lincoln with tinted windows and very annoying music blaring. She got out of her car and approached his driver's side window so she could grill him in an instant.

    "How did you know I stayed with my daddy?" She immediately wanted to know.

    "Let's just say, I did my homework. Come around and get in." He demanded.

    Standing there as if she wasn't just ordered to do something, she was uneasy about even sitting in his car. What if he tried something? Looking around at her surroundings, she was more than sure that she had landed herself a 'boy in the hood'.

"What do you mean, you did your homework? What is your name?" She asked.

"I mean that once I got your number, I asked a few people about you. I remember you from the studio and you run around with Kash. I'm cool with her cousin. I know you a baby, in my eyes. You just broke up with your ex after years of puppy love. I like you and I like your name. It's different. You different. My name is Teddy but they call me T." He stated, all in a nutshell.

Taken by surprise, she was actually moved by his brief introduction and considered talking to him a little longer. They sat in the car and talked for hours as he drove around, allowing her to get to know him a little better. Before she knew it, they spent the whole day together and for the first time in a long time, she didn't seem so lonely. She admitted that talking to him was a good feeling. They spoke nearly every day and fell asleep on the phone just about every night. Within a couple weeks of just kisses and hugs, she was laying in bed one night and found herself wanting to be touched by him. As if he could read her mind, she was startled by her phone notification.

Incoming : What are you doing?
Outgoing : Thinking about you
Incoming : Word? Can I come get you?
Outgoing : To go where? It's late
Incoming : Wherever you wanna go

Holding the phone, she contemplated her next message. Her honesty would sometimes get the best of her to where she could not sugarcoat things. Before she knew it, she had replied.

Outgoing : I haven't had sex in forever
Incoming : Let me help you with that
Outgoing : Call me when you have time
Incoming : I'm on my way!

Within ten minutes, Teddy was outside waiting but she wasn't schooled on the sex game like he was. She was only 19 and he was 23 with a bigger frame, plus he was a thug. She was sure she had signed up for failure. Yet it was too late and her mind was made up, so she thought. Hopping in the passenger seat, she was immediately uncomfortable and tried her hardest not to show her nervousness. She could feel him glancing over at her and when they locked eyes, he licked his lips then turned away with a smirk.

"Oh, shit." She thought, "I wanna go home, I wanna go home." She wanted to just get it over with and finally know what another man felt like. She was hoping Dylan never found out. Then a part of her wanted him to know and feel all the pain by just that one guy, as she did all those girls he dealt with. Too late to turn back, he was doing just as she presented and was about to give her what she asked for. They pulled up to The Marriot Hotel and her heart almost jumped out of her chest when he cut the car off. While he stood at the front desk getting a room for them, memories of Dylan crowded her mind. She had never slept with anyone but him. Now she was blaming herself for moving on, when she knew she had too.

Once inside the room, he made the vibe feel normal like they were just chilling. It was a big relief because she would feel like a big kid if she allowed herself to chicken out. A piece of her just wanted to experience someone else and answer her own curiosity. With only the TV on, she could see him undressing. He was really a grown man, unashamed and ready for business because he took off everything in an instant.

"Take off your clothes and come here." He demanded.

Frozen, she whispered. "I can't."

"Don't tell me you're shy. You're too beautiful too be hiding. Let me see you." He laughed.

"I'm serious though. I really can't. Like, I want to but I've never…" She stopped.

"I know, I know… you use to that high school shit and never had a thug love you. I'll make it easier for you." He stated. Cutting off the TV, in total darkness, she knew he was coming for her so she closed her eyes and anticipated his touch. He stood her up to begin undressing her, then pulled back the covers and pushed her down. Deeply kissing her, she couldn't help but give in to pleasure as he proceeded to introduce her to gangster loving. Dylan was good and satisfied her all those years. However, she now had a taste of someone else who roughly handled her so gently. That night, she slept like the baby he always said she was.

After their first time, he teased her everyday about biting off more than she could chew. Which was no denying and she could only thank him for showing her exactly what she never knew. They continued their normal talking habits, as they both agreed that's all it would be. She did let him know how much her heart was forever grateful that he was able to take her mind off of Dylan. He in return, shared with her that it was nice to just bond with a cool chic who made him laugh. They enjoyed each other for a few more months but she slowly just became more busy. If she wasn't trying to hustle up something or dodge drama, she was at home exhausted. He reached out to her on a Friday night and mentioned that he missed them kicking it on the weekend and although she missed that too, they both knew what they had was slowly fading. Not trying to catch feelings for anyone no time soon, her mind was strictly on what's best for her, so love was a foreign language.

Almost a year later, she had become so sick, all she could do was stay in bed with symptoms like she had the flu. Covered up in a blanket, sneezing and shaking, she was sure she had pneumonia. Gathering all her strength, she managed to drive herself to the nearest hospital where she waited hours for treatment. She was so hungry but she couldn't keep anything down for even five minutes without throwing it up. Feeling like it was her deathbed, she was relieved to finally see the nurses coming in with her diagnosis.

"Well Ms. Brown, we have some good news and some bad news." The petite nurse grinned. "The bad news, is that you have a horrible respiratory infection, which we will treat with meds. The good news is, you have a positive pregnancy test, congratulations!"

"WHATT!! Good news? I can't be pregnant! Noooooo." She burst into tears.

Leaving the hospital, she couldn't decide what the nurse meant but was for sure that she had it confused. Possibly, the good news was the infection and the bad news was definitely a positive pregnancy. Not sure of what to do or who to even tell, all she could do was sit in the car and cry.

"Kashhhhh!" She cried, as she called to give the news.

"Whats wrong girl, what? Spit it out!" Kash screamed.

"I'm Pregnanttttt, Oh-My-Goshh." She dramatically cried.

"For REAL? Wait, just calm down, it's not that bad. Do you not want it?" Kash questioned.

"I'm not ready for kids, I stay with my daddy. I'm on probation. I steal. I sell weed. Im not a parent figure, I can't!!!" She cried out.

"Meet us at Paris' house now, just stay calm." Kash suggested.

Once they all met at Paris' house, it seemed to be one big soap opera as everyone tried to console her from the newfound pregnancy breakdown. She knew the baby was no mistake, because she had been sleeping unprotected with a guy named Bryce. It was more so of the lesson, because she was acting carelessly and out of all the years that she had been sleeping with Dylan unprotected, pregnancy never crossed her mind. She went to the doctor and found out how far she was. She kicked herself for not noticing that she had missed her menstrual cycle for two months. Bryce had become so annoying lately and working on her last nerves, that she had started distancing herself from him. She ignored all the signs that were right in front of her eyes because she never gave pregnancy a thought in the beginning. She knew that it was a decision she did not want to make but her only option was to have an abortion.

She went to the abortion clinic the following week, accompanied by Kash, who asked her every five minutes, "Are you sure you wanna do this?" It seemed funny that Bryce had called while they were sitting there waiting her turn. Annoyed with the entire situation, she sent him to the voicemail and never mentioned to him that she was ever pregnant or that she had aborted their child. When she got to the back room, the ultrasound almost took her breath away as she saw life forming inside of her. Within an instant, she was given medicine and asked a million questions before she heard a loud vacuum sound that ended the life of a baby she was scared to birth.

When she walked out of the room, she had to be escorted to the car by Kash and one of the nurses. She felt so drained, so empty and so guilty, that she wished it was all reversible. Her soul cried for the life that she was missing. She now wanted to meet that little person she saw on the small ultrasound screen. Confused about a lot of things but she was sure that she would forever miss her unborn child.

After a while, her decision began to settle in her mind and made her act more responsible about her decisions. She had to take action and grasp a hold of her life, because she looked at everything in a whole new light now. One thing she was most certain of, was that sex was nowhere on her menu. She made a vow to herself, to cast judgment on who she slept with in the future because abortion would never again be an option.

She received a letter one day in the mail from the Housing Authority, informing her that based off information from her application, she was approved for a one-bedroom. With no children, she couldn't believe that they accepted her application but she wasn't going to question it. She found a one-bedroom apartment on the west side of town for 500 bucks a month. With housing applied, her rent costed $380 monthly, plus lights and water. She was grateful that they paid at least some of it but now her only worry was having bill money. Nonetheless, she moved into her apartment and began to furnish it, while trying to look for employment so she could stop stealing. Polo had gone to jail, so her connect on the weed for that price was a no go. After paying so many bills on her own, her money was slowly running out.

Months later, there was a shooting that involved a few guys from the hood and Kash's cousin, Vicki, truck was shot up. Everyone met in Magnolia Gardens, the projects across from a Lucky 7 mart, so they could discuss what the fuss was all about. When Loyalty and Kash pulled up, they just sat in the car and watched everything from a distance. Some guy pulled up in Vicki's truck, so they got out to see the damage that had been done to it. Observing the damages to the truck, she couldn't help but shake her head in disbelief at the bullet holes.

"Hmph Hhmp Hhmp." She stood, blowing a cloud of dro smoke.

"Hmph Hmph Hhmp." The voice from a tall, caramel colored, sneaky grinned dude mocked her same reaction. He stared with his body tilted to the side while biting his lip. He stood with his right arm folded behind his back, while gripping his left elbow.

Unmoved by his attempt to get her attention, she walked back to her car with him shortly behind her trail.

"Why you running? You scared of the projects? Slow down, let me talk to you." He yelled out.

Standing by her car, she allowed him to say whatever it was he thought she wanted to hear. Looking at him closer, he was very cute to say the least but she was already caught up in guilt from the abortion. Guys, sex and feelings was just something she wasn't trying to play with.

"What's up? Scared of what? I'm from the Northend. This IS my side." She stated.

"Yea but this is MY hood and I never saw you around here, ever! So, what's your name?" He continued walking closer.

"Loyalty." She rolled her eyes and licked her lips.

"Well, you real pretty Ms. Loyalty and I love your lips. No offense! Can I get your number or No?" He smiled from ear to ear.

"For what?" She asked, turning her back to get in the car.

"Dang." He laughed. "To call you! To see if you're the one for me." He pleaded. Standing there for a few seconds of silence, he then stated. "I'm Ghost."

"Whats your real name?" She asked.

"If you wanna get to know me, that's all you gotta say girl." He smirked.

Just then, someone yelled out his name and he told her to stay put until he came right back. As soon as he walked off, Kash jumped in and they drove off. It had been a long day!

CHAPTER 10

"Ride The Wave"

DURING THE WEEKDAYS, SHE FOUND herself just sitting around the house trying to manage the little money she did have for bills. Almost every weekend, the crew would get together and party like the sun would never come up. After their normal club hours, there was an after hours spot in Louisiana that stayed open till 6 AM. Intoxicated and full of so much adrenaline, the 45 minute ride was a breeze.

To prepare for the weekend, she was inside the mall looking for an outfit for the night when her phone began vibrating nonstop in her purse. She usually turned the ringer off when she searched around stores to avoid the attention if it rung. Once walking to the car, she pulled it out to answer the determined caller.

"Hello." She frowned.

"What's good? What you doing tonight?" The male questioned.

"Umm, minding my business. Who is this?" She was unfamiliar with the voice.

"Ghost." He bodly stated.

Rolling her eyes, she could only imagine how he had gotten her number. The nerve of him to call and try to hold a conversation like they had agreed to the phone arrangement.

"How did you get my number?" She asked.

"Nevermind all that, just know that I have it and I'm going to use it. What? You got a lil boyfriend or something?" Ghost asked.

"Not that it would mean anything to you if I said yes, but No. I don't want one either." She confirmed. She was not head over heels about talking to anyone at this point but she didn't have much to do, so she stayed on the phone making small talk.

He gave a chuckle at her comment. "Well, I'm not trying to be your boyfriend. I want to be your King. I'm headed to the South right now, maybe we can link up a little later if you not busy." He mentioned.

Agreeing to his offer, she hung up the phone and couldn't help but think of how persistent he was. A little flattered but more so intrigued, she was kind of looking forward to their next phone call to accept his invitation. Meeting up with her friends later that evening, they were parked in the driveway at a trap house while Kash talked to one of her lil boos. Listening to the radio with the seat leaned back, she closed her eyes and entered her own little world on cloud nine. All of a sudden, she was disturbed by her door being immediately opened and was demanded to get out.

"Well look who we have here, my queen." Ghost stated. "Come here baby, can I get a hug?" He asked.

Extremely high, she just laughed at his gesture and continued to stay put. Determined to get his hug, he grabbed her from the seat and pulled her to his chest. Warning her not to give him a "church" hug, he wrapped his arms around her back and gently squeezed. She could tell by his demeanor, that he was a guy who wanted his way.

"What are you doing over here? I thought you were going to the other side of town." She asked. Guys always have a million reasons why they aren't where they said.

"I already went over there. I came here to pick up my cousin so we can take care of some business. When I pulled up, I seen him over there talking to Kash. I figured you must've been sitting in the car when I seen smoke blowing out of the window. Turn around so I can take a look at you!" He ordered.

"Excuse me." Not sure if she knew what he meant.

"I want you to spin for me. Turn around like a model, ya' know." He smirked.

She looked from side to side just to make sure no one was watching and then just as he wanted, she did a full 360. When she faced him again, this time he was all smiles, as he said in one breath, "I'm gonna make you mine."

For the next few weeks, they had been doing the usual cat and mouse games. They became cool like homies and she felt so comfortable that she could be herself one hundred percent. She knew that he was a hustler and from time to time she would even accompany him when it was time to count up the money or package up. He never tried to have sex with her, which was strange. She had started to believe that maybe all he wanted was a rider and someone to be down for him. There were times when they would hang out late and she knew for sure he would make his move that night but he never did.

One night, there was a dice game at Vicki's house, that turned out to be a real live gangster party. There were so many slabs in the yard with swangers and nice interiors, that it looked like a BET video. There were card games going on in the kitchen, dice games on the porch and domino tables in the yard. Coolers were full of crawfish, sausages, corn, shrimp, and potatoes. Liquor covered the counters and dro smoke was covering the air like it was a barbecue. There was no drama or bad vibes, it was just black people having a good time.

It seemed as if she wasn't paying Ghost enough attention at the party, because he kept passing by her making smart comments. Thinking nothing of it, she continued socializing and partying like it was 1999. She walked inside to refill her cup with some ice and once she closed the freezer, he was standing there with a smirk.

"So you tryna make me mad? You don't want to do that, trust me." He said, in a low tone.

"How? What's wrong with you?" She asked, confused.

"Look, don't play with me Loyalty. You doing just a little too much smiling in everybody face. It's all good tho', we're leaving after this dice game so be ready." He walked off.

Not sure of what his problem was but she could almost bet that he had just showed his first sign of jealousy. Whether she was passing the blunt, laughing at a joke, peeling her crawfish or just standing around. He kept looking over his shoulder while he was shooting dice, just to keep an eye on her. Then just as he said, within the next hour he was ready to leave.

Once they made it to her apartment, he came inside saying that he had to get something out of the safe that he kept in her bedroom. She made her way to the restroom, then proceeded to cut on the shower to get ready for bed. He walked in behind her while she was undressing and for a while he just stood there watching. He was leaning against the door frame, then pushed himself off the hinges and began walking closer to her. Grabbing her face with both hands, he looked in her eyes before he spoke.

"If you ever get involved with somebody else, I will hurt you." He stared.

Without saying another word, he looked at her for five seconds to let what he said sink in. He leaned in to kiss her, then picked her up and placed her butt on the sink. Standing in between her legs with his arms fondling her entire body, he gave her a few more kisses, then backed up.

"I'll be back. I'll lock the door with my key." Then just like that, he left. She wanted to call and ask him to come back but she was tired from partying anyway. So she took her shower, then jumped in her sheets for some sleep.

The very next morning, before she could even wake up, she heard him come through the door at about 9 AM. She blew the candle out that had been burning on her nightstand during the night and put the cover back over her head. She felt him get into the covers then he pulled her close, holding her so tight her ribs were starting to ache. They drifted off to sleep for about two hours, then his phone began to ring back to back before he powered it off.

"I love you Loyalty." He genuinely stated. "You love me?"

"You don't even know what love is, Ghost." She replied, feeling that there was more to his life than he mentioned.

After her response, he turned her over to lay in between her thighs and began licking on her breasts. He watched her eyes close into bliss as he began to make love to her. It felt so good and it had been a while since she had sex, that a tear escaped the side of her eye.

Right after their first love session, she fixed them breakfast, then they hit the streets and resumed their usual Bonnie and Clyde routines. She noticed that his phone would ring often and he would only look at it, then set it back down. Being that they had never crossed that bridge, the thought of him being involved with someone else didn't seem to bother her as much as it did now. Without hesitation, she turned down his radio and asked him.

"Do you have a girlfriend?" She questioned.

Not taking his eyes off of the road, he remained looking forward and replied. "You want me to lie to you?"

Pissed off by his remark, she replied, "No, I want you to stop lying to yourself." Turning the radio up, she pulled out a blunt from her purse and sparked it up, annoyed with his presence.

Noticing her attitude change, he turned the radio back down so they could have a talk that was long overdue. His only argument was that he never lied to her because she never asked.

"Look, alright. I do have a girl and we've been together a little over a year now. For awhile I thought I loved her but now I don't even trust her. I care about you a lot, which is why I took my time going there with you. I didn't want to hurt you, so please don't be mad." He pleaded.

Looking out of the window, so many thoughts ran through her mind. Even though she never asked, she still thought he should have mentioned it. Yet now that they were so involved, the question she kept asking herself was… Did that even matter now?

"So, who is she? Do I know her? What does this mean? I can't believe you have a girlfriend Ghost! I should really be mad at myself though, because you seem so sneaky anyway." She pouted.

"It doesn't mean nothing too us and it won't change anything either. I love you now. I'm glad I waited on the sex because you just blew my mind. I hope you don't hold this against me or think that you're about to walk away. Just give me time. I promise to break it off and be with you. The right way." He convinced.

"Is that your baby mama? I really feel like you are a liar now, I'm confused. I want to go home, just drop me off man." She demanded, passing him the blunt.

"Damn! I didn't lie and she is not my baby mama. I told you my son's mother don't even stay out here. You know that! Eve is just my girl and she has kids of her own but I do love them like mine. Can we move past this? I'll bring you home if that's what you want but I'm not leaving." He stated.

During the ride home, they didn't say much else to each other as she soaked in all the information he had just informed her of. He said they didn't know of each other and more than likely never ran in the same circles. A part of her thought to walk away, feeling that he just wanted a girlfriend and a chic on the side, like most men do. The piece that had already fallen for him, was telling her heart to do the total opposite, which was to just wait it out. She saw so much of him and they did so much together that it seemed he had no girlfriend at all. Since they had been so close, he picked up the responsibility of paying her bills. He supplied her weed habit and even made her pick up another hobby, sipping promethazine with codeine. It was something he loved to do, so he had 2 cups of ice when he came over and 20 oz sodas for them both to be leaning all night.

After countless more sexual episodes, two months later, she found herself curled up in the bed with the worst stomach ache ever. Unsure if it was menstrual cramps or just a bad stomach virus. She stayed in bed all day and hoped it would get better. The next morning, the pain had gotten worse and she couldn't even stand on her own 2 feet without limping over in agony. She called Kash to come and get her, because at that point she definitely needed to see a doctor. However, the news was something she would have never expected and definitely something she had not prepared for. When they walked back to the car, she contemplated how she would explain this to Kash. She needed some sort of discussion to gather her thoughts before she called Ghost.

"Well, what they say? Why are you looking like that? Pregnant for Ghost? Miscarriage? You start your cycle?" Kash bombarded with questions.

Unsure of how to say it, her eyes filled with tears and she softly replied. "I have chlamydia."

"FOR REAL? I know you are so pissed off. LOYALTY! Call Ghost. You wanna go ride by the trap and check him?" She stated, amped up.

"No Kash, let's just go get my medicine from Walgreens. Then take me home so I can take a bath and lay down. I feel so horribly disgusting. I feel dirty. I feel stupid." She sobbed.

"It's okay, at least you don't have AIDS. I think any disease is better than that, right? I'll buy you something to eat and get your meds. We'll go to your house and watch movies or something because I definitely need a blunt now!" Kash tried to comfort.

She waited all day for Ghost to just pop up at her house like he normally would, then she could tell him unexpectedly. Yet he never showed and she never called, she just waited. Kash stayed over and they laughed all night long about the past and reminisced about old fights and club events. It was definitely what she needed to take her mind off of feeling like a walking STD. When Kash left the next morning, she soaked in some hot bath water and cried just thinking of how he must had been carelessly sleeping around with other girls. What should she have expected? After all, she was sleeping with someone else's boyfriend. Just when she walked out of the bathroom in her robe, she could hear Ghost walking into the house. She sat on the bed and waited for him to walk into the room. Wasting no time, she immediately filled him in.

"Well, I haven't heard from you in 24 hours. It's nice to know you are alive and healthy, so you think! You know what really gets me? You claim to have a girlfriend and you don't even know what status your dick have. Do either one of y'all get check ups?" She spoke calmly while looking at him with disgust.

"What? What's wrong with you?" He frowned.

"I have chlamydia Ghost and that means your selfish ass gave it to me. What is your response? I'm waiting." She teared up.

"You tripping! On my mama, I only been messing with you and Eve. I mean, I fooled around with this other chic a few months before you but that was a long time ago. Give me credit." He argued.

"You calling me a cheater? You saying it's me or you think I would make a big deal over something that is my fault?" She yelled.

"Calm down baby, NO, I believe you. I'm sorry. So, what you think? I been having it? Me and you been messing around for like 7 months now, right? That means we've been passing it back and forth. Please forgive me. I'll go tomorrow and get clean, I promise." He pleaded. Leaning back on the bed, he took a deep breath and placed both of his hands over his face. "Man, thank you for telling me so I know now. I'm ashamed! I'm embarrassed and I know I hurt you."

He stayed for a while so they could discuss the things he needed to do and where to go in order to get treated. She mentioned that he needed to tell his girlfriend because she as well was in need of the same medication. Their relationship or at least their involvement together, seemed to stay the same but she noticed that he was definitely in the street more than usual. She tried to tell him that some of the decisions he was making seemed a bit stupid and careless because you can't trust everybody when you're all playing the same game.

About a month later, she went out with a few friends and towards the end of the night she was ready to go home but she remembered she left her keys inside Ghost's car. She called him nearly 20 times, back to back and never received an answer. She found that weird because even when he had claimed to be around his girlfriend, he would still pick up the phone to see what she wanted. She rode by a few places she thought he may have been hanging out, but to no avail, she never spotted him. All she wanted was to go home, so instead of playing "Where's Waldo", she decided to just ride with Kash home and stay the night at her place. Early that morning, the phone call she received had quickly changed her life.

UNKNOWN CALLER

"Hello, who is this calling me blocked?" She answered.

"This is a collect call from an inmate at Jefferson County Jail, to accept this call dial 7 or hang up now. To block calls of this nature, press 0. This is a collect call from an inmate at Jeff..." The automated message repeated.

Pressing 7, her heart dropped when he spoke.

"Loyalty, listen to me, I got picked up last night. They got my car and you know I was dirty. I won't be here long because they placed a federal hold on me. I need you. You hear me? My safe. This is why

I gave you the code. I trust you. Take everything out and call my mama. She gonna know what to do with it. Go home now! Where are you?" Ghost rambled off.

Already in tears, she replied. "What, when are you getting out? How much do they need? I stayed the night with Kash. I'm up the sidewalk but I don't have my house key, it's in your car. I'm scared. What did you do, Jordan?" She stated in panic, waking up Kash and Kali who had stayed the night as well.

"Listen to me, forget about my car. I won't have a bond. The feds picked me up last night. I was set up. Figure out how to get in your house because if they come there, they will lock you up. You know what time it is. Oh, take the trash out! I love you." CLICK

She jumped up once she heard the dial tone, reality sunk in when he told her to take the trash out! That meant the police were coming and she had to move fast. Lord knows what her house had looked like once him and his careless friends left. Luckily, they had already discussed the 'what ifs' before, so she knew exactly what to do. It just hurt that the day had finally came to play.

"Kash, Kali... let's go... Quick!" She ordered. "The feds picked up Ghost last night and my crib might be where they end up watching. I have to clean house NOW!"

Without any remarks, Kash and Kali jumped up, slipped on clothes and they were out of the house in 5 minutes. Loyalty went to her front office and had the maintenance guy unlock her apartment because she had lost her keys. When they got inside, the girls had to move quick because Ghost left out everything. By him saying he was set up, it seemed as if he was right and left in a hurry, because he had never left the apartment in such a mess. There was dope, weed, syrup and money just scattered. The microwave was open with filth and the stove was full of residue so they each had their hands full. She remembered all his little hiding spots, so she collected all the drugs and dumped them into an empty shoe box. Moving on to the safe, she took everything out and bagged it all. She called his mother and told her that they needed to act now. Within 15 minutes, she was outside the complex. Loyalty walked out with a back pack and shopping mall bag, then placed them both in the backseat.

"So, what he say? The big boys got him?" Mama Jewel asked.

"Yea, I can't believe it. He said somebody set him up and he only told me to take the trash out, then hung up. Be careful, I'll call you if he calls back." She stated, then walked back to her building.

Just when she saw Mama Jewel pull out of the complex, two blue unmarked cars slowly creeped in. She kept the same pace as she strolled to her apartment and told the girls that it was time to go. They had really came through for her, because the apartment was clean as a whistle and no trace of Ghost at all. She packed a bag because he always told her don't stay home for a couple days if something were to happen. They only took about thirty minutes to leave the house and when she opened the door, there was an eviction notice. Snatching the paper off the tape, she read it out loud to her friends.

"I'm being evicted. Dear tenant, you are hereby evicted from our rental property, reasoning to conducted criminal activity. You will need to vacate your unit by November 30." She read in disbelief. "That's two days, are they serious!"

"Man they tripping but don't even try to dispute it. Just incase they know more than you think. We'll help you pack tomorrow. Let's blow some dro, this is too much for one day!!" Kash stated, walking off to the car.

Locking the door behind her, Loyalty just sulked in her own existence as too much was just unfolding at one time. She had not been boosting because he was soaking up so much of her time and helping her with bills. Money was not her worry when he had his freedom. She remembered that he had just given her $400 a few days ago, so she used that to move out of her apartment and just took things one day at a time.

She was starting to become worried, pacing back and forth at her dad's house, waiting on his collect call every day. She told Mr. Ralph that she had to move out of her place and he welcomed her back home where everything was still in place in her room. About a week later, she was sitting outside under the carport smoking a blunt when she received another call that made her feel even worse. Accepting his collect call, she braced herself for the news she felt was going to break her heart.

"Hey babe, how you doing?" He asked, sounding hopeless.

"I'm okay. What about you? What's next?" She asked.

"Look, I'm a man. So I don't need you pretending to be down when you got your freedom staring at you everyday. I'm not coming home anytime soon. They tryna stick me with that dope, plus a gun. Giving me a 10 year sentence off top. That gun was a state charge months ago but since I got caught up, they tryna run it with my fed time. I need the best lawyer, my mama know who to get and she got the money already. I'll let you go, just know I loved you." He stated.

"Wait. Wait. No, don't hang up again. I can't forget about you, Ghost. How can I move on and leave you stuck in there like that? I promise I'll write you everyday and I'll mail a letter tomorrow to show you. Even though you had a girl, I fell in love with you before I knew that. That didn't break us, so jail time won't either. I love you rise or fall. Don't hang your head down because of what they told you, God has a say too. I'm going to pray for you everynight and you do the same. Talk to God about your case, not another inmate, because they're all crabs in a bucket. I'll wait for you. Love is patient, right? Ghost? Jordan?" She called out.

"Yeah, I'm here. I just never met someone like you and I thank God you're in my corner. I knew you were a queen when I met you. I know you're down for me but just let me know when you get tired of riding the wave and I'll accept that. Ok!" He stated.

"I'm riding till the wheels fall off. I love you." She reassured him.

They talked for the next few minutes until the recording came on to disconnect the call. She told him that she took care of everything and was evicted, now she was living back with her dad. He told her if she needed anything, Mama Jewel and his brother would take care of it just as if he was home, so don't hesitate to ask. CLICK.

Holding the phone in her left, with her blunt still lit in the right, she knew that it was time to get her life together. She was unemployed, broken-hearted and a fool in love with a federal inmate. Yet, she was not about to let any of that claim her life forever. GAME FACE

CHAPTER 11

"Just Be Loyal"

FIRST THINGS FIRST, SHE KNEW she had to land herself some type of job that was doing immediate hiring. Seems like when she desperately needed things to fall into place, lo and behold, doors would magnificently start opening up. Every since those charges were pressed against her for assault, she had accumulated a marijuana and trespassing charge along the way. Her chances for getting a job at a decent place were slim to none if the final say was based on her background. Not to mention, she had just got caught stealing from the mall trying to make some extra money about a month ago. Knowing that she had a possible theft case pending, a job hunt became her only hobby for the next few weeks.

One morning, she walked into a corner store to pay for her gas, along with a chocolate milk to drink with her fresh Shipley's donuts. When she approached the cashiers' register, the clerk was getting ready to post a few 'Now Hiring' signs on the windows. She couldn't help but take one last look around the place, then decided to settle for whatever she could get and take it from there.

"Good morning. Can I work here?" She greeted.

"Hello, how are you? Can you work or are you just trying be cute selling lottery tickets and beer all day?" The lady fired back for an immediate response.

"Nah, I'm a good worker plus I really need this job. Is your manager here?" She asked, paying for her items.

"I am the manager. Do you have an ID and a Social Security Card? As long as you can pass the drug test, you're good!" The clerk announced.

"Okay, cool. So when do I come back? I can do it today if you like!" She suggested, knowing that she could get someone to take the drug test for her.

"You start tomorrow at 9. Wear blue jeans and comfortable shoes." She stated, handing Loyalty a shirt.

Waiting on the gas to finish, she leaned against her car and began to stare into the sky with a smirk. She didn't know how to express her emotions at that point because she was heavily flawed and so perfectly imperfect. Yet someone beyond the clouds definitely had a soft spot for the kid, because this was one of the many times where she felt blessed and highly favored. Sure she was the average sinner but she was truly a believer who believed in a prayer and a plan. She couldn't even cry about the situation with Ghost that had spiraled completely out of control. Overall, she felt accomplished, so she headed to IHOP for some breakfast. It was a rainy day with nothing else productive to do, so she went back home to smoke, eat and sleep the day away.

One night while leaving the club, she and her homegirls were walking to the car when they heard someone calling out her name. They were unsure of his vibe because it had been so long since they'd all seen him but it looked like he came in peace.

"Loyalty! Yo, Loyalty. Girl you hear me talking to you. I can't believe you acting all Hollywood now. Like you upgraded your life and don't recognize anyone. Stop the BS girl, for real." He stated.

"What? Who is he talking too? Wait, girl that's Dylan. Look Loyalty!" Kash pointed out, making her notice him and respond instantly.

"I cannot believe you trying to talk to me. What's up, Dylan. How's life? Horrible, I hope." She smirked.

"Life is good, its all good but I do miss you! I haven't seen you in forever. You left, then completely changed lanes and switched the game on me. Forgot all about us. I thought we were just on some sort of 'break up and make up' type of time frame but you never looked back. Whats up with you? Change ya' number on me and everything. That's cold girl." He laughed.

"Keep it real with yourself, you know you were the reason I couldn't take it anymore. I was one hundred percent with you and you thought I was obligated to always understand the lies. I did love you but I'm glad I was able to actually move past that stage. Because boy let me tell ya', it wasn't easy sleeping with a broken heart. Now that I'm over it, it feels good to look at you and walk away without crying all night. See ya later!" She attempted to walk off but he grabbed her arm and insisted that they talk.

She allowed him to say whatever it was, telling him to meet her at Paris' house. He understood that she did not want to be seen with him because an unnecessary rumor about nothing would spread. Hopping inside his car, he was already smoking a blunt while the AC blasted like snow. As soon as her butt hit the seat, she immediately started to demand a few things.

"Dang, you tripping. How can you smoke a blunt in this freezer? You not about to give me chest pains. Your lungs are gonna fold on you, seriously." She laughed.

"Come closer, I can warm you up. You scared of me now?" He asked, taking a sip of his drink.

"No, of course I'm not scared of you. Just know that we're not doing any touching, hugging, kissing or pretending right about now." She replied, taking the blunt.

"I wasn't trying to bug you are anything but I hadn't seen you in a long time. You are as gorgeous as I remember and it reminds me of how much I miss you being around. On the real, after all this time, I still want you. I miss you like crazy shawty, I can't lie. I'm bugging that you are actually considering putting your life on hold. Will you really wait for some dude you claim to be in love with, while he serves a multiple year sentence? Not to mention, he was actually someone else's boyfriend. Is that about right? Why are you throwing your life away? Do you love him that much Loyalty?" He stared.

She couldn't believe he had the guts to bring that up but listening to his remarks about it, she stared right into his eyes to respond. Gathering her thoughts before she answered, looking back and forth then left to right. Her eyes pointed towards the floor of the car, as she paused for a moment. Looking at her Nike slippers that she switched into from the club, her mind instantly thought of Ghost and his needs. What kind of shoes were they allowed to wear in there? He said it was better than serving time in the county because of the food, plus he knew more people in the feds. A few weeks after he was charged, they later arrested his older brother, Murder Mike, as well. He was brought in on similar charges and was due to be on the unit next to Ghost by the end of the week. It had been months since he had been in federal custody and had a limit of how much money she could send for his commissary a month. She thought about what he asked her to do so they could make some cash while he was in a unit with flexibility.

Hitting the blunt a few times, she lifted her head and glanced over at Dylan, to give him the well-thought of response. Not wanting to sound vulnerable or confused, she spoke with a smile and courage in her voice even though it was killing her softly.

"Yes. Yes, I love him. Before I started loving him and became involved in a sexual way, we had already started hanging out. We bonded. He was like the sweetest homie I ever had. He looked out for me and came through when I needed him. I can't just walk away and turn my back on him now, he needs me. I'm not throwing my life away! I also can't see myself walking away without second thoughts. I was dealing with him when it was all good, so I can hang around when it's all bad. At least until he's sentenced, because he says that's the longest wait in life. A person waits for the judge, hoping he doesn't give you a football number and have you locked away uncomfortably for the next 10-15 years. Dylan be honest, if that were you in prison, would you want the person you were rocking with to just forget you because you're not winning anymore? Some people you wouldn't expect to stay solid, have better intentions than the ones you give the most credit too. They're the ones who God place in your life to open new doors. I'm not sure if this is a blessing or a lesson but only one way to find out. I have to be there for him and I actually don't feel bad about waiting. The Bible said, love is patient." She spoke.

"You're right, all that is so true. I hate that I messed things up, babe. You're a good girl and he got himself a good thing. I know he will be proud once he realizes what he has. I hope he treats you good because I feel like even if he doesn't, you're going to stick around anyway. Just don't accept less than what you're worth, trying to prove how loyal you can be to a man that doesn't deserve a woman like you. I promise, I'm going to miss you. Shittt, I've missed you every since that night you and your homegirl tried to beat me up." He laughed at his last remark.

"You are wrong for remembering that!" She giggled.

"I missed your laugh." He stared out the window.

Placing his cup into the cup holder, he leaned over and kissed her forehead as he parked in front of Paris' house. She finished up the last bit of her bacon, pancakes, eggs and french toast from IHOP. After the club, full of liquor and completely exhausted, that breakfast meal always made her night.

"Take it easy. I'm not sure if I'll see you anytime soon but just hit me up if things don't work out. Even if I have a girl at the time, you're still a great person to have as a friend and hang around. I respect that we can't be anything. You owe everything I took for granted to someone else now. That's crazy. " He laughed.

She joined his laughter. "Dylan, shut up. I can't even deal with you and the childishness. You take care! Thanks for the food and drugs!" She laughed again. "Thanks for understanding and not tryna force anything but just listening to my situation. I know it may not make sense but you know what they say don't you." She stated.

"No, enlighten me." He challenged, smiling as he folded his arms and waited for her response.

"Everybody plays the fool, sometimes!" She walked away, laughing and twisting, singing and shouting as she harmonized the lyrics, full of that weed.

Ghost had convinced Loyalty that he would be able to get tobacco, weed, cash money and a cell phone inside with him if she was willing to help make it happen. He would use the money to pay off the guards and the rest of the items were for sale. He would have her meet the inmates folks to pick up the money or sometimes they would just make it easy and add it to his books. She agreed since her role was pretty simple and all she had to do was get the packages ready to go inside. At visitation, they talked about what door she was to park by and who would come out to get it. He explained to her in detail, how to saran wrap each Buglar tobacco pack so that it would stretch and make enough cigarettes worth the risk. She would place just enough marijuana inside the grinder to have the correct amount of dro to fill a balloon the size of a quarter. Tying them each into a knot and then cutting off the loose ends, she would always make enough so that he could keep at least one or two for his own addiction.

Not only was the extra money helping him survive in the inside but it was also putting extra back into her pockets. It allowed her to save more money so that she could move back out on her own. Her job at the gas station was only enough money to say she had income and a far cry from being enough to pay some bills. Yet, there really was no need to talk to anyone else because she still had Ghost financially. Physically, she missed him but looked forward to him being transferred to a different unit where they had contact visit. Being able to see him at visitation was better than nothing at all because it outweighed phone calls and reading letter after letter.

Within a few months of working at the corner store, she received a call back from the local travel center in town where she previously applied for a cashier's position. At the interview, she was offered the position immediately and was hired on to work the fuel desk at the truck stop. They agreed to only work her for the night shift, considering that she had her day job at the corner store. She began to work so much that Ghost added her work number to his call list to be approved for inmate calls.

When it came to visits, she informed each job that Fridays and Saturdays from 12PM to 3PM was strictly for visitation and she could never work during those hours. She would sometimes get in touch with Ghost's baby mama, Valerie, so that she could pick up his son, Pop, as well. Pop was only about seven years old and no stranger to reality. Every time they attended, he was fully aware of what was going on and what they were there for. At first, he would always just sit in the backseat and look at her side-eyed while she glanced at him in the rearview mirror every few minutes. She always started small talk with him about the basic stuff like his hobbies, school, interests and just life. The more she picked him up, the more she learned him and began to love him. She helped out as much as she could with things he needed since Ghost was not around to play the part.

Everything was not peaches and cream but she knew her situation could have been worse so she was trying to keep her chin up with a clear mind. Between both jobs, it was very seldom that she had an off day. Yet when she did have a chance to hang out with her friends, they would all link up and pull an all nighter. She was such a down to earth person with a big heart and beautiful spirit. Like the average, maturing young adult, she was still making bad decisions and learning. She was not a person to bully anyone or keep up drama with unnecessary conflict. If she had mad love for you in any kind of relationship, then she was flat out as loyal as she could be. Knowing that no one is perfect, she was a person of patience who believed in second chances. Just how many second chances do you give someone who keeps disappointing you? She definitely believed in the quote one of her highschool teachers, Ms. Dixon, would always say, *"Be the type of person, you would want to meet"*. She felt like she could accept a few lies and depending on the circumstances, she swallowed the fact that most guys were not one hundred percent faithful. She would rather be hurt by owning up to the truth, than to be fed lies because there was one thing she did not like to feel and that was *'played'*.

It was during the week and she finally had a day off from the corner store. She had to work the truck stop that night so she was enjoying the day with her usual hobbies and chill spots. Every since Ghost had been locked up, someone had been playing on her phone calling from a private number. Ghost told her that his girlfriend, Eve, had been questioning him about who she was. The dark had finally come into the light on Ghost's behalf, because she was not down to do any explaining to another female about a guy.

Before Ghost was arrested, he called Loyalty and said that he had a flat tire on his way to the beach. Confused, she gave him an ear full because he had told her he wasn't attending the Kappa Beach Party in Galveston. Being a man, he kept trying to explain a point that made no sense at all. Pleading the fifth, he conveniently forgot all about the annual beach party that weekend as if he was just driving 45 minutes to look at sandy beaches. The insult to a womans intelligence with the lies some men give just has to be some sort of thinking disorder. Yet and still, she had Arin knock on Eve's door for his rim so they could bring it to him. It was late. It was cold. She was pissed off but her dude needed her, so she came through.

Now that Eve had put things together that tied Loyalty to him, she began to make it known that she had a problem. Riding with Kash, the two of them were casually rolling through the city when she noticed his silver Cadillac and instructed Kash to pull into the store. A few days before, she had seen Eve in the mall with her sister, who walked up and exchanged words in an attempt to fight for her. For whatever reason, the altercation did not lead to anything physical. Since that day, she knew a fight would soon follow. Ghost would always tell her to ignore it and try to avoid the confrontation but she was growing tired of the games. She took it as an opportunity to just get the fight over with while it was early in the day and no one was around.

She strolled into the store and walked up to the counter where Eve was buying a few things. She didn't know if she wanted to just hit her or calmy approach her to just look and see if the hype was real about them fighting on sight. Instead, she stood at least four feet away and greeted her.

"What's up, Eve? You ready for that?" She looked her up and down.

"Come on now, girl. You know I been waiting to see you again." She replied, grabbing her things.

"What you talking about then? Let's go. Right here!" She challenged, now standing outside the doors.

"Hold up. I'm about to go do something, then I'll catch you later." She walked towards the Cadillac.

"Awe, man come on." Loyalty stated as she smacked her lips. "You about to go get a crowd and make a scene. Whatever man, it's good."

Nearly twenty minutes later, they came across his Cadillac again. Only this time, Eve had passengers. Kash noticed the car of girls going in and out of traffic to catch up with her and Loyalty.

"What you wanna do? We can just stop and see who actually tryna fight! Even if they try to jump us, we can handle it. What we're not about to do is just let her chase this car around like somebody in here is scared. Let's just pull up somewhere and get out." Kash suggested.

Just then, Kash's cousin Vicki called and they changed the topic to quickly inform her of what was going on. She told them to pull into the Toys R Us parking lot, because she had just finished shopping and was now outside standing by the car.

As soon as they pulled up next to Vicki and parked the car, Eve's older sister quickly approached Loyalty and began to question her.

"So, you the one messing with Ghost?" The sister asked.

"Why? What's up. You act like he was your man or something. Why can't she speak for herself? You always got something to say. Do you want to fight or wha…" She ranted on, until she saw the first lick coming from Eve's sister.

It made her even more upset that Ghost couldn't even control his little girlfriend. Now she was having a fight with some chic that had nothing to do with the situation at all. That was the only lick her sister landed because Loyalty was all over her in a second and would not let go. Vicki and Kash attempted to break it up until she heard Eve yelling out for them to let go of her sister because she was pregnant. That statement alone sent her over the edge because they initiated the conflict from the beginning. Did they forget she was pregnant when she got out the car? Loyalty snatched away from the fight and gained her focus on Eve as she approached her with her fists held up for striking. Warning her that it was time for them to get it over with, then she leaned in on her for contact. She got the chance to swing several times before Eve put her in a bear hold to where she couldn't move an arm or leg if she wanted to. Wrestled up, Kash broke them apart and the crowd of people went there separate ways. Loyalty felt her phone vibrating in her back pocket and noticed it was Ghost calling. She placed him on speaker phone so that Eve could hear how her supposed-to-be man was on the line.

"Wait a minute boo, here goes our man calling. Let me tell him we don't get along." She joked, as she began to tell him about the incident.

"Girl you wack. You like sharing a man, huh? He don't even want you." Eve argued.

"Sharing? No, I'm admitting. Maybe you should try it. Just know these dudes for everybody, whether we like it or not. Girl BYE." She yelled.

Mother's Day weekend finally approached and Ghost had been telling her that his mother was going to be coming to visit for the holiday. She totally understood and since she rarely had free hours during the day, she took it as an opportunity to go have some fun. Sitting on the porch with a blunt at Kash's grandmother house, they discussed their plans and prepared for a mall run. She decided to go out since she didn't have to wake up for visit early Sunday morning.

Once they made it back to Grandma's house, she received a call from another chic who she had switched numbers with at visitation. It caught her totally off guard and she was not sure of what to do, other than drive there for herself.

"Hey girl. What's up? You and Ghost mad at each other or something? Another girl was here today and it wasn't his mother that came before. This was a younger female and they had conversations he wouldn't be having with his mama." The girl informed.

"Word? I'm glad they're still there. I'm getting in the car now, so I should be there in about 15 minutes." She hung up.

She told Kash what happened and that they needed to pull up at the jail house pronto. Once she arrived, she saw Eve's car in the parking lot and her heart almost fell out of her ass. He had been lying to her, about everything! He told her that sometimes his mother came to visit but now she was wondering if that was even the truth. He was only allowed one visit but if she walked fast enough, then she could at least open the door before she was put out.

Visitation was practically closed anyway, so the two of them were sitting towards the end booth when she walked in. Ghost spotted her first and the color seemed to have drained out of his face when he saw her standing there full of disappointment. His facial expression made Eve look back and all Loyalty could do was laugh. She took a moment and snapped back into the real world because this dude was really trying to play games like she was obligated to be there for him. At least you can be honest, since you can't be free. The nerve!

"Really Ghost? Like for real? Your mama? This not even your real baby mother, let alone the mother that birthed you. You know what? You out of there! I did't ask you to be faithful Ghost… I wanted you to be real. With nothing else to offer me since you are the one locked up, I'd think that wasn't too much to ask. Look at you, can't even do that!" She walked away, feeling pretty.

She bumped into Kash on the way out, who was coming inside to make sure they were not fighting or being arrested. She couldn't believe he would betray her trust and lie about something so small. She had been taking penitentiary chances and working her butt off at two jobs to make sure things were taken care of as much as they could. If he thought she was some kind of dummy, he was sadly mistaken. Their bond before the feds picked him up was what carried her so far. He made her feel so loved before their fate lied in the hands of some judge. Was she willing to forget about him now? Should she allow what he was doing to dictate her actions or change the way she felt about him? It was a tough call but she was ready to ignore him for a while.

Before they even reached the redlight, he must've ended the visit quickly because he was now calling back to back. The thing was, he called over five times every 60 seconds if that was even possible. Guys just don't know how good they really have it, until they come close to losing it. Which in his case, the kind of things she would do for him was truly a modern day 'ride or die' that stood right before his eyes. Unlike most, he was able to handle her attitude on top of dealing with her constant changing personality that was full of life and flaws. His calls became annoying, so it was time that she answered to give him the reaction he knew was coming. Her mouth was the most deadliest thing on her body and it was indeed her favorite weapon.

"What do you want? Closure?" She answered.

"Closure? Man, stop playing with me. What's wrong with you? I'm sorry, alright! I promise it won't ever happen again. You have my word. I'll do whatever you want, just don't walk away on me. Please accept my apology baby, I choose you. I'm not playing this time." He pleaded.

"You are such a pretender Ghost." She sighed.

"What? Don't forget who you're talking too." He warned.

"Whatever, look, just don't call me anymore. Go work things out with the girlfriend you claim is not your girlfriend. I was tired of you being with someone else when you were here. So you think I'm going to tolerate it while you're gone? It's cool, no pressure! Don't think I'm forcing you to decide or choose, because I'm not." She laughed.

"Just chill, you really over there sounding like you're mad but I was just being a man, as you say. Now, I'm ready to just be your man. It's over between me and her. I promise you that. Can you forgive me?" He asked.

"I need time to think and think again, then think some more. I can't say what will happen because I don't know Jordan. The things I thought I knew, mean nothing to me now. Call me tomorrow." CLICK. She powered off her phone.

A few days later, he decided to pick a fight about her going to the club. She began to state her argument, being that she has never gave him any reason to doubt her loyalty or question her love. Perhaps it was because of the rumor that surfaced around about her talking to Tory, a guy she would be in contact with in the past. He knew her and Tory's relationship had never gotten serious or reached the next level, so it never bothered him. Yet now that he was incarcerated, it changed the entire situation that made her out to look sneaky and untrustworthy. Anytime that he mentioned it, she would always reassure him that it was just a rumor and no one else stood a chance as long as he had her heart. Not sure what type of test it was but she was definitely surprised when she noticed Tory's number come across her phone screen. It was late and she was working a graveyard at the truck stop when she found herself answering for him to see what he wanted.

"Hello, who is this?" She answered, already recognizing the number.

"Like that? You deleted my number?" He chuckled. "How you doing Ms. Loyalty? This Tory."

"Hey, what's up? The number looked familiar but you know I deleted your number because we haven't talked in forever. Thought you forgot about me!" She may have flirted just a little. Yet because she didn't have much to do at work and Ghost kept showing signs of deceit, she just enjoyed the conversation for what it was.

"Nah, you're the one who forgot about me. I'm sorry if you felt that way but I only sit back and chill if I'm not chasing a check. Ya' know! What's been good with you? You must be bored because you talking to me like you finally ready." He seductively stated.

Almost turned on through the phone with just the tone of his voice, she could only imagine the presence of him. It had been months since she had been touched by a man, let alone hugged by anyone. They talked on the phone for at least two hours until she realized that she had to stock the coolers before her manager came in at 4 AM. She had never talked to him about so many different things before, so to hear his opinions, only made her want to answer for him again the next time. However, the piece of her that was in love with Ghost took up too much of her heart to even attempt or indulge in leading someone on. Locked up or not, Ghost was still her dude so she couldn't just sleep with someone else and pretend that she wasn't. Crazy part was, she felt horrible for just the thoughts that ran through her mind and they were only thoughts.

She always had a thing for Tory but they never had sex. Although everything about him said 'yes', her integrity kicked in and continuously said no.

"Well, I have to go. It was nice talking to you but I have a lot I'm dealing with right now. I'm always like extremely busy." She explained.

"You really working like that?" He laughed. "That's cute! Look, Im tired of playing with you. We've been doing this for too long. What time do you get off? I'll come over or pick you up." He stated.

Stuck for a moment, butterflies filled her stomach as her body cringed at the thought of having sex with someone else. Although she needed to be touched and wanted so badly to give in and just live in the moment. She couldn't bring herself to tell him no again. He was the cutest thing ever with chocolate skin and always kept the freshest set of braids. He smelled good with a thug-gentleman deamenor, plus he was getting money like a bank.

"Okay. Okay. I get off at 7 but I know you're going to be sleep." She said, knowing that she was going to ignore him afterwards.

He laughed. "That's a few hours away, just answer the phone." He replied. As they said their good byes, all she could think about was Ghost.

Ghost was incarcerated and still being unfaithful, not to mention a liar. She hated that she felt so attached to him because no matter how he treated her, it never changed her character. Eve had already moved on and a piece of her wished that she had been the one to take the easy, less stressful road too. Tory did just as he said and called her around 7, which shocked her to see him showing so much interest again.

It was now Christmas day and Tory had called at least three times making it very tempting to answer because he was calling on such a grand holiday. On New Years he was still calling but this day he only called about three times then gave up. She laid in the bed that night and cried herself to sleep because she wanted to feel love and get affection. After all that time she had waited on Tory to push harder in the past for her attention. He waited until they stopped talking and she was involved with someone else to finally decide he was ready to take it to the next level. She figured it was a test of faith and her loyalty, so she kept her morals intact. Tear after tear, she wanted to call him and just explain the whole situation. Instead of stirring up troubled waters, she laid in bed and flipped her pillow over to the dry side. She fell asleep and was okay with her decision to survive his sentence faithfully, alone.

CHAPTER 12

"Wife on Duty"

DAYS GREW EXTREMELY LONELY FOR her, as she found herself crying more than usual at night. Being at work was the only thing that kept her mind off of Ghost, so she needed another job to save her sanity and benefit her financially as well. Deciding to quit the corner store day shifts, she managed to find a warehouse job with decent pay and weekends off. Since the checks started coming in every week, she laid back to save some money but was low key stressing over everything. Mama Jewel had been paying his lawyer fees for the federal charges. Yet, he instructed Loyalty to seek another attorney who would be able to dismiss the gun case that popped up after his arrest. Once she hired an attorney, it took nearly three months to pay the new fees. Court date after court date, she wiggled her way around both jobs to make sure he had her support and seen her face at every court appearance. It would warm her heart every time the officers appeared with him from behind those closed doors. She would tell herself each time that he was always one court date closer to receiving his sentence. While the judge talked and read off each statement, she watched closely as he scanned the court room trying to spot her face.

After paying attorney fees, she was now preparing her mind and finances on the new town home her sister was approved for. Since she had gotten into more trouble, it made her unable to apply for most things that consisted of passing a background check. Having a close relationship with her sister always came in handy because she helped her when needed. Lucky seemed to be the only sibling that understood her more and accepted the rough edges she couldn't sharpen if she tried. It seemed to be no hassle, once she learned that her little sister had once again needed her help out of the hole she fell into. Sure, she would always give the "keep a clean background and good credit" speech. To no avail, it went right through her ears as she mentally calculated each new charge on her record. On top of things, Lucky had also helped with cosigning for her a new Nissan since her credit score was higher. She was very appreciative that her sister was willing to help obtain the things her own name wouldn't allow.

Once she got settled in her new town home, if felt like that was all she had. Sleeping on an air mattress for the first few weeks until her mother came through and provided a bedroom set, that only left her to purchase a mattress. Within a few months, she had enough cash to purchase a living room set with the matching dining table. She waited until Black Friday, which is the popular price cut sales day after Thanksgiving, to purchase two flatscreen TVs. She literally patted herself on the back when she recognized that she had fully furnished her own place and made it home sweet home. Of course with the good, there comes the bad. Her savings was now completely dry and she found herself living paycheck to paycheck. She was still making trips for Ghost so that he could continue to eat but it was becoming more strict so she knew that it was about to come to an end. Besides, the extra money she got from him was only enough to pay her car note. It didn't take a rocket scientist for her to figure out that she had to briefly return to her old hustle, boosting.

Ghost had been in jail for over a year and still not had received his sentence. It left her no choice but to show up at his lawyer's office once a week for some sort of update. She hated going to visit without any good news to give him because she could sometimes see the worry in his eyes.

"What's good baby girl?" He said, hugging her tightly.

"Missing you in my world, that's it." She replied.

She was so happy for contact visitation once he was transferred to the Beaumont Medium Federal Prison near Port Arthur, Texas. Every time she made that drive, her stomach would fill with butterflies as she anticipated touching his skin and filling the warmth of his body. He felt so different due to the committed work out most guys seem to have once they are surrounded by those prison walls. They sat and talked for the entire two hours, as usual, as if they had so much to discuss. They never ran out of things to talk about because he admired that her mind was full of knowledge.

Since she was no longer able to assist him with getting things inside and it began breaking her pockets to keep up with his commissary as he was used to. She put $150 on his books every Friday since she was working two jobs but her rent was $750 a month. Along with her car note being $480, insurance $130, not to mention other bills like water, lights, cell phone and definitely her weed habit. She hated to go in there complaining or sounding like she was close to giving up but she was thankful that he allowed her to vent.

"I mean, besides all that. I still need my nails done, my hair kept up and I have to buy tennis shoes. After I take care of what's important, I'm broke. I haven't had time to run in the mall but now I have to make sure that I'm okay without needing anyone else." She stated.

"Look ma, I don't want you stealing, it's a bad look. Plus, we both don't need to be behind bars. Just send me whatever you can every two weeks instead of every week, I'll be cool. I just bought new sweats and shoes, plus my locker is filled with food. You've been doing a good job and I take my hat off to salute you. They call me everyday for mail even if you send a letter or just pictures with a card. You never slacked up with that. You come up here looking and smelling good every week. Besides keeping up with my lawyer, you even look out for my son when he need you. If you didn't tell me all these things that worry you, I wouldn't know because you make the struggle look good. Damn good!" He replied, holding her hands tighter.

"Thanks babe but I won't change anything I've been doing. I just have to pick up more hours or go get it the only quick way I know. I'm going to meet Kash when I leave from here because her and Arielle been making a killing." She convinced.

"Ok baby, whatever. Just be careful because you know the phones up here cut off after 9. The mall will be closed and I'll be up all night wondering if you made it home." He sighed.

"I just love you!" She smiled.

"I love you more." He kissed her again then slowly walked away with the guards.

She made trips to many different malls within the past few weeks and was able to save up enough money to reduce her struggle. Between job paychecks and her extra money from boosting, she was living more comfortably by each day. She began showing up to visitation so exhausted that he would just let her lay on his shoulder the entire time. He allowed her to sit in silence and just relax her mind because he knew the streets were a beast. The thought of her facing it all alone made him want his freedom even more.

As a normal routine, she only had a few hours before she had to clock in at the truck stop. She managed her time wisely by meeting up with Kash and Arielle to hit up the mall for some extra money. Not actually being in the mood to steal, if that made any sense. She went anyhow because money was always needed and she was her only provider. It didn't take long for them to get the things they needed for a successful mall run. However, she noticed a black male who kept following them around so she brought it to her friends attention.

"Man, I know I'm not bugging. This dude keep looking at us and following us around. Even in the girls' section! He's pretending to shop, so I feel like he's a cop." She warned.

"Chill out, Loyalty. Don't start! Did you smoke a sweet before you came in? You high?" Arielle asked, ignoring the warning as she headed for the door.

"What do you mean? Like, a real cop? A badge cop? A cop-COP!? Stop playing." Kash questioned with a tone of worry and doubt.

Smacking her lips. "Nah, like Robo cop. Duh, a real cop! Stop acting slow. Y'all tripping! I'm ditching my bag. Let's just go and come back tomorrow or something." She suggested.

"Be serious. You have over 600 bucks in your bag within 30 minutes! You can drop yours if you want but I'm walking out regardless." Arielle stated, as she began to pick up her speed.

Once they got closer to the door, so was the suspicious male as if he was done browsing the store. Just as she suspected, he tried to grab Arielle but she snatched away with Kash right behind her trail through the doors. He attempted to grab Loyalty's arm but she dodged his reach, then threw her bag at him. It gave her an opportunity to get away, so she took off down the aisle. She ran right into the arms of another cop, who walked her to a vacant room and shut the door behind her. She was so pissed because the lesson taught her to always follow your first mind. She knew that she should have left out of the store when she saw all the signs of him being an undercover police. Her friends couldn't convince her otherwise but instead of listening to herself, she let the money in her bag guide her feet towards the door.

The cop left her unattended, which gave her time to think of a plan. The officers went in the opposite direction in search for Kash and Arielle. A store associate appeared in the doorway with the bag she had thrown at the officer. Taking the risk, she flew past the worker and never looked back. Making it to the parking lot, she noticed the car was gone and she had no getaway vehicle. So she did the only thing she could think of next, which was to keep running. Her wind was becoming shorter and her legs were growing tired. She felt weak from the unexpected chase she was under but didn't let that stop her.

It came to an end once she made it to the opposite side of the freeway. She took a look back and noticed the cop she had jerked away from was right behind her in a blue F150. He had the nerve to stand straight up on the pickup bed like he was hunting, while another officer drove. Knowing that she couldn't outrun the speeding pickup truck, she just sat on the curb and waited for him to approach her. If he thought she was going to walk up to him in defeat, he was definitely wrong. He had come this far, so who was she to make his job easier.

Assuming that she was going to run again, once he was within arms reach he grabbed her from the back and bear hugged her. Unsure of the feeling from his physical contact, it caught her off guard because she had not been held by a man in years. Not to mention, he had rich chocolate skin, smelled good and was well built. She was not a fan of cops, so the idea of him turning her on was embarrassing to admit. Instead of placing her in handcuffs or inside the patrol truck, he walked with her back across the intersection. It was kind of ridiculous because now that she was captured, she wanted a ride in the AC.

"Why did you run from me?" He asked.

"That's kind of a stupid question sir. Why did you chase me? Clearly you couldn't keep up so you had to fetch some wheels. Very unfair! Don't they put y'all through some kind of training camp or something?" She sarcastically replied.

"You're kind of funny. You should've been a comedian instead of trying to be a thief because it doesn't look like you're really good at it." He snapped back.

"I'm better than you think. Can we walk a little faster though, it's hot as hell out here. I'm hungry and I really don't feel like going to jail Mr. officer, so just let me loose. Give me a warning or something." She bargained.

"Now you want a favor? After you made me chase you 5 miles! Well, 2 miles since you said I fetched some *wheels*. Just sit in here and hang tight for me while I go get the stuff you tried to take." He stated.

They made it back to the mall and he brought her inside a room that looked similar to an interrogation room. He returned with the bag they confiscated while she was running. The workers only wanted their merchandise back, mentioning she would also have a no trespassing ticket, banning her from the mall for a year. She was already thankful that once again she was spared from the trouble she couldn't stay out of. Yet it was up to the officer whether she went to jail or not due to the items in her bag totaling more than $200.

"Ms. Loyalty Brown." He stated, looking at her driver's license. "You're definitely no stranger to trouble. I see we have you in the system more than a few times. Why are you stealing when you have enough money in your purse to pay for these things?" He waited for a response.

Folding her arms, she sat back in the chair and looked at him as if he already knew the answer. Once again, cops can ask some very dumb questions. He had been nice to her though and he was rather cute with a nice body, so she kept it polite as possible.

"That money in my purse is for bills. Those things in my bag were for me to make more money after I go broke paying those bills. Look, I have a job. I actually have two jobs but it's hard out here when you're doing it alone. I understand I have a trespassing warning against me now, so it's my word that I will not be back inside this mall." She answered.

"Well, I hope life gets better for you. Jail is no place for a pretty lady like yourself. If you keep up the same actions, your background is going to get far worse. I won't take you to jail this time because I hope you take this as a lesson. Not every cop will let you go so easy, so get yourself a better job and some new friends." He preached, opening the door as he signaled for her to get up and leave.

"I'm free to go? Thank you, thank you, thank you. God is going to bless you. By the way, you almost broke my ribs, that was no way to handle a lady." She laughed. "Have a good day my brother!" She pumped her fist.

He couldn't help but laugh himself, as he winked then closed the door behind her. Once she returned to the parking lot, she remembered that her friends had left and she needed a ride. Forgetting that her phone was on vibrate, she pulled it out and saw there were so many missed calls. Just as she was about to call Kash back, her phone started vibrating, it was Robin.

"Loyalty? What's up! I saw the law man walking you to the building but looks like they let you go. I'm about to pull back around so you can hop in. Kash and Arielle had to leave because they already have warrants. They told me what happened and that I needed to pull up for you." She explained.

"Cool, whatever. I'm standing outside by Dillards, so come on. Oh wait, I see you. Girl this is some BS, I can't believe I got caught up. Thank God he let me go." Loyalty stated, getting inside the car to enjoy the AC.

"Everything happens for a reason boo. Just work your two jobs and spend your money wisely. I know it's hard out here but your situation could be worse." Robin replied before passing the blunt.

There was so much to think about because she did not want to spend any more days running out of the mall. After cleaning her house, she took a shower then prepared a pot of spaghetti, corn, fried chicken wings and corn bread. Wrapped in a blanket, she drank some kool-aid while she sat on the couch watching "Waiting to Exhale" until she fell asleep. Her phone rang, waking her from a 45 minute nap that was well needed.

The operator began to speak. " This is a prepaid call from an inmate at a federal correctional Institute, if you accept this call please dial five, to block calls of this nature please dial seven."

"Hey babe." She answered.

"KNOCK KNOCK." Ghost stated, obviously in a playing mood.

"Who's there?" Rolling her eyes with a smirk across her face.

"Love." He whispered.

"Love who?" She smiled.

"Love-ing you, is easy cause, you're beautiful. Do do do do doooo." He harmonized.

"Ahhhhhhhhh." She joined in to complete the tune before they burst into laughter.

"What's up queen, you sleep?" He started conversation.

"I was taking a little nap. I got jammed up yesterday but he let me walk, so I take that as a lesson. I'm just gonna chill on the mall issue and try to pick up some extra hours with both jobs whenever I can." She gave him the run down.

"What? I'm glad you're okay baby! Most importantly, I'm glad your mind is on the right track and you're deciding to leave that alone. You're so much better than stealing! Just let your purpose catch up with you, cause what's meant will always find it's way." He replied.

After discussing a few alternatives to make sure that her finances were in order, they ended the phone call with a few more laughs and positive vibes. She found herself waking up every morning praying and talking to God about the things she could no longer fix. The things she was trying to solve on her own but had the slightest clue where to get the answers or find the guidance. Spending her spare time at home and seeing less of the people who occupied most of her time, was definitely a start towards the person she wanted to become.

Hurricane season came around again and the city announced mandatory evacuation with such short notice that she had to move quick. This time, it was Hurricane Ike that had everyone in an uproar and she felt horrible that she couldn't take Ghost with her. Packing everything she needed, someone had advised her that the jail house had relocated the prisoners in the area. It was shocking and must had been without notice because she knew Ghost would have called to let her know where they were being transported. She called every number she could think of to get in contact with someone who could give her details. Never receiving an answer, she knew that it was too late and had to leave the city without knowing.

They were able to shelter safely in Houston at Liberty's house while the storm passed. She was horrified that night as she listened to the angry winds move through the city. It literally had them up all night, expecting the unexpected. It practically felt like the two story home was rocking from side to side while little rocks of hail slammed against the windows.

The next morning, she contacted nearly every number associated with the federal prison until she received the answer she was looking for. Ghost had been transported to a jail facility in Conroe, Texas. She put the address in her GPS and got on the highway in hopes to see him in good health. Some roads and exits were blocked off, so what would have been a hour drive turned into taking nearly two hours to reach her destination.

When she finally arrived, she signed in and went through a very strict security check. She was not even a little bothered by the long wait, as she anticipated seeing his face to know that he was fine. Time flew by and she heard her name being called, so she purchased a few snacks and walked into the visitation room. Looking around for his face, she knew he had already spotted her once she noticed his priceless grin.

"Man, I'm so happy to see you baby. How did you know I was here? They shipped us so quick baby, they wouldn't even let us make a phone call. I been thinking about you non-stop. I really love you girl. How is the world looking out there? They say the storm was really bad. You looking good shawty." He stated, hugging her tightly.

"Hey, baby! I'm fine, the roads are messed up but Hurricane Rita hit us harder. We should be able to enter Beaumont in a few days. I'll stay out here at Liberty's house until they transport you back. I figured you were unable to call but you knew I would find you. They let me put $50 on your books when I got here. I'm so happy to see you babe." She stated, gripping his hands.

They were allowed a hour visit and within that timeframe she was able to catch him up on most of the things that were going on with her life. She also told him how she planned on actually moving to Houston herself because their hometown seemed like a dead end to her. She felt like she wanted more out of life than to just dwell in the same city forever.

"I feel you on that. I promise I'm coming with you, for real. I want to change too! Our visit is almost up and the system does collect calls over here. If you can, put some minutes on the phone so I can keep in touch with you that way. I been in here over two years now, so I pray once I get my sentence that I won't have much longer to serve. My lawyer said I'm looking at five years, so I'm cool with that. What about you? I been wanting to ask you something. I know this may be a little selfish of me or you may think this is jail house talk. Just take me serious because I don't ever want to lose you. The guards transporting me, only made me think more about the distance and time separating us. I want you forever. Will you marry me Loyalty?" He asked, waiting on her response.

They discussed how she would always be there for him and that marrying her wouldn't define their love. She was only 22 and had nearly her whole life ahead of her. From what she thought at the moment, there was no one else she wanted more than her bestfriend, Ghost. She expressed how a jail house marriage would deprive her of the dream wedding she always wanted. Yet instead of filling her own head with doubt, she answered him without hesitation.

"Of course Jordan, I love you… I pray we live happily ever after." She kissed his lips.

That wide smile spread across his face again as they stood and hugged each other for almost two minutes in silence. He kissed her once again, then she announced that she had a surprise engagement gift.

"Here you go husband!" She slid off her thumb ring and told him to wear it back home. Since their federal unit had gotten so strict, she wouldn't be able to give him anything once he was transported to his main facility.

Smiling harder by the minute, he replied. "Loyalty, your thumb ring? Really?" He laughed. "Thanks baby, it fits tight but I love it. I already feel like the luckiest man on Earth. See you later, wife!" He picked her up off her feet for the biggest hug ever.

Once she got back to Liberty's house, she felt like it was some good news that she would share with her family because after all, she was excited. The fact that he was an inmate who had not been sentenced but she was willing to stick by his side was crazy. For someone who wasn't in her shoes or did not live by the code she lived by, the whole idea of marrying a man behind bars was ridiculous. Of course everyone expressed their concerns and totally disagreed with her decision exactly the way she knew they would. Respecting her family's opinion, she only told them that it was her life and she was not living to please anyone but herself. Yet in her heart, she felt and believed that their opinion was more of a fact. How could she marry someone who will serve the next couple of years in prison? Unsure of how to explain her reasons, the only thing she had the answer to was her love for a man that she had just agreed to marry.

By the next month, she went down to the courthouse in their hometown and paid for the marriage license. She had to wait hours before she could see a judge who would approve their jailhouse matrimony. The longer she waited in the halls, it gave her more time to think. She was very afraid of what the next step would be after she made it official. She truly loved him but she did not want to spend the first few years of her marriage alone. Living in the moment, she was mentally prepared to give up her last name to become Mrs. Jordan "Ghost" Dawkins. She chose to make the permanent decision 'till death do them part.' Notifying his parents, Mama Jewel and Dollar Bill, came to the courthouse for the support of their son. Kali came to stand as Ghosts' proxy in support of her friend's decision.

Once the judge approved the ceremony, he read off a script and asked Kali to repeat the words just as if she was Ghost. Loyalty repeated the same scripting, then he pronounced them man and wife. Both girls couldn't help but burst into laughter. Standing behind them was Mama Jewel and Dollar Bill, as Loyalty showed them the marriage certificate with a face full of joy. They hugged their new daughter-in-law, then Dollar Bill proceeded to pull out a box from his pocket and placed a gorgeous ring on her finger. The feeling was so surreal and unexpected that it made tears form because who she wanted most was not present.

After it was over, they drove off to meet up with Kash for drinks at her favorite restaurant, Pappadeaux. Kali caught her staring out of the window the entire time looking up at the clouds. She noticed her glance at the ring on her finger then focus her attention back on the empty sky. Kali couldn't help but ask her friend what was on her mind.

"You ok? So, how do you feel? Married?" Kali asked.

"I feel different. Like, I know that I got married to you technically." She laughed. "Yet, I also know that I just signed up for a lifetime partnership with a man who doesn't even have a release date yet." She soaked in her feelings.

"It's not that bad. Some women walked down an aisle in front of all their family and friends to marry for all the wrong reasons. You just so happen to marry a man for what you believe in, love and loyalty. There is nothing wrong with that! I wouldn't pay attention to anyone who tells you different." She tried to convince.

"Thanks Kali." She smiled. "Now let's meet Kash and get drunk. I need a blunt." She stated, turning up the radio while Chris Brown's song "With You", blared through the speakers.

The next morning, she was awakened by her phone vibrating on her pillow which served no justice to the hangover she was having. Noticing that it was Ghost, she couldn't wait to tell him that everything was official.

"Good morning babe. What's up?" She answered.

"I was hoping to hear from you last night but I called you like three times. You okay?" He asked.

"Yes, I'm fine. Just had one too many drinks so by the time you called, the liquor had already claimed me for the night. The bad news is, I have a major headache and I feel this hangover trying to ruin my day. There is good news though… "I's married nah." She replied, as she mocked the line from the film, "The Color Purple".

"For real? Stop playing. You serious? You're my wife? I'm a husband? Why didn't you tell me yesterday? I can't believe you really love me and made that happen. We're in this for better or worse, right?" He bombarded with questions.

"Forever! I love you Jordan! Just be honest with me about anything and my trust will always be with you. I always wanted to grow old with someone who loves me unconditionally, despite everything. I'm not a liar and I don't expect to be married to one. I won't betray you so don't ever question my loyalty. When you get out, there is no more hustling or taking chances in the streets that could cost you your life. I'm with you for rich or poor. They say the richest thing a man can have is love. Nothing is greater than that." She genuinely stated.

"You are a wonderful person Loyalty. One day, you are going to be great at whatever you do. I just pray that I'm apart of that so I can watch you grow old too. I'm about to go celebrate, I have a few homies I want to brag too. You're a treasure that I found, like a diamond in the mud. I'm glad I spotted you before someone else ruined the greatness in you." He continued.

The remainder of their 30 minute phone call was as close to a honeymoon as she would get. Discussing what life would be like once he was set free, she could only close her eyes and imagine the perfect picture he was painting. Convincing herself that she would honor their union even though they did not stand before each other to recite the vows. The only reward she got for being loyal to a man behind bars was his total appreciation for all she did. He would acknowledge every move she made while applauding her trustworthy behavior. Now that they were legally married, she dedicated every extra minute of her time to focus on his lawyer because she now needed that release date more than ever.

A few more months had gone by, marking three years since he had been locked away in federal custody. Her attitude was becoming nasty and savage, yet she still had a heart of gold. She was so irritated with her life and the things she could not change, it affected the way she felt about everyone around her. The slightest things annoyed her, mainly because she was sexually frustrated and yearning to be physically loved. Yet there was nothing she could do but sit back and wait for the only man she wanted to receive it from.

The more time passed, her hormones raged dangerously out of control causing her to keep a heavy chip on her shoulder. It was so easy to get a reaction out of her since she was not dodging any conflict.

One night, the girls met up for drinks then shortly decided they should go clubbing to celebrate Joy's birthday. It was one of the most decent clubs in town, so they went and changed into party attire. Meeting up in the parking lot, they spotted a girl named Demi, who was a fling of Ghosts' back in the day. For no logical reason, she kept giving Loyalty ugly stares to make it obvious that she had a problem. Once the girls caught a whiff of it, they each reacted on it and made sure Demi knew the beef was now mutual. It doesn't take much to get a crowd hyped when liquor is involved. Especially when tension is in the air and lil Boosie rap songs are blaring through the speakers. Weeks before, she had an altercation with some other chic behind Ghost which made her upset that they waited until he was locked up to surface. She was far from naïve but she was a person to trust what someone told her, expecting everyone to keep it real. Although reality made her believe; without hearing it from his mouth that he was dealing with more than just her when he was dating Eve.

They were making direct gestures to Demi and her friends while the song continued to play. Shortly after, the lights came on to signal that the club was over and it was time to head to the parking lot. Loyalty was the driver, so they all hopped inside her car and began discussing the shenanigans that just took place inside the club. It was more than funny because from what she had known, Demi and her group of flunkies were not about the action they were trying to create. Pulling out to the street, she noticed a car that was driving recklessly behind them swerving from lane to lane. Once she realized it was Demi, she began to drive a little slower, attempting to call her bluff.

Instead of creeping behind them, Demi decided to go around and proceed to do the same thing, swerving from one side of the road to the other. By the looks of her car, it seemed to be worth the dramatics she was putting on. Everyone inside was ready for the altercation they knew was about to take place once the cars stopped. Enough was enough, so she maintained the same speed, staying in her own lane. The liquor had already decided for her that if Demi swerved in front of her again, she was going to smash the back of her car. Just as she expected, the tiny car Demi was driving recklessly flew past them again. Instead of trying to dodge her, she rear ended the vehicle, violently slamming into the trunk.

"LOYALTY!!" Everyone yelled at once, looking at the wrecked cars.

Speechless and nearly frozen, she just looked forward with both hands still on her steering wheel. It came to the point of no return and her only argument was, it was not her fault. Within a second, she saw her friends all jump out of the car as one big confrontation took place in the middle of MLK Blvd. The traffic was backed up down the intersection while spectators walked up to watch the fight unfold just as they saw it coming. Once Loyalty walked up to the crowd, Kash was already fighting the passenger from Demi's car. Even though Kash was about 5'5 and weighed every bit of 115 pounds, she was always the first one who was down for whatever. She had Loyalty's back no matter what, right or wrong. The girls were a joke and unknowingly signed up for something that Loyalty and her crew lived for. ACTION.

Demi walked up and asked for Loyalty's insurance while a few elderly people approached the wreckage to make sure everyone was okay. She advised her there was no way she would hand over her insurance. She told her that the car was already old, so she should just buy another one. Informing her that she initiated what just happened, so she had better move around before the situation got uglier than what it already was. Club security had walked down the street, attempting to break up the big girls fight that took place.

Warning them that the police were coming, everyone attempted to walk back to their cars until they noticed more unfinished business. Demi was walking off, she continued to run her mouth from afar, not noticing that security had already walked back to the club. When Loyalty noticed no one around to stop it, she calculated each step as she walked up to her opponent and began swinging. Not sure if it was the Hennessey or just her built up emotions but she took every ounce of anger out on Demi. She could hear her friends excitement as they cheered from the side, while screaming out in thrill that she was winning. Once the girls got wrestled up, she heard Kash and her other friends warning Demi to let go of her hair. Maybe she didn't do it quick enough. Maybe they just wanted to jump in anyway but everyone began swinging until the police arrived. Loyalty only received a ticket for refusing to give up her insurance and failure to control speed. It had been one crazy night as the girls drove off in her car that was now wrecked in the front. She figured her dad would help her come up with something, after all, he always came through when she needed him.

A few months later, gossip and mess got out of hand with her friends which caused them to have friction when they were around each other. Even their body language was full of bad vibes. When you knowingly cross someone who trusted you, you deserve the consequences. She did not discriminate or choose sides when it came to integrity. Each day of feeling played, was slowly making her more of a savage than she wanted to become. Friends can definitely mistake your loyalty for weakness, yet there was nothing weak about her when it came down to fighting.

At that point, with the rumors and chaos that was unfolding between them, she had to address the pillow talking that was jeopardizing their friendship. Once Arielle learned of the things that was brought to her attention, she immediately became defensive. Not one to argue over what she already knew to be true, she shoved Arielle as hard as she could with a stiff push to her chest. Arielle attempted to charge back at Loyalty but there were people who got in between them to stop what was escalating. Before she walked off, she warned Arielle that a fight was inevitable the next time they saw each other.

A few weeks later, she spotted her inside the mall getting a few things from Victoria's Secret. Once they made eye contact, it was confirmation that their time had finally come. She walked right up to her and initiated the first contact that started the fight. Kali and Kash were warning Loyalty that the workers had called mall security and it was time to go. The brawl eventually led to the next store while everyone stopped and watched the girls slam from window to window. After the girls broke them apart, Loyalty snatched up Arielle's shopping bags because she knew she had merchandise for sale inside. Not done with the confrontation, she advised her that if she wanted the things she had taken from her, she was going to have to fight for it. Surprisingly, Arielle was up for the challenge as she attempted to reach for her bags. It led to a second fight right outside of Forever 21, while the girls continued to fight as if they had never been friends before. To Loyalty, being friends didn't mean anything once you crossed the line like an enemy. You deserve to be treated accordingly!

The next month, she found herself in a similar altercation with Kali. She was just not accepting anything less than what she was offering. If you couldn't be her friend the right way, then she didn't want the friendship at all. Word got out about the abortion she had years prior and no one knew that kind of information but her friends. Getting to the bottom of it, she confronted Kali about the betrayal she felt. Reminding her that you cannot talk your friends' business to every guy you deal with. Denying the accusations, Loyalty disregarded her explanations and told her that there was no way she could allow her to walk away without a fight.

Similar to the situation with Arielle, she spotted Kali walking into the mall one night with a few girls. She walked up to her and advised her to put her things down so it could be a fair fight between them. Kali pleaded the fifth and began to express how she did not want to fight because they had been friends for so long. She wanted to define the meaning of friends for Kali because apparently they lived by two different definitions. It hurt her as well that it led down to a physical altercation between her and a best friend that she'd known since ninth grade. However, there are some things as a friend that you should not do or say out of respect. Once you cross that line, everything else is null and void. Realizing that she could not avoid the conflict Loyalty was insisting, she slowly dropped her mall bags. Loyalty felt so relieved after the incident even though they say fighting solves nothing. It gave her ease knowing that she was not about to let anyone play her, no matter what title you held in her life.

One afternoon, they had been chilling all day just riding around smoking and running the city streets. Sometimes, the munchies will have you pulling over at every store you see or any place that's serving some good food. The girls pulled into a parking lot at one of the popular stores in town so they could get snacks and more Swishers. When they parked, Kash began staring at a guy outside who looked familiar. Loyalty noticed he had the perfect caramel skin, with a nice build as they exchanged stares. He wore the tightest shirt that complemented every muscle with the demeanor of a Boss.

"Wait a minute! Girl, I can't believe he finally out. That's Kokaine, Eve's baby daddy." Kash informed her.

"For real? I never saw him before. He cute! Dang, he looking over here! You get out Kash, I'm too high." She stated.

"You act like I'm low!" Kash sarcastically replied. "Man, I got out at the last store run. It's your turn."

"Whatever, trick!" Loyalty smacked her lips and slammed the door.

Now, the history between Ghost and Kokaine was simple. Kokaine had been locked up for five years and Eve immediately started dating Ghost when he was jailed. It had the streets talking about the rumored beef between them and although she had never seen him, she wasn't trying to either. Her heart almost jumped out of her chest when she heard him speak to her.

"What's up ma, how you doing?" He yelled out.

"I'm good." She stated, picking up a little speed in her walk.

"Slow down. Can I talk to you for a second?" He asked.

She turned around because she realized he truly didn't know who she was. Since they never encountered one another, it was believable because their past had never collided. Figuring it wouldn't hurt to say a word or two, she turned to let him know.

"You really don't know me, do you?" She asked. Looking at him was a mistake because he was even more handsome now that she was closer.

"Nahh but I'm trying too!" He boldly stated.

"I'm Ghost's wife but nice to meet you anyway. Welcome home!" She began to walk off, knowing that she did not want any bad blood.

"Oh! That's cool. I respect that. You have a nice day baby." He stated.

When she got back to the car, Kash informed her that he had been locked up for the last 5 years and had just gotten out weeks before.

On the day of his release, Eve was coincidentally arrested on charges that associated her with a crime her current boyfriend was accused of. What are the odds of that? It's like they did a prison swap and she was now walking in the same shoes he had been in when she left him. Hearing of the news, she felt terrible for Eve because she had kids that needed her. Although they weren't friends, she wouldn't wish a jail sentence on anyone. Especially when Loyalty had been around Eve's kids a few times herself. Her heart instantly went out to them. One thing she believed in was to treat others how you would want to be treated because karma has a long term memory.

CHAPTER 13

"Welcome Home"

CALENDARS ALWAYS MADE HER EMOTIONAL when she looked at the days in a month and noticed the twelve long months in a year. Each hour she survived made her realize that pain and stress could really drive someone mentally ill. Sure she had her sanity but her heart was in pieces and each step began to hurt more as she walked all over them. She had done all she could do for Ghost but his future was now in the hands of a judge who did not favor African Americans, by far. That thought alone, caved her shattered heart inside her chest even more as she began to slip in and out of faith. She recalled the pastor saying at church that you only needed faith the size of a mustard seed. That one thing in particular stuck with her because she could feel herself losing hope in all the things she had been praying for. Yet, she still had enough fight in her soul to keep kneeling down for prayer. Gathering a pile of photos she could find of Ghost, she laid them on the carpet as she sat on the floor next to her bed. Being that she prayed every day for the same things, she had ran out of words to say and didn't want to bother God with a repetitive prayer. Crying out for help, there were only thoughts racing through her mind as she soaked in her sorrow.

"God, please help me! I've been attending church, paying my tithes, honoring my vows and growing this relationship with you.

Please, help me! I've done all I can. You have to take it from here. Please take it from here. Please!" She cried.

The next morning, she woke up in the same position she had been in all night with pictures laying on the floor. She got up to take a shower then proceeded with her day, preparing for work as if she had not been crying all night. Her mom would always say, *'to never let a stranger identify your pain but let them recognize your strength.'* So with that, her chin would be held up while her chest would stick out as if nothing in her life worried her. She would only vent to her friends about the agony and suffering she felt taking over her at night. After a few drinks and a blunt, it would sometimes numb the ache so that she could drift into a peaceful sleep.

That following Monday, it was now time for Ghost's federal court date that she had been dreading. It had a huge impact on her future, so she prayed for the best but still braced her heart for the worse. When she arrived at the entrance, the security guard immediately stopped her in her tracks to warn her of the dress code she was in violation of.

"Excuse me? How am I supposed to drive back home and make it back within 30 minutes? Please, can I just wear a jacket? I can't miss my husband's trial, sir!" She explained.

"Your blouse is not appropriate, I'm sorry. You have to leave." He advised.

She walked away as quickly as she could when she noticed his father pulling into the parking lot as well. She stopped to inform him that the dress code was very strict and that she had been turned around for her shirt. He said that he would text her if it started before she got back and that was a big relief for her. She went to the closest store, purchasing a more suitable blouse from Target that was within their dresscode policy. She changed her top once she got back into the car, then quickly headed back to the courthouse. She had been calling both of his lawyers all morning and neither answered or returned her phone calls. Arriving back to court, she was filled with peace once she noticed one of his lawyers in the hallway. Once he noticed her, he acknowledged her presence with a wave and motioned for her to come over. The anxiety began as she watched him open his briefcase and flip through court documents trying to explain the events that were about to take place.

"I just need a payment today as you promised because I have delivered everything you asked. Things are looking terrific for Mr. Dawkins and before they put him in transit to the courthouse, I had a visit with him this morning. I made him aware that the gun case has been dismissed because there was no solid evidence. It was thrown out by the D.A and that's what I've been fighting for. He has cooperated and did as I asked the entire time. A very humble and nice guy with a heavy attitude. Now, the judge has offered ten years and Mr. Dawkins has declined. I have been working with the attorney you guys hired on but it's out of my hands on that call. Sorry!" He stated.

"No, thank you so much! I really appreciate it and I'm sure he was thrilled to hear that the gun had been thrown out because that was his biggest worry. I can't wait to speak with him!" She stated, handing him the last payment as they sat on the bench and continued to discuss the possibilities.

When she walked into the courtroom, she sat near the front row so he could see her without having to search the aisles. Just as the officers opened the door to the left of the judge, he appeared from the back with a pleasant smile. Seems that he was just as pleased that the day had finally come and was ready for the remainder of his time to be a cake walk. He would say that doing time is easier when you know your release date but doing day for day without a sentence is torture. He stopped asking if she knew his court dates or if she was attending because she started to know before him. She continuously reminded him that it was an insult to ask if she would be there to support him. It seemed self-explanatory that she was there no matter what but this moment was definitely about to decide their fate for the next few years.

His lawyer handling the case walked in once Ghost had been placed at the table, so he strolled over next to him to take a seat. When Ghost mentioned to her that his lawyer advised him that he could get him off with no charges, she knew that was just a dream. She kept informing him that the feds do not arrest you because they "think" you did something. Either they know or they have been watching long enough to have reasons to arrest. He would be a fool to allow the attorney to set his hopes up for failure because he was under the assumption that he would be released after court. She told him that if the small ounce of faith he had in his lawyer didn't go as planned, then he had better accept whatever number they give. Refusing it again and taking it to trial was not an option because the number would be larger than the initial offer, which he knew that. He argued that ten years was too much time to agree on without some sort of fight.

The judge began to read off each charge as he approached the bench. His eyes were glued to the man's forehead, not missing a word. He then started speaking to the judge as if he was beginning to plead his case. Stating how he wanted a better life and with a new chance he will no longer participate with distributing drugs to the streets. She couldn't believe how intelligent he sounded and the things that escaped his mouth sounded so truthful. Yet knowing Ghost, he was not one ounce close to being sorry for his hustle. The Judge began reading off some type of scripting about being a better individual as he asked Ghost to repeat each line after him. Then immediately after the statements, he announced that he was being sentenced to five years in a federal institution. Each word after that seemed to be a blur as tears formed in her eyes. He looked back instantly to see her reaction as she blew a kiss, signifying that she was happy with the outcome.

She dreaded to watch him go but now knew that it wouldn't be long before he would be free again. Walking to the parking lot, she was approached by his lawyer as he apologized for not returning her calls. He explained that he did not want to get her hopes up high on something that he wasn't for sure would take place. He mentioned that he knew the judge very well and it took some time granting him the five years they were awarded with. He gave his best wishes for their future as he walked off to his vehicle.

She sat in the car and laughed while tears were slowing escaping her eyes. She thanked God nonstop because no matter how imperfect you are, God will still show you favor. His parents were thrilled as well that one of their sons would finally be granted freedom again. The rest of her day was a celebration once she met up with Kash and Arin to get some liquor.

A big worry of hers had finally been lifted off her shoulders and her focus was now on his release date. She had began buying clothes, hats, shoes and practically anything she saw that he could use. She could not believe that the time had come closer to where she could finally start hanging up clothes on his side of the closet again. She made sure that her bills were paid on time each month so she wouldn't be behind or play catch up so close to his release date. He had been incarcerated four years now and she had to pat herself on the back for her own patience. Her horoscope seemed to have nailed her personality because she was loyal when it came to those she loved. She had not been intimate with anyone since the last time Ghost touched her and her desire for romance was driving her crazy. The bigger picture was that she only wanted sex from one man, so anyone other than Ghost didn't stand a chance.

When she got home, there was a letter as usual from Ghost but this letter was one of the sweetest as he thanked her for riding the wave with him like she promised in the beginning. Confessing that he had never met a woman so strong in her beliefs, he acknowledged that her word was really bond. Admitting that he did not believe such a woman existed who could stick by her man through such a storm. Sometimes people around you try to hide jealousy and destroy a relationship by lies, claiming to have truth about who a person is. While others make false accusations to destroy who a person is not. He continued to state that he paid attention to her actions, gestures and patterns to judge her answers. All things done in the dark come to light, so whatever a person doesn't catch you doing, it will surface sooner or later. It was one of the reasons he thanked her for discussing her past and telling him about who she was before life allowed them to meet. That let him know who he was dealing with and gave him the option of whether to accept the real her or not.

Once she was done reading his letter, she put out her blunt in the ashtray then grabbed a paper and let the pen do it's thing. Her only thoughts were that he should've known better to doubt her this entire time. Seemed as if he confessed that he questioned her loyalty in the beginning but towards the end, time taught him that she was solid. She put a few pictures of herself inside the envelope that was pre-addressed to him, then slid the one page note inside that stated lyrics to Monica's song, "You should've Known Better."

She knew from the very beginning that she would've never been able to forget about him being behind bars. She never understood how any person who claimed to love someone, could go cold turkey on them because handcuffs caught them by the wrist. When you stick with someone while they are winning, the worst thing you can do is leave them when they have already lost their freedom. If you can't be loyal, then you could at least be honest or keep in touch every now and then. Ghost always said that a person in jail is "outta sight - outta mind" because people don't remember what you done for them once you're no longer able to do it.

A few months had passed and it allowed her to have enough money to pay his surcharges, which would finally give him the opportunity to obtain a drivers license. He was so excited when she told him she had taken care of the fees so that he could walk into the Department of Public Safety office and take his driver's test. He never had a drivers license and stated that no one ever cared enough to help him get one.

She began creating a resume, so that he could apply for jobs that interested him. She made it clear that hustling could no longer be his source of income, because everyone was now telling on each other and it was just a big cycle of returning to prison. She was not signing up to wait for him again while he serves another prison sentence for the same mistakes. He agreed and advised her that he just wanted to have a baby girl and focus on making a decent living without surviving financially through the streets.

The time had finally come as she sat in the parking lot of the federal prison that housed Ghost. It had been four years and eleven months. Now that it was all over, time had passed quicker than she thought. Her hormones were raging out of control as she sat in the car for over two hours waiting for him to walk out the doors. She wanted to get out so badly and question the guards on whether or not he was being released. The paperwork stated his release date and time, along with the address for the halfway house he was too report to by noon. It was going on 11:30 AM as she began to get irritated because she at least wanted him to come home first. She woke up in the middle of the night to start baking his favorite desserts and made a fresh batch of his favorite lemonade. She left the house with candles lit and trails of rose pedals leading to the bedroom. Every inch of the house was clean while a R&B cd played with a hot meal on the stove. She had baked chicken with potatoes in the oven, with a few sides of yams, pinto beans, macaroni, cabbage, dirty rice and cornbread. Now the prison was running behind on his scheduled 9am release time and nothing went as planned.

She looked down at her attire again as she sat completely naked under a black Polo robe that she had purchased for him. Her hair was curled and pinned up just right as she started to become impatient. Just as she was about to call the front desk of the prison, she saw the doors open and out came at least six inmates. It felt better than anything she had ever experienced once she saw Ghost walk past the guards with a box in his hand.

Parking towards the back of the parking lot was purposely. She hopped out of the car and waited for him to come closer. He opened the door and tossed his box inside, then picked her up off the ground for the tightest hug ever. She laughed and begged him to put her down because she felt her robe strap was loosening. Once he placed her back on the ground, he kissed her lips then went under the robe with his hands.

"Babe, what the hell do you have on? I thought this was a jacket! Girl, you standing out here butt naked in a dang house coat. You want me to kill you? You already trying to put me back behind those walls." He laughed.

"It's been five very long years, so I wanted to make it easy! What? You don't like what you see?" She smiled, kissing his lips again.

"Let's go. I'll show you! Man, it feels good to finally leave here with you instead of watching you go. You looked so lonely when you left sometimes and it ate at me the whole day. Now, I'm home baby! I promise I'm never going back." He stated, as they drove off into traffic.

She informed him that the directions she was given to the halfway house had bold letters on the top that stated he must be there by noon, no exceptions. He thought there was some sort of time frame between his release so they could go home to enjoy each other for awhile. She explained to him that his release was set for 9am but they let him out so late that it interfered with their play time. She promised that once she dropped him off, she would come right back to bring the things they allowed him to have and a plate of food she cooked. There were candles still burning at home, plus she was naked so it was a must that she returned back to the house. It was their first argument and he was not giving up without making his point.

"Look, I'm not going. I'll tell them I had a flat or that we ran out of gas or something. Babe, I'm coming with you. I want to see the food you prepared and the roses. Plus, you're sitting here naked, come on man. Don't do this!" He pleaded.

"Jordan, listen to me. This paper CLEARLY STATES that there are no exceptions for you being late. Please follow the rules before they lock you back up. I promise I will come right back. My word!" She convinced.

"I want to make love Loyalty. I'm already feening for you babe. Please." He softly stated.

"We're already here! There goes the other guys that were released with you. Don't be the only one who didn't follow instructions and give them a reason to make an example out of you. I want to make love too but we've waited this long, a few more hours won't hurt. I'm not jeopardizing that for anything." She replied, kissing his lips.

With no response, he opened the door with a pout across his face then walked inside slowly and never looked back. It hurt her that she had to tell him no and go against every flutter in her body that just wanted to give in. Most guards in the halfway house are worse than the correctional officers in prison. She drove off and headed home to do exactly what she stated. Once she took a shower, she put on some fresh clothes and fixed him several plates of food. She packed his bag of clothes, along with the entire pan of brownies and pecan pie.

Returning to the halfway house, she noticed that the set up was similar to visitation in prison, only a little more freedom. She was able to sit with him for three hours while he ate his food and shared his dessert pans with the guys he knew. He had a few more visits come in while she was there, which was expected because she knew word had gotten out that he was home. She was happy just to see his excitement as he laughed with old friends he hadn't seen in years. Once visit was over, they said their farewells and she advised him she was heading home to get some rest. She had been up all night preparing for his return, so she was exhausted. He told her to take a nap, then come back around 9pm to pick him up. He was told that there was a drug class everyone had to attend that night but he happened to know the guy that was leading it. All he had to do was sign in and the guy was going to let him leave for an hour.

She went home and immediately fell off into her nap that was very much needed. Her alarm went off around 8, so she showered and slipped on a dress with nothing under it. Heading to the halfway house, she got a call from Ghost advising her to stop and get the closest hotel room near the halfway house. Going against her own mind, she agreed to his command and pulled on the side of a building downtown. Looking at a few cars, she noticed that at least two other guys were sneaking away as well. When she noticed him walking to the car, butterflies filled her stomach instantly. Jumping in the passengers seat, he wasted no time making contact with her body as he pulled his shirt off, touching and kissing her during the short drive to the hotel.

Before they could even get through the door, her dress was off and his clothes were on the floor. As they pleased each other sexually, this moment was everything she had been needing, mentally. Her mind was going blank, as her soul escaped her body for just a short time. It seemed as if she was giving up her virginity all over again. She had to remind him several times to take it easy, because he started off handling her small frame rather rough. Breathing heavily, he could only apologize, as he continued to slip into ecstatsy.

She was beyond satisfied, while he perfomed as if he was trying to make a baby that night. Just as she was about to remind him that he only had a hour to spare, his stroking became no more as he passed out next to her and instantly began snoring. She thought he was pretending, so she started pushing him by the shoulders and calling his name repeatedly. When she kept getting no response, she yelled a little louder and pulled the covers completely off of him. Noticing the time, he jumped up, as they began to rush out of the room within minutes.

By the time they made it back to the car, it was already past the one hour window but he had to sign himself out of the drug orientation class. He seemed to be nonchalant about it and as usual, she took on the worry and asked him one thousand questions about the possible consequences. Brushing past the topic, his focus was coming up with a plan to make a way back inside the halfway house. Just his luck, he noticed the instructor for the class was still putting a few things inside his car. Kissing her lips goodbye, he told her to let him out and that he could take care of everything from there.

"Hey, what's up bro? I appreciate you for letting me have that hour to be with my wife. I heard the fellas saying it was some sort of sign out sheet but I may have missed that." He stated, approaching the instructor's car.

"No problem Jordan, Welcome home again! I'll walk you inside so the security guard will allow you in. Don't get yourself into any trouble, because this place is pretty strict and you won't have many chances to do what you just did tonight. An important thing I tell most of you around here, is that nearly 85% of you guys either end up returning back to incarceration or finding a new home in a graveyard. Sad part is son, that number is calculated from the first five years of their release from prison. Don't become a statistic young man! Do something different with yourself and don't be afraid to trade your old life for a new one. Find you a job, take care of your family and make sure you watch out for everybody in those streets." The instructor contined to give Ghost a small lecture about how he should change his life in a positive direction.

He gave Ghost the rundown on a few halfway house rules and allowed him a chance to sign the sheet he missed after class. Walking him into the building, the guards checked him up and down as if they were airport security or an episode of COPS. Once he was allowed the chance to make it to his bunk, he only had a few minutes to shower as the guard announced that it was almost time for all activity to cease. He got a chance to go through the bag Loyalty packed for him. He laid down and cut on the cell phone she had purchased and it was no surprise that she prestored the only numbers she figured he would need. He clicked on the contact number stored as *Wife*, while he turned on the mp3 player trying to figure out how to search through the music.

"Hey husband, I see you found your phone and noticed the little contact list too!" She began to laugh.

"Girl, you something else. I miss you! Are you in bed? Thank you for coming back shawty, that was just the medicine I needed to sleep like a baby. I wish I could be laying with you but it's all good. They say we get to leave during the week if you have a job. So you know what that means right? Yea, I need a job that I can start tomorrow." Drowsy, his words were almost in a deep whisper.

"I wish you could start tomorrow too, trust me! I can't wait to see you in somebody's uniform." She laughed.

"What you mean, somebody's?" He laughed. "I'm not working anywhere corny, so you can forget it. I want to start off with a real job! You know, like a hard working man's job. I am the man, ain't I?" He continued.

"Yes baby, you're *the man!* I'll start looking for those manly jobs ASAP." She continued to laugh.

"What's so funny girl? You laughing like you don't believe in my work ethics. Just have my snacks and food for my lunch in one of those big orange suitcases." He stated.

"Ghost stop, they're called lunch boxes. That's why we have a long way to go before you can even get an interview but I got you baby." She laughed uncontrollably.

They continued to talk for the next 15 minutes until he stated that he had to go. He was told they could only use their personal phones during the day. He laid down and allowed the R&B songs that were saved to the mp3 player soothe him to sleep. At home, she slept all over the bed as she gave into the comfort and peace that allowed her hormones to find it's balance again.

A few weeks later, after applying nearly everwhere she could think of for Ghost. They finally received a call back from the truck stop where she previously worked. Once he came home, she was so busy getting him situated and readjusted that she had to quit working two jobs. She was still pretty cool with several workers, so she applied for him a position at the Tire and Oil Shop. Now, he had never worked that particular position but he mentioned to her that 18 wheelers interested him. She thought he may like servicing them as well, then possibly move on to another interest.

Great thing about working, was that the halfway house had put in a request that allowed him to start the transition from their facility to house arrest with a monitor around his ankle. He could only go to work and then head back home because the halfway house would definitely call to check. If he was lucky enough, he could leave work early and have a little extra time to play in the streets before he had to start heading home to accept that call. He seemed to love being on house arrest and she made sure that he was set up with everything he would need while she was gone.

She was now only working at the warehouse because it was day shifts during the week that allowed her to be home for him at night. He knew that she wasn't out messing around on him but he simply just wanted her at home all to himself. He had always been the jealous type and hated that she was a well known person, so if someone even spoke to her, he would always add his two cents. She didn't mind. She simply just enjoyed the moments of him having to stay in the house, because that was way better than him being granted to hang in the streets.

A couple weeks went by and he started calling in, explaining to her that he must had gotten a sinus cold or the flu. He was for certain he was sick and could not stand in the heat changing oils and tires all day. She started leaving work during lunch because she would begin feeling sick as well. By Ghost being at home with cold symptoms, she would rush back to snuggle in bed and they slept the day away. Waking up during the night to talk and watch movies, they would start making breakfast at three in the morning. This night in particular, he mentioned that it was something he had been meaning to say.

"Ya' know, I meant to tell you this morning that you feel so different. Like, it's a new feeling. It was so good, I had to tell my bro about it and how crazy I am over you. Anyways, he said you might be pregnant." He ended his statement with a smile.

"What?" She looked puzzled. Actually tripped out because once again, pregnancy never crossed her mind.

"You know, with a baby!!" I told my mama I was gonna tell you to take a test, so I asked her to bring us one." He informed her, walking off to go get the package.

"Really Jordan?" She burst out in laughter.

"Come on babe, take it. Man, I'm telling you. I just know I'm right. They say the sex will tell you everything and last night it was talking to me." He laughed. "Just take it when you have to pee." He stated, walking off to go shower.

She laid back down and thought about all the little signs that she really paid no mind to before. Her breast felt full and tender to be a handful. Also, she had been feeling a little nauseated when she ate breakfast for the past few days. He had only been out for three weeks and she didn't think a baby would be the first thing they would journey into before enjoying just the two of them first. Yet, there was a strong possibility just sitting at the pit of her stomach, literally.

Once he stepped out of the shower, she instantly had to use the restroom but it was coming out of her mouth instead. She made her way through the hall and swung the toilet seat up to quickly vomit in the commode. He stopped in the middle of drying his body off with a towel and stood there frozen as he watched.

"I knew it!" He shouted.

He ran her some bath water, then went to the kitchen to fix her a glass of orange juice. He grabbed a bath towel, then gently placed her in the tub and bathed her. He couldn't help but talk the entire time and tell her how excited he was about having a baby, speaking as if she had already taken the test. Once she was out of the tub, she brushed her teeth and laid back in bed until she had to pee. Walking to the bath room, he was right on her toes so that he could watch her every move for a positive result.

"Make sure you pee right on the little piece it says to pee on. Read the instructions that said to make it your first urine of the day." He stated, looking around. "So, it's morning… and we slept the night away…!" He began harmonizing the R&B tune.

They placed the cap back on the tip of the test and laid it flat on the counter top. He began to hug her, then led to kisses and then led to his daily dose of the love she had been missing for those five years. She loved the way he would hold on to her while he slept and just to watch him with his eyes closed, she actually gave a smile at the thought of their own child. It made her mind refocus on that pregnancy test, so she slipped out of bed and walked into the bathroom.

She stood in front of the sink for just a few seconds before she dropped her head to stare down at the white pregnancy stick. When she looked down at the word, it made her laugh because Ghost made sure he would understand the test by making his mom purchase the one with words. Maybe the laugh woke him up because he then appeared in the doorway, disturbed from his brief nap, barely holding one eye open.

"What does it say baby? It's a girl or what?" He asked.

Laughing at his question, her giggle only lasted for two seconds before she looked directly back into the mirror to tell herself it was real.

"We're pregnant." She whispered, smiling at her reflection.

CHAPTER 14

"Roll With The Punches"

MORNINGS, WERE BY FAR THE worst part of the day. The nausea was unlike any stomach virus or common cold symptoms she had ever experienced. No matter what she would drink or how light she would eat, it would all come out of her body the same way it went in. She had missed over a month of work at the warehouse, making them aware that she was simply in bad shape. There was no other diagnosis or any prescribed medication and the only advice anyone could give her was to just wait it out. She was only two months and couldn't bare the thought of feeling horrible for several more weeks.

Ghost was tremendously helpful around the house by keeping up with the laundry, cooking and cleaning. There were days when she couldn't do anything but sleep. The times she lay awake, she dreamed about being sleep. If labor was anything near the morning sickness she was going through, she knew for sure it was nothing she wanted to experience again.

As with anything, some men grow tired of being in the house for so many hours during a 24 hour period. Since he had no choice but to remain confined to there townhome, he was starting to become a monster. He continued to work during the day and with his change in behavior, that was exactly where she preferred he stay. When he wanted to engage in any sexual activity that involved her full participation, she just simply could not shake off the nausea. Understanding how long he had been deprived of sex during those years of being incarcerated, she would try her best to please him anyway.

Despite the way she was beginning to feel about his change in attitude, the love she had for him remained the same. He noticed she was becoming committed to her personal space and began to show his rage like never before. When he started daily arguments behind it, she calmly explained that it was her body changing and not her heart. She would go from sleeping in the bed, to sleeping upright on the couch at night. Then maybe the next few days, she would find herself curled up on the bathroom floor because she constantly had to vomit. She expressed her feelings to him about the changes pregnancy caused and what she needed most was his understanding and support.

"I've been a faithful wife to you while you were away. Now that you are here, I just ask for a supporting husband to do the same. I don't want to argue about a pregnancy that I can't control. You think I like not being able to keep anything in my stomach? Do you think I like missing work? I want my checks just like I did when you were gone. Don't think for one second I'm going to sit around getting fat and lazy!" She explained.

"I don't give a damn about all that. When a husband needs love, it's your job to give it to me. You need to shake that morning sickness excuse off quick because I'm starting to lose my patience." He snapped back.

"Excuse me? Patience? Did you just say, patience? Wow, imagine that! After a few months of being granted your freedom, you all of a sudden losing patience. I should have lost patience a few months after they locked you up, then you wouldn't be a factor now." She bodly stated.

"What?" He got up and walked over to her.

"Let me guess, now you losing your cool? HA! That's funny because at the rate you're going, you better watch it before you lose your wife. You have some nerve to tell me you're losing patience. You about to be losing alright!" She remained standing, waiting for him to approach her.

Once he was within arms reach, he slapped her across the face. She didn't have time to think anything because her reflex kicked in and reacted for her. As she started throwing punches, it caught him completely off guard as they both fell over a chair next to the dining room table. She rushed up before him, feeling her uneasy stomach taking over the moment again as she hurried to the restroom in need of the commode. He stood in the bathroom doorway and continued his argument, making no valid points at all.

"Ghost, shut up and walk away. Leave me alone!!" She weakly stated.

"You still want to be disrespectful huh?" He grabbed her by the arm and pulled her out to the hallway.

She laid on the floor feeling weak because nausea claimed the remaining energy that she desperately needed. That was the only advantage he had over her, so he used it. Telling her that she would learn to keep her mouth closed and to respect him. He squatted down to sit on her legs while he pinned her arms down under his knees. With one hand holding her forehead, he began to squeeze her cheeks together so tightly that her teeth started to cut the inside of her mouth. Screaming, squirming and yelling for him to stop, she could only let her thoughts get her past the moment. She couldn't believe he was purposely inflicting such horrible pain while she was carrying his child. Tears poured from her eyes as the pressure from his grip got tighter and tighter around her cheeks and jaw bone.

He finally loosened his grip and stood to his feet, telling her that a smart mouth would get her nowhere but in trouble everytime. He walked down the stairs in their home, then sat on the porch and smoked a Newport. When she heard the door slam, she slowly got up to her feet and walked into the bathroom. Her face appeared to be fine besides a few scratches from his nails. Her skin tone was so light that his finger imprints were still visible. Once she tried to open her mouth, the pain shot down her throat like poison. The blood was leaking onto her gums, so she parted her lips and let it drop into the sink. The ache inside her mouth would not allow her to fully open her lips, so she pulled them apart with her fingers. Looking at the cuts inside her cheeks and the lines of blood between each piece of hanging skin, was unbelievable. She couldn't help but let tears roll down her face as she splashed cold water to her mouth to stop the bleeding.

    She finally got in bed after a long bath and watched a few episodes of *The Game*. She loved Melanie and Derwin's big circle of a relationship, even though they had it rough, she couldn't judge anyone's situation at that point. Ghost finally came upstairs after sitting in the living room for hours. He showered, then climbed into bed and slid his body towards hers. He grabbed her from behind, then planted soft kisses on her back before he drifted off too sleep. The touch of him made her body cringe but she never moved. Her feelings towards him were changing right before her very own eyes and she was not good at pretending.

She had faith in his commitment to work but just as she was starting to expect, he began to call in from work for any reason. At times, he didn't even have a reason other than he did not feel like going, which was the only excuse he needed. By this time, her nausea had subsided and was truly a blessing because she could finally return to work. She couldn't work the entire ten hour shifts but for the most part, she was just happy to leave the house and get away from Ghost. Her cheeks were healing up pretty good and she began to eat certain things that sat well with her stomach.

    A few weeks of him missing work, he eventually quit all together and announced that he was back hustling. As if he had just made the best decision of his life but all she could do is look at him with confusion.

"I quit that job, Loyalty. I'm tired of waking up every morning to go clock in but still have to wait every two weeks for a check. I can't even take care of you like I use too, plus the bills and still have enough to buy what we want. We can't even shop or go hang out! All we do is pay bills. I rather take chances for the money the best way I been surviving." He explained.

"You call getting locked up, surviving? You call taking chances and gambling your life, surviving? That's not the best way you know how, Jordan, that's the only way you knew how. Now that you are getting older, put away childish things and grow. Develop into something more other than running back to the streets." She stated, rolling her eyes.

"I won't be standing on the corner. I have my lil' cousin doing stuff like that for me." He replied.

"You just missed the whole point." She sighed.

"Nah, I get what you saying but you loved me when I was doing it before. You were down with me then and never complained about the money! You always spent it with no complaints." He argued.

"Yea, you're absolutely correct. Only thing is, we were not married and you had never been to the feds. I'm trying to grow with you, not take chances with your freedom. Looks like I'm the only one concerned about your freedom though. Hey, what do I know? Do what you want!" She stated, throwing her hands in the air to surrender the argument.

"You act like you down for me, so be down for everything. Right or wrong!" He continued.

Turning around to face him again, she replied. "Look, life is about growth. If you don't give up who you use to be, you will never become who you're destined to be. I'm sure that just went over your head as well. So I'll say this, I want better for my life and I thought you wanted better for yours. I married you because I love you, not what you had to offer me before you were locked up. You are still infatuated with the street life and they say it's only two ways out, a cell or a casket. I want more for you and you should want the same for yourself." She left him sitting on the porch to be alone with his thoughts.

Just as he wanted, she was riding with his decision to continue his prior hustle but she did not like it one bit. Support can go a long way, so she helped him do everything she could between meeting people and counting the money. Everytime she met up with someone, she would say a prayer in regards to the encounter not being a set up that would land her in the same place he just came from, the Feds. She had no choice but to meet people he had business with because with him still being on a monitor, his curfew interfered.

Sometimes she would take so long coming back, he would accuse her of creeping with the guys she met. As if she wasn't pregnant and wrapped up in so much distress to focus on anything else. Besides, she always told him it's not her fault every woman he had in the past wasn't loyal and betrayed him. People have a bad habit of accusing you for someone else's actions, when majority of the time they are guilty for the same accusations.

One day, she was out doing a little shopping with Lucky who had purchased her car seat and stroller as an early baby shower gift. Once they left the mall, she realized she had spent all the money Ghost had given her, so she made the phone call she dreaded. Assuming that he would be upset with her for blowing so much cash, her only defense was that it was for the baby. She shopped up an appetite and was ready to feed her tummy.

"Hey babe, what ya doing?" He answered.

"Um, nothing much. Just got some new things to start decorating the baby room. I find out what I'm having in a few weeks. Lucky thinks it's a girl because I've been so sick." She replied.

"I hope she right because I want a baby girl so bad. Especially if she looks and acts like you, I know she gonna steal my heart." He stated.

"Hey, we were going to eat somewhere but I ran out of cash. Can you meet me for some? I'm hungry." She asked.

"Yea, that's cool. I'm about to meet my homeboy by the corner store near the mall. Give me five minutes and I'll be there." He stated.

Just as he stated, in five minutes she hopped out of the car to talk to him. She walked to the passengers side and leaned through the window to tell him about the baby items. Once she got ready to walk off, he gave her the money and told her to come around to his side for a hug.

"Damn, you look gorgeous shawty. I love you!" He admired, before embracing in a hug.

"Thanks, I feel pregnant and out of shape." She laughed, before noticing the gold condom wrapper. "What the hell is that Jordan?" She asked, tears already forming in her eyes. "You haven't been out six months and you already being a hoe."

"First, watch your mouth. Second, that ain't mine. Must be for my homeboy cause he just got out the car. I'll call him for you to prove it, just stay right here." He tried to convince, picking up his phone.

Before he could even make a phone call, she slapped it out of his hand and walked off. Hopping back in the car with Lucky, she tried to keep her composure. She attempted to hide the pain that was forming more and more, every two seconds. She didn't want to mention what just happened, simply to avoid the drawn out conversation about all men are dogs, especially one that was just released from prison. No matter how much a guy expresses his love for you, there is always enough room that allows his temptation to surface and explore any given opportunity. She could answer every question she had, with no help. It's just that she thought the cost of loyalty was priceless and anyone with a sane mind would not gamble that.

Ghost must've literally called her phone one hundred times, so she put her phone on vibrate mode. After her and Lucky came from eating, she got dropped off to Kash's house and chilled the rest of the night. She couldn't believe Ghost was about to attempt some bogus lie and have a friend cover for him. One thing she hated the most was an unnecessary liar.

She had Kash bring her home later that night because she wasn't in the mood for an argument. She had done no wrong but she braced herself for the fight that was brewing in the midst of his actions. Her mind was telling her that she could be by herself and take care of things just fine without him. She had proven that to herself five years ago and did not need a man unworthy of her love to validate anything she stood for. The thought of him laying with someone else was a turn off and left a disgusting taste in her mouth.

Then there she was again, found her body laying on the bathroom floor in front of the toilet. To her surprise, he didn't have much to say about the incident or where she had been. He switched his attitude and tried to make things pleasant again but the damage had already been done. The vibe she once had for only his love was fading through the cracks of their own home.

A few days later, she received word that his son's mother was not too pleased with their marriage or unborn child. Tension was present between her and Ghost because she refused to argue over an irrelevant issue. He dismissed her assumptions, stating it was impossible for Valerie to be mad because he hadn't touched her since their son. Regardless, she knew girls were petty over the smallest things. Sure enough, she took it upon herself to address the situation that she knew nothing about. Its one thing to be mad for a legit reason but it's another to just start drama because you're hating. Either way, she was up for anything that came with the beef because she was sick of it.

Later that night, she was laying in bed and heard a bunch of noise outside the gate of her townhome. She got up to take a look outside and noticed that it was Valerie, which was funny because they knew Loyalty was nowhere near afraid. The two girls had a slight misunderstanding before but it never went anywhere. Yet now that she was pregnant, Valerie had the audacity to pull up to her home and put on a show. They may have thought by Loyalty being pregnant, that would be an excuse for the fight not to take place. She had the right idea but definitely the wrong chic. She could hear Ghost downstairs on his phone cussing her out and trying to figure out why the mess started. That was neither here or there as she slipped on her airmax and walked downstairs. When Ghost noticed she had on some sweat pants, a muscle shirt and some tennis shoes, he instantly blew up.

"Where you going? This shit has gotten out of hand for no reason. You think I'm about to let you fight while you carrying my child?" He asked.

"What? You don't think about your child when you fight me. Do you? It would have never gotten out of hand if you would have checked it when I brought it to your attention. You allowed this to happen! So, I can handle it from here." She replied, walking past him.

He grabbed her arm but she jerked away from his grip. He could see the rage in her eyes as he stood to the side and let her walk by. Once she got to the gate, he picked her up from the back and wrestled her into the house. He was still on a monitor, so he couldn't walk past the car shed or the sensor would go off. She pleaded with him not to wrestle with her because she was already pregnant and needed to save her energy for Valerie. Disturbing her friends sleep at one in the morning, she told them to come over as she quickly explained the situation. April and Paige pulled up first, then Robin and Kash showed up with two of her cousins. When she realized Valerie and her friends had left, she called her cell phone to come back and finish what she started. It took longer than expected but the car of girls finally pulled back up and stood around.

Loyalty walked into the middle of the crowd and waited for her opponent to come closer for their match. Once Valerie had a clear path, she charged at Loyalty like a raging bull. With her feet planted, Loyalty remained still as she watched the charging female race towards her. Once she was within arms reach, the contact began and Loyalty knew it was an easy fight. What affected her most was the braids being yanked from her scalp right before they began to wrestle. Kash and Ghost separated the two girls and the situation was never entertained again.

A few days later, she wasn't speaking to Ghost at all. She walked around the house and completely ignored his presence. When he noticed her distant ways, he finally came out and asked what the problem was.

"You want to be a kid all day?" He picked.

"Does age define a kid or does actions? The only kid in this room is you! Ya' know, I find it funny that you sit here and pretend all day like you're married. Then you go out in the streets and turn into a dog. Well guess what Jordan, I don't have anymore bones to throw you! Anything else?" She stated, folding her arms across her chest.

"So what, you wanna leave me now?" He asked.

"Leave? I'm not going anywhere! If anyone should leave, you better start beating your own feet. I worked hard for everything in here and even fought to keep up with this bullshit union I thought was a marriage. Nobody was there for you but me, now you chasing sluts that couldn't put a stamp on an envelope. Oh, how quickly we forget!" She replied.

"I'll take your life before you leave. Yea, 'till death do us part. How quickly did you forget!?" He snarled, walking closer to her.

"Look, you can go right back out those doors and continue doing what you've been doing. Just remember every dog has it's day. Just to make it clear, when I get tired of putting up with you, you can kiss our matrimony goodbye. This is the worst and it's not getting any better. You wouldn't know anything about vows because you weren't even present when I said them. This marriage is a joke!" She flipped her hair.

When she attempted to walk off, he instantly grabbed her by the back of her neck and swung her to the ground. The grip on her neck was so tight that her face was starting to turn red. She wiggled to face his body and opened her mouth wide to bite the side of his leg. Surprised, he yelled out in pain then lifted her from the floor by her hair. She placed her hands on the wall in an attempt to stop him from dragging her upstairs but his strength over powered her. Step by step, she was forcefully being yanked upstairs by her hair.

Once they made it to the top, he let her go and instructed her to unpack the bag of clothes he had found in the closet. She looked at him in such disgust as she sat on the floor next to the bed, thinking of ways to end the marriage she signed up for. He walked back downstairs to the living room, then she finally got up and headed to the bathroom. Suddenly, she began having back pains and her stomach was aching with mild cramps.

She hopped in the tub because a warm bath was definitely needed at the moment. She took two Tylenol and drank the bottle of water on the nightstand before she slowly eased in the tub. She sunk down a bit and relaxed in their oval sized garden tub then closed her eyes. She leaned all the way back to attempt some quiet time. Sitting peaceful for about five minutes, she opened her eyes and reached for her phone to play some music when she noticed spots of blood in her water.

She assumed that he must've scratched her somewhere or she may have been poked by something on the carpet when he pulled her. She began examining her arms and legs to look for a cut when she began to see more blood. Pausing for a moment, she opened her legs and saw the trail was flowing from her vagina.

"Jordan!" She screamed in panic. "I'm bleeding!"

She could hear his footsteps rushing upstairs and when he appeared in the bathroom doorway, she was already standing. He noticed the blood dripping from her vaginal area and immediately became worried.

"I'm sorry. I apologize. I promise I'll never touch you again. Let's go to the hospital. I don't want you to lose my baby. Hurry, let's go! We have to get some help. Let me call the halfway house and tell them I have to rush you to the hospital. Come on, just put these on." He suggested, as he helped her dress.

He handed her some sweat pants and a big t-shirt, then she slipped on her fluffy house shoes. Slowly walking down the stairs, her cramps were becoming more intense. She told him to place a pad in her underwear because she could feel the blood continuing to leak. She was afraid of what may happen as well. A part of her was beginning to regret that she had even married Ghost, let alone have a baby for him. Yet now that she saw blood flowing from her vaginal area, her only thoughts were hoping that their baby was still alive.

When they arrived to the hospital, she was able to be seen immediately because of her condition. The nurses began taking blood from her arms as soon as she was placed in a room. There was no way they could stop her from bleeding but by taking her blood, they could determine if she was threatening a miscarriage. The second nurse walked in and mentioned that she would perform an ultrasound just to take a look at the baby. She stated she would begin with the heart monitor, as she placed a long belt around her back then strapped it across her belly. Placing the cold gel on her stomach, the nurse positioned the medical instrument towards her lower abdomen. Instantly, they heard the heartbeat she had been wishing for as they focused their attention on the TV monitor. The nurse informed them that they wanted to check the movements of the baby, then let her rest for awhile until the blood work came back.

"Looks like she is still bouncing around just fine in there." The nurse guaranteed.

"She?" Ghost repeated.

"It's a girl?" Loyalty asked.

"Oh, I'm sorry. Did you guys want it to be a surprise? Me and my big mouth." The nurse shamefully apologized.

"Oh no, you're fine. We just didn't know the gender yet. I actually go to the doctor for that this Thursday. Thank you for telling us! I already have girl items at home. That's great news!" She replied with the biggest grin.

"Ma, guess what. We're having a girl, I can't believe it! Didn't I tell you…" Ghost stated, already on the phone with Mama Jewel.

The nurse walked out after the ultrasound, as the two of them sat in the room for over an hour. Ghost sat bundled in a cover next to the bed, snoring so loud it disturbed her sleep. She unwrapped herself from the blanket and tapped him on the leg in an attempt to end the awful sound.

"Jordan! You sound like you haven't slept in three days." She stated, hitting his knee.

"My bad! I'm tired and it's colder than the *world* in here." He replied.

"Why don't you grab us something to eat from the cafeteria. I'm starving!" She mentioned.

He walked out of the room, as she laid back down to enjoy the peace while he was gone. Within ten minutes, there was a knock on the door and the first nurse returned to give the blood work results. She sat upright in the bed to give her undivided attention because she did not want to lose the baby girl she always wanted.

"Hello again, the blood work looks normal. Your pregnancy is still progressing and moving forward. Only blood work can test those things we were looking for but you are fine. We suggest bed rest, also continue prenatal vitamins and no sexual activity for at least a month. Follow up with you doctor immediately if you begin to feel any pain or experience any sign of spotting. Other than that, you guys are good to go home. Take it easy." She informed, then left the room.

Just then, Ghost returned as she told him all about the news from the nurse and how lucky they are to still be granted the pregnancy. She expressed to him that the things he put her through were not healthy for her or the baby. The only thing she wanted to do was take it easy and make sure she gave birth to a healthy baby girl in a few more months. He agreed and she gave him a chance to speak without an argument. Although he gave his apologies and took full blame for the situations that got out of hand, she still made him aware that her feelings towards him were not the same. She looked at him differently now. He understood, given the circumstances and considering all that he had done to her within the short time frame he had been released. Yet, he made promises that he would do better because he did not want to lose her or the family they were starting. They sat for awhile to discuss a few things as they ate their food then headed home in peace, for once.

His probation officer called, stating that he was in the area performing home visits and was about to stop by. That instantly made him hop out of bed and start cleaning anything suspicious. He put away any sign of him hustling and woke Loyalty so that she could help him prepare. He wanted a quick and pleasant visit without any hold up to have his PO sticking around any longer than he had to. He walked to the mailbox next to their building and put his drugs inside, then locked it back with the mailbox key.

As promised, his probation officer arrived within the hour and took a short tour around their home. Seeing that the townhome was more than comfortable living, he stated that he wouldn't be much longer. They sat on the couch to catch up on his employment and discuss how things had been with the halfway house concerning his monitor. Ghost informed him that they cut his hours at the truck stop, so he eventually stopped working there altogether. He gave an update about a moving company that hired him on but he was just waiting for his background to clear. His PO applauded his progress and behavior, acknowledging that he had not been in any trouble since he had been released.

Walking him out, Ghost winked at her for helping him make the first home visit from his PO a success. She smiled back at him and continued to prepare one of his favorites, loaded nachos and tacos with chili cheese burritos. He came back inside so they could watch a few movies before they took showers and headed for bed.

Next morning, he woke up well rested and headed for the bathroom to brush his teeth. Placing a hot towel across his face to wipe the sleep out of his eyes, he noticed the time from the clock on the bathroom wall. It was almost noon, which made him realize he never went back to the mailbox to grab his things. Running out of the house barefoot, he rushed to the side of the building and opened the box to only find the light bill. His heart sank as he looked around for the mail lady to question her about the brown bag he put inside.

Loyalty was in the kitchen about to fix breakfast when he came into the house slamming the door extremely hard. She knew he was furious and was hesitant in asking him what was wrong because she didn't want to add to his problem.

"I can't believe this shit! I got jacked by the damn mail lady." He yelled.

"How? It's always someone different, seems like they switch up so much. What did they take? You mailed something?" She asked, confused.

"I put my brown sack in there before my PO came because I didn't know what to expect and didn't want him to find it. I thought they searched your house or brought other people with them. Anyway, I locked it in the mailbox and forgot to get it out after he left. Now it's gone! Damn! I was just about to be comfortable with my money and now this pushed me back like I'm just getting out all over again." He stated, punching a hole through the wall.

"Ok! I understand, I'm sorry." Is all she could say before she walked away. She truly felt bad for him so she left him alone to deal with his frustration.

Hearing of the complications with his wife's pregnancy and plus good behavior, he was granted to be off the monitor to roam free. A few days later, he began to complain of his side hurting extremely bad. The pain was so excruciating that it had him hunched over in agony. Although she was exhausted, she stayed up with him watching TV until he fell asleep. The pain was so severe that he tossed and turned for hours until she just couldn't watch him suffer any longer. He kept complaining, so she convinced him to take a visit to the emergency room.

Loyalty's tummy was huge and often made her uncomfortable, so she did not physically feel up to sitting at the hospital for hours. She had ran out of solutions at home and could not get him to feel better by herself. Upon arriving, there were at least eight people ahead of him and his patience was at zero. After about two hours of waiting, he lost his cool and demanded that they leave. He was more comfortable at home dealing with the pain instead of sitting in a hard chair for hours. Still, she suggested that they stay for at least another hour before he made the decision to leave and waste the time they had already been there.

Just as he got up and was about to confront the registration clerk, a nurse appeared from the side doors and called his name. That was like music to their ears and a life saver because she knew he was about to act ignorant. Watching him walk, she couldn't believe that the illness had him so drained. She prayed that it was something the doctors would be able to solve immediately so he would be back to his old self in no time.

Once he began telling the doctor his symptoms and overall condition, they suggested to perform an immediate CAT scan. The nurse came back in to draw his blood for a few test and handed him a cup to collect a urine sample. Loyalty was pleased with the overall service of the staff because she was positive that with all those tests ran, they would get to the bottom of it. He lay in bed feeling weak and slept for an hour with her sitting next to him until the staff returned. Coming in at once, the nurses returned with a surgeon who explained his diagnosis.

"Hello Mr. Dawkins, you must be feeling pretty bad. Well, I'm going to have to perform surgery on you tonight. When is the last time you ate or had anything to drink? I'm glad you came in because your appendix is about to rupture. It looks pretty bad! No worries, I have over twenty years experience and I also perform this particular procedure more than most." The surgeon informed, handing Loyalty a consent form.

"How long has this been happening? He was fine a couple days ago, then all of a sudden ends up in surgery? What about recovery, how long? Can I go in with him or stand by the window and watch?" Fear began to take over as she asked every question that came to mind.

"Appendicitis is usually detected through a physical exam or if a doctor checks for high white blood cell count that indicates infection. In Mr. Dawkins case, he hasn't been sick so it's something that over time has caught up with him and immediately got worse. You can sit in the nearest waiting room and I promise to come and get you when we're all done." He stated, patting her shoulder before walking out.

Ghost sat quietly with no expression as if he didn't hear anything the surgeon said. She could tell he was nervous because he kept taking deep breaths. The nurses came to take him to the operating room for his surgery when he called his parents to join Loyalty in the waiting room.

"I trust God. I'm glad we came tonight so that you will feel way better by tomorrow. I'll be right here waiting when you realize it's over." She assured.

"Thanks baby. I never had surgery before. Don't let them kill me!" He stated before they shared a quick laugh and kiss.

The three of them sat in the waiting area for at least three hours before the surgeon appeared in the doorway. They always give that pleasant smile as if they are greeting you with the best news ever, only to deliver more options. Noticing him in the room, they stood to their feet and eagerly listened for the update.

"Well, he is fine. We removed his appendix and it looks like we had done so just in time. The issue now is that we've spotted a small but dangerous clump of cells that have formed in the lining of his colon. It is closely attached, so I suggest that we remove it now because it is cancerous. Although in doing so, it will remove a third of his colon, causing his bladder to become weakened. I'm very positive that this will prevent any future problems and also keep him from having to wear an colostomy bag that holds feces." He explained.

They were all speechless, as she could see the tears forming in his father's eyes while Mama Jewel fell back in her seat and began a loud prayer. The decision was pretty simple because she knew he would not want to end up with a 'shit bag' for the rest of his life.

"Do what needs to be done! I'm positive that he will not want to walk around with a colostomy bag. Let's just solve the problem now and I'll explain it to him when he wakes. At this point he has no choice but to remove it." She stated.

The surgeon walked away with the consent to remove a third of Ghost's colon. The three of them remained in the waiting area as she laid across the bench trying to camouflage her tears. Dollar and Mama Jewel sat in chairs across the room and she could still hear her talking to God, asking for favor and healing over her son.

Two hours later, a nurse walked in with the surgeon following right behind her to share the good news that everything was a success. They gave a list of prescriptions he would take during his recovery while explaining the things they would need to help him do. He was admitted for seven days because it was necessary for the medical staff to start the healing stage.

Minutes later, they returned with Ghost on the same rolling bed while he laid there moaning in pain. To hear him suffering and calling out for her instantly broke her heart. Dollar assisted the staff and helped them lift his son from the rolling bed to the clean bed. Hearing his father's voice, he began to question why they let the doctors put him through so much pain.

"They took care of you son. Now you have to heal but we got you!" Dollar reassured.

"Be careful how y'all handle my son. Take your time! He's hurting and can feel everything you're doing." Mama Jewel instructed.

"Babe, you're better now. I'll clean you up and get you a popsicle since the nurses said that's all you can have now. Just relax, everything went fine." She convinced.

For the remainder of that day, he slept like a baby after she gave him a sponge bath and the nurses issued his meds. Later that night, he gained full consciousness and demanded answers. He wanted to know exactly what had taken place with his surgery. He was upset to see that his cut stretched from his pelvic to his chest. The doctors referred to it as a 'zipper' across his stomach and by the looks of it, he totally agreed. She explained to him that his bladder was now weak because they had to take a third of his colon. So from that day forward, each time he had to use the restroom would be urgent because he could not control it.

He started making progress in the next few days and was now able to stand with help. He was only allowed applesauce and Jell-O, which made her eat in the cafeteria so that her plate wouldn't tease him. One night after she had lotioned him down, she began to brush his hair when she noticed a tear sliding down his cheek.

"What's wrong babe. Are you hurting?" She asked.

"I'm in a little pain but I just can't believe I'm in this predicament. Thank you for being here! Really for still being my wife even though I haven't been acting like a husband. I'm in pretty bad shape right now and I can't do anything about it but just lay here." He replied.

Not quite sure of what to say, she stopped brushing his hair and carefully climbed into the hospital bed with him. Positioning her belly comfortably next to him, she held his hand and dimmed the lights as they drifted off to sleep.

Months later, she was at work eating breakfast when she suddenly started having bad cramps. Only this time, the cramps were getting worse and more intense every few minutes. She went to her supervisors office and began to tell a few coworkers that something was definitely wrong. It was becoming harder for her to walk and each step she took felt like her baby would just fall right out between her legs. When she made it to the bathroom, there was blood in her underwear and the pain started shooting through her spine. She managed to walk back into the office and told everyone that she needed help because she was in labor. Paris walked in and mentioned that they called Ghost and he was on his way. By then, she had stopped responding and began to brace herself every few minutes for the pain that was never ending. Instead of waiting, Paris asked a few of the male coworkers to assist her with carrying Loyalty to her truck. She decided to drive her to the emergency room just in case she dilated more than they expected.

Paris stayed with her for a few minutes until Ghost rushed into the room to take her place. Mrs. Daphne, Lucky and Kash showed up within the hour. Unfortunately, she had only dilated 2 cm but her contractions were a 20 on a scale of 1 to 10. They gave her meds to numb the pain and advised her to walk the halls, climb the steps or even sit in some warm water to speed up the delivery.

The next morning, she was given an epidural and hours later she finally reached 9 cm. Everything suddenly scared her when she watched the nurses lift the bed and turn on the bright lights above her head. Everyone reentered the room, as they all began to coach her through the painful delivery. It took nearly 15 minutes and six big pushes for her to feel the pressure that tore through her vagina like a ring of fire.

Looking down at the tiny face and fragile body, she had never felt so instantly responsible in her life. She was now someone's guardian and she could feel the difference in life by holding the tiny hand of someone she had never met. Women go through so much pain to push out such a little person who brings them so much joy. Feeling accomplished, she could only smile as she looked up at everyone while Ghost placed his arms around her.

"Hi Journei. I'm your mother!" Allowing a single tear to escape her eye.

CHAPTER 15

"Starting Over"

PARENTHOOD WAS A NEW BEGINNING! She not only had to take care of Journei but making sure she kept herself up was a job as well. It was hard to do sometimes since she was exhausted by staying up late all night. She had not worked for over a month, so everything she needed was solely provided by Ghost. It was starting to make her feel less than a mother, which made her realize that it was time to bring more to the table than just a chair. Finding a babysitter was harder than she thought and being that her newborn was beyond spoiled, it made the struggle more difficult. Once she found someone who would take care of Journei for a couple of hours, it was all the time she needed to run in a few stores.

Just when she was trying to help out around the house financially, Ghost seemed to make matters worse for their marriage. He would always complain about her spending money but was now making a fuss about her trying to make some money of her own. Her house duties never slacked up, even with the baby being born. Once her stitches healed and she went for her six weeks checkup, the old habits immediately came back as she found herself rolling a blunt.

After giving birth, she was eventually back on speaking terms with Kali and Arielle. Then just like the old days, the girls linked up for a money mission. She had to admit that during the time frame of them not being friends, she missed them like crazy. Not only were they back getting money together but they were back to hanging out and having good times like old times. Even though Ghost didn't like the fact that she was back stealing, nor the idea of her hanging with her friends, he respected that she was trying to help their family survive.

Journei had just began to crawl, which was the best-worst thing that could've happened because she had to baby proof everything. Every morning, she would fix bottles then find herself jumping right back in bed to rest. She began asking Mama Jewel to look after her grandbaby while she did nothing more than catch up on her sleep. Waking from a nap that evening, she felt sick and had no idea why she had gotten so ill all of a sudden. She took a relaxing bath and her breast felt so tender. It made her realize that her period only came once since Journei had been born. Freaking out, she eased out of the tub and begin to search for the pregnancy test she had underneath the cabinet. It was the same package that Mama Jewel purchased a year before when she was pregnant with Journei. Taking a deep swallow, she placed it on the counter top and proceeded to the kitchen for a drink of water. Within the next thirty minutes, she was ready to take the test. Her heart almost fell in the toilet when it read *Pregnant*.

Sure pregnancy is a beautiful thing but she wanted to enjoy her body for a little while before turning back into a hippo. She wanted to cry but was too weak, so she laid back into the sheets and fell asleep. Shortly after, she heard movement in the living room and decided to tell Ghost about the new baby. Looking at her face, he could tell she had something to say so he kicked off the convo.

"What is it? What do you want to accuse me of now? Being hungry?" He asked, fixing a plate of food.

"Nothing really, I just wish you were the one eating for two and not me!" She replied.

"What? You pregnant?" He asked.

She sighed. "Feels like it, although I'm not ready to look like it."

"I hope it's another girl, just eat those vitamin things so you won't get so sick this time." He stated, walking passed her with his plate of food.

"Vitamins? That won't stop nausea! Besides, I just don't want to push another watermelon out of a lemon. That was the most painful thing in my life and I just wanted to get back on my feet before having another baby." She stated, flopping down on the couch.

"On your feet? Let me worry about the bills and you just worry about taking care of home. Stay in the house with your baby and do that mother-bonding thing. I'm about to head out after I eat this plate to take care of something. I'll pick Journei up from my moms' on the way back." He muffled through his chewing.

"Whatever!" Done with the conversation, she walked back into the bedroom.

A few months later when her morning sickness slacked up, she was back in the stores to make some money. She returned back to work but with Journei staying up so frequently at night, it made her call in almost every other day. Her body was changing by the minute and it seemed as if she was gaining five pounds every two days. It was beginning to slow her down in the stores but she was starting to love the extra money in her pockets. Ghost had warned her that he didn't want her inside the mall shoplifting because she was pregnant and needed to behave that way. Really not seeing the point in that statement, she kept doing her same hustle with no regards to his command.

Leaving the mall one night, she sat in the back seat with bags full of merchandise as Kash and Arielle drove around to sell their items. Things sale pretty quickly when you pull up to the right areas and bump into a few folks with money. While she was selling her things,

Ghost called and demanded that she go home because it was late. She saw no reason for the big fuss he was making because Journei was fine at Mama Jewel's house and she was using her spare time to get money. She told him that after she was done getting rid of the bag she had, then she would go in but the night was still booming right then.

After they finished making their rounds, the girls pulled in front of Kash's grandmother house to jump in their own cars. Before she could even grab her things, the door flew open and she was pulled out of the car by her t-shirt. Her instinct made her arms do the talking as she proceeded to throw punches wherever they landed. The smell of liquor reeked from his clothing as she could tell that he was wasted and looking for conflict. She couldn't understand for the life of her why he wanted to fight her so much. Was the hate that strong or was the love never real? Either way, she always fought back, in hopes he would eventually grow out of it.

Kash and Arielle walked over to them in an attempt to break it up when he shoved Loyalty away to charge at Arielle for talking smack. She saw things about to reach a whole new level so she jumped in front of him and started fighting again. It was one thing to fight on your wife but what you will not do is fight her friends for trying to help. It was only right she took the heat from the rage Arielle would have felt had he gotten close enough.

She managed to have enough chill in her for a second that led him to walk to the car, waiting for her to get in. The girls began asking if she felt safe going home with him and even though her response was yes, she knew it was far from over. The drive home was quiet, while he drove slow the entire twenty minutes it took to get there. As soon as she unlocked the bolt and turned the knob, he slapped her harder than ever before. It was so forceful and unexpected, it actually knocked the fight out of her. She stayed in the same position for a few minutes to evaluate her life and rethink the decisions she had made that led up to the marriage she was beginning to hate. He walked past her, then went straight to the bedroom where he passed out across the bed into a drunken sleep.

The next morning, she noticed he was gone. She rushed out of bed and gathered some things to leave for a few days. Kash pulled up in an instant, waiting for her to come outside so she could attempt to flee. Unsure of what she wanted to do, she just knew for sure the life she was currently living was not one she was going to continue. She wanted her marriage but did not want to accept the terms Ghost was living by. Making it to Kash's mom house, Mrs. Brenda, they sat in the living room discussing her current situation and options. Noticing her face, Mrs. Brenda and her boyfriend shared a little advice about being pregnant and marrying so young. Everything sounded logical but some situations are harder to fix than others. It was true, she couldn't get rid of him or just think he would let her walk away. So, she decided to move away from the environment that seemed to stagnate her life. She wanted more. It seemed that if she didn't change her circumstances, then it would claim her future forever.

After hours of calling her phone, she finally answered and informed him that she was moving to Houston. She didn't have a plan, other than packing up all her things and figuring out her next step when she got there. He disagreed for so many reasons and a part of her wanted him too. She told him that her mind was already made up. After hours of going back and forth, she told him that he could run the streets as he pleased because nothing mattered anymore. She was tired of hearing rumors of him and other women, especially women that couldn't equal up to half the solid woman she was. She stretched out across the bed to watch television, as her mind replayed the past year and a half of her life.

The next day, Kash brought her home to start packing her things. It was definitely a decision she was sticking with. Life was no longer just about her, she had kids to think about. Making a healthier life for herself, would bring about a more successful life for her children. In order to allow growth in your life, you have to start by changing the things, people and places around you.

Loyalty went to her job at the warehouse to let them know she was moving. Basically, telling them something had to give. She thanked them for the opportunity of letting her work there for the past five years but she had to move on to better things. Everyone was so understanding and supportive by wishing her luck as she headed down a new path.

When she arrived home later that night, Ghost had already packed up a few of his things. He said if she felt the new quest was going to better their family, then he was all for the change. Even though she was still feeling distant from their marriage, just to hear him say that made her feel they had hope. Maybe he actually wanted better but had never known any different. Everyone needs a little push sometimes to bring out the best in themselves. She was honored to be the one to motivate him. They piled the important things in the car and the three of them jumped on the highway to head for Houston.

Her mother was waiting for them to arrive and prepared the guest bedroom just for them. She was the kind of mother that loved helping take care of anyone. To know that they were moving for better opportunity, she was all for it. The room they occupied was attached to it's own bathroom and was already pre-setup with a bed, computer and television. They unpacked their things and showered. Prepared for bed, she said a prayer that she hoped would guide their next steps.

The very next day, she turned on the computer and created a resume for each of them. Trying to find a decent job was harder than it seemed. Within a few weeks, Ghost was hired at a mechanic shop that serviced diesels. Once they read over his resume and saw he had prior experience from the truck stop, the job was all his. He was beginning to like the idea of wearing a uniform that had his name stitched on the patch across his chest. She would laugh every morning he got dressed because he would say, 'any man with his name on a uniform is a man that knows how to do his job'. She always let him boost his own ego but in actuality, everyone's uniform had their name on it where he worked.

It was nearly a month later, when she finally received a phone call and was hired at a local call center. During her interview, she was escorted around with a guy named Rich. She absolutely loved his positive attitude and bold demeanor, so she knew it was a good start to meet the right kind of people. He mentioned the training would not actually start for another couple months once the department was finished being remodeled. That was perfectly fine with her because she was due any day now with her second child.

After the interview, she waited a couple weeks and received a confirmation email that she had gotten the job. Once she had taken her drug test, it was by the Grace of God that they overlooked her background and decided to give her a chance. That was a big relief for her because now her focus was on finding a day care, plus a nice apartment. Everyday Ghost went to work, she would wake up to search all the places she found online until she spotted a two bedroom apartment that was perfect for them. Once again, Lucky had to apply for the apartment since her background was squeaky clean. Once it was approved, he paid the deposit and first months rent, leaving them to patiently wait for their move in date.

Having things set up in their new home, they went back to Beaumont and started boxing up their old apartment. It felt good to see her friends and chill with everyone, because absence makes the heart grow fonder. In the midst of things going good, something will always try to steal your joy. That day, she received a phone call saying Ghost just had an altercation with some guy who tried to pull a gun out on him. When she heard the news, she called him to see what was going on. He made her aware that he had just bumped heads with Reggie, the boyfriend of some girl who tried to make herself relevant when he was released from jail. It didn't make since to her that the couple wanted attention like there was some hidden agenda behind the fued.

He told her that he was on his way to pick her up and drop them off to his aunt's house. Once she got in the car with him, he mentioned that he was about to ride around and see if he saw Reggie again so they could handle the bad blood. He decided to bring Journei over to his little cousin's house to be out of harms way. She told him to bring her by Kash's house and she would chill there until he came back. He agreed, so they stopped by the store to get her some snacks first. She told him to be careful and make wise decisions because they had a lot more to lose than their opponent. They were not a factor to her and she wished he had felt the same way. She tried to convince him that as long as no one was a physical threat, there was no harm in letting the enemy admire from a distance. He insisted the guy threatened him, saying that if they fought he would kill him. With those words, he felt he had to go and get his own gun from his homeboy around the corner.

"Say man, I need to get that hammer I let you borrow last week." He informed his friend.

She couldn't believe he was really considering shooting someone after he had just gotten out of jail. Yet, she couldn't talk him out of it. Sitting in the turning lane, Ghost was about to turn into the corner store for her snacks when she pointed out the guy he was looking for. She didn't know if telling him was a good or bad thing at the time but she was glad they spotted him first.

"There he goes babe, it's Reggie. That's his car right? That's definitely him walking out of the store." She stated, making sure he spotted the guy.

"Yep, that's him. Let me see what he does first. Talking 'bout he gonna shoot somebody." He giggled.

"He see us, babe! He saw us, look! He's walking fast to his car, watch him!" She warned.

"Chill baby, don't panic. Be cool." He calmly stated.

"Jordan! You see it? He grabbed a gun! He does not want to fight!" She yelled.

"Damn, baby! This clown might try to shoot while you in the car. You gotta get out! Go!" He instructed, slightly shoving her arm.

"No! What are you gonna do?" She asked.

With no time to respond, he sped off rushing back towards his cousin's house to drop her off. She kept her eyes glued to the back window to keep a close watch on Reggie's car, when she noticed him weaving in and out of traffic. He got ahead of them and made his car spin, then slowed down in mid 360 with his driver's side facing the front of their car.

"Jordan, he's gonna try to block us off. I don't even have a gun of my own. It's two guys! What if they shoot the car for real?" She panicked.

Never saying a word, Ghost turned the wheel and angled the car just right to open fire several times towards the spinning vehicle. The guys car immediately jumped the curb on its right side, sending them swerving through the grass.

She was in such panic and her adrenaline was at an all-time high. She had never been in such a near death experience and it was the closest she had ever felt in harms way. Before Ghost started shooting, he told her to duck and she did so in an instant before covering her ears. The shooting was so loud, it made her feel as if a bullet was going to pierce through her own skin within seconds.

She began to pray that Ghost had missed the guy because she didn't want to lose him again through the courts. The fact that it was broad daylight, she was sure the passing vehicles heard or saw what happened. She told him they should get out of their car until they figured out what was going on with the scene they just fled. Driving a little faster, still not saying a word, he pulled to his cousins house again and told her to get out.

"Why? Where are you going? What if you missed him and he's already looking for you? What if he's dead and the cops are already hot? Think!" She calmly stated.

"I am thinking, that's why I want you to get out. Now!" He yelled. "I'm gonna check the scene out myself, it's too late to change either way it's handled now. Come on, get out!" He demanded.

Shutting the door, she walked inside his cousins house and tried to remain calm until he returned. She kept looking out of the blinds getting more paranoid by the minute. About two hours later, she noticed him walking up the sidewalk. She walked outside to greet him and get the info, hoping that he had some decent news to share. He saw tire tracks through the grass where the shooting happened but that's it, so the guy was still alive. Once he knew that much, he drove to his friends house and switched cars to pass by Reggie's crib. Unable to locate him, he stated they had been cruising around the whole time but hadn't seen anything. Reggie kept calling but Ghost simply told him there was nothing to dicuss over the phone. He preferred they encounter each other again on the streets. They sat at his cousins house for a second, then headed back to Houston because he still had to get up for work in the morning.

Months later, they woke up and began preparing for Ghost's birthday dinner when she started feeling contractions. She didn't want to drive all the way to the hospital, only to be there for 24 hours again before giving birth. She started to walk up and down the sidewalk until the pressure in her lower abdomen grew more intense. She went inside to bathe in some warm water, then packed her bags for the hospital stay before telling him she was in labor.

"Labor? Right now? It's my birthday!" He looked puzzled.

"Well, it's about to be your daughter's birthday too! Let's go, I'm really in pain!" She stated.

He jumped up from the couch and grabbed the bags, then picked Journei up from her high chair and headed to the hospital. Upon arriving, the contractions had gotten so bad that she knew it was almost delivery time. Once the nurses had everything set up, she gave birth to a healthy baby girl named Jream Jewell. Holding his newborn daughter, he was so excited that she was amazingly born on his birthday. He couldn't take his eyes off of her while he kept repeating to Loyalty, how much she favored him was like looking into a mirror. He was infatuated with their newborn for a second, so she took the opportunity to drift off into a much needed nap.

Two months after giving birth, the training for her new job started right on time. She toured many child care facilities, until she stumbled across one day care center that she absolutely fell in love with. They were finally situated into their new apartment, so it seemed as if all things were finally going good. Ghost was back working a full time shift but he wanted more money without being tempted to hustle. He began working with his cousin's moving company and soon that became just another reason for him to hang out more. She knew he was going to enjoy life when he was released from jail but she figured he could've balanced family and streets. Her hands were always full dealing with a newborn and a toddler, so the only free time she had was at night when she fell asleep. Working full time hours were exhausting for her as well, so she did not complain when he would leave to hang out with his friends. The only thing she hated was when she wanted him to watch the girls, he would rather party all night.

She began to complain to him about his ways, so their arguments eventually led to their reoccurring cycle of physical altercations.

He continued to stay out more and she was starting to love the peace. His actions were becoming disrespectful and she finally had to confront him about his shenanigans. There was some girl she found in his cell phone who he had been texting, talking and creeping with. She read the messages and viewed his call log until she confirmed her own assumptions. Validating what she knew to be true, the feeling of disgust was back floating at the pit of her stomach. She couldn't imagine him sleeping with other women but just that thought alone was a turn off for any sexual desire she had with him.

"If you're going to cheat, at least you can do so respectfully and have some standards about it. Guys choose to destroy trust and union for some of the most dusty looking females that aren't even worth the nut. I hope you are happy with all the decisions you keep making because your actions are responsible for the way I feel about you. I waited five years for you, day by day, when I didn't have that to do. I could have went on with my life but NO, I let love decide for me. While you sit here and allow that tingle in your nuts to do the thinking for you. That's not good enough for me!" She argued.

"You've been unable to have sex babe! You had stitches from the labor and then you had to wait awhile for your six weeks exam. I can admit I messed up before but I left that alone because I knew you would find out anyway. I don't want to lose you or my family!" He pleaded.

"That is a lame excuse Jordan! Don't blame the stages of pregnancy for the reason you can't be faithful to a wife who's been there for you. You don't have any respect for that! You made the decision to forfeit your sexual episodes in this marriage when you started sleeping with trash. I don't even know how to trust you or believe that you even love me!" She stated, then walked away as she left him sitting with his elbow on the table, scratching his head.

One afternoon, he was walking in from work when she asked him to keep an eye on the girls for about two hours. Explaining to him that she wanted to attend a rally that was being held for a teen who had been shot in Florida by some neighborhood watch guy. She had been keeping up with the story for the past two days and she overheard on the radio about the rally in town. She was off that day and was just waiting for Ghost to get home so he could tend to the girls.

"You're not going to that, it's dangerous! I'm not watching them while you be apart of something that could turn ugly. You can chant from the couch but you are not about to walk into trouble. No!" He ordered.

"What? Dangerous? There is chaos around the world over the smallest things but this is something big to me that I want to be apart of. I see marches on TV all the time and now there is one not even thirty minutes from here. Sitting at a trap house is dangerous! Hustling, carrying guns, fighting people and etc. is dangerous! I rather get hurt at a Trayvon Martin rally, than sit around a chill spot shooting dice all day in the midst of trouble. Check your own actions before you try to dictate mine! Everybody out here dying for nothing, yet nobody waking up!" She walked off to the bedroom and slammed the door.

The distance between them was growing. Although she had no interest in sexual activities, she still took care of things around the house as usual. She remained his wife as far as house duties, taking care of the kids and making sure food was still prepared. Fixing his lunches for work, having his uniforms cleaned, and watching the bills like clockwork. Yet, they were becoming strangers under their own roof because her conversation faded while his attention remained else where. You can't change someone who still has an itch to go back and scratch something in their past. It has to be outgrown! That person should make a decision that will better there life and live according to that. A piece of her truly believed he loved her but he wanted her to remain a perfect full-time wife until he was done being a part-time husband.

Her little brother, Rome, had mentioned to her that his girlfriend was involved in some foul play with Ghost. Rome tried getting to the bottom of it because he noticed something different about the two of them. Once he went through his girlfriend's phone, he saw multiple text messages and phone calls between the two of them. It was even more embarrassing because not only was he cheating again but this time her family would know about the betrayal she was humiliated with. Loyalty called the girlfriends phone from her brothers cell and questioned her about their involvement. Of course she denied everything, saying that the few times she did talk to him, it was only conversation. No one usually admits their faults when they're caught red handed, so she expected her story to change once they spoke. Either way, she explained that it was inappropriate and not acceptable for them to have even exchanged numbers. Some people have no morals or values when it comes to boundaries. Respect should always come first!

When Ghost came home, she let him shower, eat and get all comfortable on his favorite sofa. He was smoking a blunt with a shot of Hennessy next to the ashtray, when she calmly sat on the couch next to him and began repeating what she found out. He started looking crazy, never taking his eyes off the TV, yet listening to every word in disbelief. He attempted to deny it until she showed him the screenshots from the girls call log and inbox. There wasn't much he could say but own up too it. He apologized repeatedly then dropped his blunt into the ashtray before he took a seat next to her and held her hand. She explained the embarrassment he constantly put her through was becoming too much to handle. She was ready to walk away from him and all the lies.

Her thoughts consumed her days and he noticed the change in her spirit because she was no longer wearing the same smile. He tried to start dating her all over again by going to the movies, parties and events but nothing could make her look past the mask he was wearing. She no longer trusted anything about him and it killed her softly to know that old feeling was gone. The man she was once in love with did not hold the key to her heart any longer and he felt it. She could never see herself cheating on him but she was starting to think about it all the time. She began to think that if she ended her marriage and found peace again, then her life wouldn't be so depressing. Love was not supposed to keep you down all the time or continuously stab you in the heart with the same sword. She kept telling herself that things would get better and a piece of her faith was actually looking forward to that brighter day. So she stayed and remained faithful to a marriage that only she was faithful too.

When the tension between them remained the same for weeks, he tried to change his behavior in a way that caught her attention. When he came home during the day, he would pull out her Bible and sit on the bed to read it. Unsure of his sudden change in attitude, she figured he was just going through more than she cared to find out about. She was in the kitchen cooking when she noticed him walk to the bathroom to take a shower. She went to the bedroom to flip through the Bible he was reading, just curious to know if he had any notes, bookmarks or something that meant anything. Finding nothing, she continued cooking and began feeding the kids when he walked into the dining room to ask if she had turned the pages.

"You touch the Bible? Why? I'm not where I was because it doesn't look or sound familiar to the last thing I was reading. So, what's up?" He asked.

"Jordan, please! Now you want to act all Christian, like you not out there sleeping with the choir. Don't sit in here and play with God just because you want me to think you're not the same man you were two weeks ago!" She stated, preparing a bottle for Jream.

"I'm not changed, you're right but I'm trying too! Maybe we can go to the marriage classes at church like the pastor was saying one Sunday. If you give me another chance, I won't mess it up. I promise! Let me have your heart again and I won't fumble the ball this time. If you want to work it out, I'll work for it just like you." He replied.

Unable to find words for his proposal to start the marriage classes, she figured that wasn't such a bad idea. Yet still, she was not going to agree so suddenly and forget the deceit and humiliation he had just caused within the past few weeks. Within the next couple days, he mentioned the counseling classes again, stating that he wanted to work on the marriage before she decided to give up. She agreed and decided to look into the scheduled times so they could attend the next session. It was a new experience for them to be around elderly couples who had been married for decades, share their stories on a marriage full of mistakes. Somehow, the ugliest situations led to some of the most beautiful years of their life. Marriage is all about effort, patience and commitment. You must be willing to put forth the effort in working through your problems and have patience to understand that things won't change when you expect them to. Stay committed to one another and allow nothing to damage the sacrifices you both have made.

Although the feeling was not the same, she tried harder everyday to block out the wrongs he had done. It made things slightly better for their intimacy because she tried to see the change in him instead of his past façade. That opened the door a little bit more for romance and the friendship they had before things turned so sour. Nevertheless, she was at least giving things a try because he was the father of her two daughters and she still had love for him.

CHAPTER 16

"Expect the Unexpected"

SEVERAL MONTHS PASSED, WHICH ALLOWED her to find herself again because she had somehow lost that person along the way. Keeping a journal, she wrote down the things that bothered her instead of verbally bringing it up to anyone. She had pages and pages of a fantasy life that she had all mapped out in just a short period of time. She told Ghost about her plan to make something of her writing one day and his only reply to her was that dreams only last for so long. Meaning that her words were simply a waste of conversation because they were only a wish. If she would have graduated from college years ago like she planned, then she would have been some sort of counselor by now.

She was beginning to gain weight and noticed that her appetite had increased in the past two weeks. Realizing she hadn't had a period since they started making up, her anxiety began to kick in. Although she hoped pregnancy was the last thing that could be wrong with her, there was a voice in her head saying that it was going to be a positive test. She just had to check for herself and settle the denial that was already taking over. A baby was the last thing she wanted at a time like this in their marriage. Things were more than shaky between them and she did not want to continue bringing innocent children into a bad situation.

On her way to work, she stopped to get a pregnancy test to find out before her shift started. Finishing up her second bottle of water, she headed straight to the ladies room, impatiently wanting the results. Fixing her clothes, she looked in the mirror and tried to keep her head forward until the answer was ready to show. A minute later, she focused on the small display screen with the word *pregnant* shown across it. She calmy took deep breaths and tried to slow down the anger that was rising. No parts of her wanted another baby to go through the same cycle as her last two pregnancies. The arguing, fighting and lies were just too much for any good woman to deal with. Usually, babies are the best thing a married couple could ask for and a blessing to those who repeatedly try to have planned pregnancies. She was not thrilled because her past experiences with carrying a child was bittersweet.

A part of her didn't want to tell Ghost until he noticed it on his own. She felt it was going to be a very stressful nine months but she prayed time would fly by as it always does. She just needed a little more time to decide if her marriage itself was healthy enough to bring another child into the equation. Of course her usual symptoms kicked in faster than she hoped because a few weeks later she was calling in sick to work every morning. She finally told him she was pregnant and that she would make a doctors appointment in a couple days to find out how far along she was.

So many things interfered with the times they would set aside to attend the marriage classes that they eventually stopped going. She could still sense that things were not peaches and cream, as if they had ever been but she still wanted help. She purchased a book from church and read it nonstop until the message was clear. She mentioned to him that he should read it as well. Trying to fix her marriage, spiritually, she was doing all she could to heal the wounds that were still open. She assumed that her hormones aligned with her thoughts because her lack of trust in him made it hard to become sexually aroused. Being intimate and genuinely enjoying the pleasure is a mind thing. Once the feeling is gone, so is the desire. Some women lay with their significant other every night with a fake smile to comfort their bleeding heart. Pretending was just not her thing, if it was something she did not come out and say, then her body language would confirm the feeling.

She let him come and go as he pleased but the reality of her pregnancy with a cheating husband was beginning to get old. He never understood from her first pregnancy that the stages and things that comes along with carrying a child is not a cake walk the entire time. If he had given things a chance to move along accordingly and just have patience in the process, there wouldn't be such turmoil. Things take time to get back where they used to be after a womans body is put through such transformation. As a husband, she felt it was only right for him to stick by her side through each step, not temporarily walk with someone else.

All things done in darkness will come to light and it seemed as if his dirt was getting filthier each time. He had been sleeping with his phone nearly tucked under his pillow every night, which confirmed he was trying to hide more infidelity. Yet she never would've imagined that he would play so close to home, again. It was true what they say, to never let someone slide because they'll start to ice skate all over you. She always questioned herself for not leaving him when he was caught with her brother's girlfriend. Now he was begging to get dismissed by playing scandalous games and destroying friendships.

She received a few calls from folks in her hometown saying that Ghost had been dealing with Kash. Hearing the news, she tried to make up excuses on why the two of them had conversations she knew nothing of and sneaky meetings. The idea of them actually sleeping together never crossed her mind, so it made her sick to hear about the rumor. Some things can be perceived the wrong way, so to get to the bottom of it, she decided to ask the both of them immediately.

"What's up wife?" He answered.

"I'm going to ask you one time and one time only. Jordan, are you sleeping with Kash?" She paused, waiting for his response.

"What? Kash? What I look like messing with your homegirl? Come on, who would say something like that?" He replied, raising his voice.

"It's nothing to get upset about yet, unless it's true! One fact I know is that you're a liar. I want you to bring my kids home and get your things. We need some time apart. You do not honor or value this marriage, so maybe you can appreciate it once it's gone." Without giving him a chance to respond, she hung up.

He had taken the kids to a carnival and stated they were about to head for some pizza then back home. She wanted some space and needed time alone to sort out the pros and cons of being unhappily married. She had called Kash several times and received no answer, so she sat on the phone with Kali until her line beeped. When she saw Kash's number come across the screen, she clicked over in Kali's face to start an unbelievable conversation she never dreamed of having.

"Kash, what's up? I know we're way better than that! Is what I'm hearing true? You gonna let him manipulate you at the cost of our friendship? You out of line!" She cried.

"Girl, are you serious right now? You think I would sleep with your husband? Come on now! All I can say, is that he has been texting me and calling a few times. At first, I didn't think nothing of it but then he started to make little comments and coming by my house. I wanted to tell you but I didn't want to stress you out more. With the pregnancy and other things you mentioned that y'all are going through, it seemed like a bad idea. Nothing ever happened and I'm sorry for not being able to tell you what he has been doing." Kash replied.

"WE ARE BETTER THAN THIS KASH! I just don't even know what to think right now because there is no way a rumor should involve the both of you, ever. I feel played! I've been loyal to the both of y'all since day one. Now, the two people who I trusted the most have betrayed me the worse. We have nothing else to discuss!" Hanging up the phone, she cried for hours until Ghost arrived.

She had a few bags packed for him, so she met him at the porch with his things. Once the kids walked inside, he stood there in an attempt to explain himself. Immediately, she threw an open bottle of lighter fluid directly at him that was next to the barbecue pit. He tried to dodge the punches she began throwing at him but her rage was dominating his peaceful vibe. For once, he wanted to argue without getting violent while she was the aggressor. She managed to grab the bottle from the ground, then splashed him with the remaining liquid. Grabbing the matches that were sitting on the lawn chair, she striked match after match and repeatedly tossed them towards his damp clothing. He jumped around the porch like a grasshopper, trying to dodge each unsuccessfully lit match. Seeing that she was temporarily out of her mind, he leaped off the porch and walked back to his car. Picking up his bags she had thrown out across the yard, he kept shaking his head in disbelief as he hopped in the car and sped off.

So far, it was possibly the worst day of her life and all she could gather up was enough strength to cry. Their actions were below the belt and there was absolutely no excuse that could justify the accusations. She rather had been alone than to continue being played like she was some sort of flunky. Where is the integrity in some folks? Where do you actually draw the line between what you feel is right and what you know is wrong?

The rumor was spreading more and the story of what actually happened or did not happen was twisted each time she heard it. The stress of dealing with the drama and the history of their relationship had Loyalty losing weight she could not afford. Her baby was not getting enough oxygen and her blood pressure stayed low. The OBGYN prescribed her meds that helped keep everything balanced. The depression was horrible and she had not spoken to anyone in weeks. After putting him out, she packed up her things the following weekend and moved out of their apartment. She was making a decision to remove herself from a man who was not healthy for her heart. Out of all things and people, they had done the ultimate. Sadly, it was not something she was going to forgive or forget, any time soon.

    She paid for a storage and had all their things moved until she figured out her next move. Things were changing right before her eyes and she couldn't keep up with all the pain. She took another leave of absence from work to focus on her health and strength that was affecting her unborn. Nearly a month later, her appetite increased and she was starting to feel better. Lucky let her and the girls move in with her until she was able to find somewhere reasonable to live without having to depend on Ghost. She allowed him to pick the girls up on the weekends, which gave her time to rest. She made it clear to him that she did not want any communication if it wasn't about the kids.

    Being at Lucky's house gave her time to think and plan life from a different perspective. Things were not going as planned and what blew her mind was that she never expected them not too. The only vision she had for her life when Ghost was released, were rainbows and sunny days. Sure she knew that a storm would pass every now and then but sitting under the rain cloud itself was not apart of the fantasy.

    She thought her love was irreplaceable and he would cherish the way she rocked with him. She thought he would come to his senses and realize you can't continue to misuse a good woman. How could she explain to her daughters that she was an example of love, if she couldn't show them what to stand for? Yet, things fell apart and she blamed herself for never thinking that they would. Second chances are earned but not appreciated when they are granted. Letting someone walk all over her was something she could never tolerate. Her mouth was too wicked and her attitude was too snappy for someone to mistreat her in a way that was not equal to her own vibe.

She felt horrible that she had to separate from a man she accepted as her husband. She thought about him almost every second of the day but her self-worth was more important than her feelings. She had to listen to her mind this time. She stopped trying to repair the lies that she played no part in. He was not understanding the fault in his actions because he made so many excuses for his deceit. She explained the principle of love and respect for your spouse, not to mention the value of loyalty. Overall, people won't accept your definition of their wrongs because they act without meaning.

She felt bad that he had no place to stay, going back and forth from his moms or any chick he dealt with. He lost the job working with diesels at the motor company but shortly after was hired on in the oil field. Comfortable with her decision, she was still looking for residence without him. She wanted him to grasp that hustling was something not granted forever because a few of his friends had gotten locked up again with a two digit sentence. Not to mention that half the street population was committed to snitching, so maintaining employment wasn't a bad idea.

Trouble seems to find you anyhow, a few weeks later she received a phone call from Ghost in jail. He had gotten caught up in a murder case but was truly innocent. She yelled at him every second the pre-paid phone call could spare because she couldn't understand why he thought life was a game. She went to check out the charges and evidence, then found out he was actually telling the truth. She advised the police that he was not in his hometown on the day of those murders. She had proof of him being at work, then picking up the kids from school. She couldn't believe he had not thought of those things himself but she went through the details of his day in questioning. After she ran down the information, the police pulled the recordings from the school and gas station where he pumped gas. Everything checked out fine and he was released without any charges. She met up with him to get some money for the girls and have a conversation about his life that kept drifting off in the wrong direction. She told him to start paying attention to the signs and learn to recognize a blessing or a curse.

Freedom can be taken so easily and life can be snatched from you in the blink of an eye. Those were two fates she did not want to see him end up with, regardless of their situation. That moment gave them a reason to get on a better note with each other and put their differences aside to have a decent conversation. He use to be her bestfriend, so to get back on speaking terms was a good feeling but his betrayal never left her mind.

She began listening to gospel music and praying all the time to find calm in the middle of chaos. Preparing for her new baby and making space for a total of three children was a challenge when she had so many problems pulling her in a million different directions. She had not spoken to any of her old friends in months but one day she got a call from Kali, just checking on her. It felt good to talk to someone who had a few problems of their own. She would talk to Lucky every day about her situation but didn't want to keep the same topic relevant night after night.

Finally came the finish line of her pregnancy and her due date was days away. She had been in such a rush to get it over with, from doing jumping jacks, squats and a little walking up the sidewalks. Nothing helped speed up the contractions as she remained dialated at 3cm for over a week. One night she was sleeping, the pain became so intense that she rolled out of bed and headed straight to the hospital.

She called Ghost and told him that Rome was dropping her to the emergency room. He met her up there, along with Lucky and Mrs. Daphne, as they sat around watching the clock. No matter how many times a woman goes into labor, there is nothing that will prepare for the pain it brings.

It was such a relief to get past her last delivery because three kids definitely seemed like she reached her limit. She did not hold her baby girl until she bathed and changed into her personal pajamas. She buzzed the nurse into the room after eating her food and they returned with her new bundle of joy. Placing her into Loyalty's arms, the nurse began to read off a list of do's and don'ts as if it was her first rodeo. Gently touching her newborn's soft skin and thanking God for a healthy baby, she smiled and kissed her tiny nose.

"Sleep in peace baby girl 'cause this a cold world! I love you, Klover!" She softly stated.

Returning back to Lucky's house with Klover was uncomfortable she had to admit but she was not ready to take Ghost back. Although she missed her own space and needed to get her life back in order, her heart was still broken. He made it his business to mention every chance he got that he would take care of everything if she took him back. He kept insisting that all she had to do was take care of the kids and allow him to be apart of their life. Saying that it was ridiculous to live with her sister and continue being ugly towards him, when she could've been in her own apartment. She didn't know what to say because she was truly ready to move out and get situated. She started the search for a new home and allowed him to financially keep his word. He loved to brag about what he did for her and what she was unable to do without him. It bothered her so much and made her not want anything from him but in actuality, she needed his help.

Within a few weeks, they moved back under the same roof without working through the problems she had not gotten over. The resentment was still there and she couldn't take him serious. She would only tolerate him enough until she found out about another sexual escapade with him and someone else. It made trusting him even harder than before, knowing he was capable of hurting her in the most disgusting way. She lost so much respect for him as her husband and she knew it would take a lot more than paying bills to get that back.

She returned back to work and began a routine for her busy schedule. The kids were all in day care during the day while Ghost had to look over them at night. He worked morning shifts, so he was able to get the kids from school then head home until she got off. Her night shift was starting to create more problems and there was no explaining to him that his help in looking after the girls was unavoidable. She knew that he didn't know exactly what to do all the time when watching the kids but she tried her best to make it as easy as possible for him. Leaving food on the stove and snacks labeled in little baggies with the girls name on them. She made sure he had movies to watch and things to do for entertainment while he sat at home with the girls.

His complaint began to be that he was tired after he got off because he worked a man's job that was very draining in the sun. He told her to quit her job or find something that only scheduled her in the morning. Her shift changed every few months and although it was a nice job with benefits, the schedule was an inconvenience to her family. Wanting his understanding a little bit more, it was just another hill they had to climb. It was apart of the selflessness and sacrifice that they work together and do what had to be done for the family. Only thing was, he still had a piece of the streets that kept calling him like a dog hearing a whistle in the rain.

There were times when he would spark up an argument so he could have an excuse to go out on a Saturday night. Seems like every

Friday he was mad about something but then once Sunday came around, he was back to feeling spiritual. She believed that he wanted his marriage but he wasn't ready to dedicate his undivided attention to their union. He always told her that any woman would be happy just to know that her man comes home to her. Whatever that's done in the streets shouldn't matter to a woman who really loves her man? He always tried to educate her on how to be a weak woman because that's what he described. He was definitely wrong if that's what he thought she may have been. There was no way she would continue to accept him coming and going as he pleased or disrespect her by sleeping around with different girls. Sleeping around with any woman but her, for that matter, had broken trust and placed a brick wall where their friendship use to be. Praying for the best and braced for the worse, she remained faithful to a man who had scarred her for life.

CHAPTER 17

"Beginning of The End"

HE SLOWLY BEGAN TO DRIFT more away from home. She simply ignored his actions and let him enjoy life. When he came in from work, he would quickly eat and shower, then head right back out of the door with a cup in his hand. Since he was hardly ever home anyway, she allowed Kali to come down for a few months and stay over. She was searching for a place to relocate to the city as well, so Loyalty was more than happy to help out. Mrs. Daphne had been staying in Dallas for almost a year but for so many reasons moved back to Houston per her request. The house she chose had more than enough space and came in handy now that she could use the extra room.

Ghost would come in at all times of the night, giving him about three hours of sleep before work the next day. He started having drinks at bars on his lunch breaks and couldn't go a day without smoking weed. She noticed him taking pictures of himself when he got home from the gym and then he would sit in the garage for hours playing with his phone.

One day, her and Lucky looked at his phone record and called back at least ten numbers. About four of them were girls and she recognized the other voices from people he hung around. Instead of telling him about it, she went through his phone while he was taking a shower that night. When she heard the curtain slide arcoss the rod, she grabbed his phone only to see that it was vibrating. It was a girl calling him through the Facebook App, so she let it ring until the caller hung up. She only had about twenty minutes until he would cut the water off and notice that she had snuck his phone from the floor, then the drama would begin. She browsed through the messages, google searches, social media, recent gps locations, then letting her last looks be through his photos. Her heart was pretty much in the condition she felt coming because there were pictures of him at clubs with two different chics. She didn't think anything of the pictures besides maybe it was girls he clubbed with that night.

In the middle of her browsing, it rang again through his Facebook App from the same chic. She wanted to answer so badly but knew that would blow her cover, besides she really had no argument for a girl who calls a guy from an App. It brought her attention to his inbox and a very quick look was all she needed to verify that he had been sleeping with the girl. By the looks of it, they hung out more than once but were trying to keep it an online thing. When a person cheats on their spouse with someone who is also in a relationship, they get comfortable. All it takes is one careless night to end up with a baby or disease. Sure enough, mostly everyone found that sex without condoms was a new trend and very popular. Looking at the girl's profile, she surely wasn't cute in the face but had a little booty that made up for looks. It bothered her in the worse way and she didn't feel so bad for not wanting to induldge in sex with him when he wanted. Knowing that if he didn't get it from her, then he would roam until he found a bone. She wanted him to learn the genuine things it took to make a marriage work after trust is destroyed and the love is lost.

He had been keeping up another sexual conversation with a different girl that was miles away who he had been sending all those photos too. Looking at it blew her mind because he simply had enough time in one day to do all that. She wish she had an extra minute or two during the day just to browse through her phone as well. Let alone entertain the thought of meeting someone else and invite them into a crazy situation. She figured that forever was more than enough time for them to fix things and work it out. Yet his actions showed her otherwise as if she was obligated to stick by his side through all the cheating. What man doesn't cheat? That's a dumb question she had heard so many times and her answer was simple. A faithful man who has submitted to God and honors his marriage.

She managed to slide the phone back on top of his clothes in the bathroom. She decided to keep her mouth closed about what she had seen because a giant piece of her heart was numb to his games. Without the words ever leaving her mouth, she showed her disappointment every day. She picked up some extra hours at work and began saving money for a girls trip she booked to Miami.

One day, he called and said that he was headed to their hometown because Murder Mike had just been released from prison. After all those years, he was reunited in the streets with one of his brothers that he talked about all the time. She told him to be safe and she could take care of the girls while he was gone. He was living life like a bachelor but she advised him so many times to stop missing work. He had been blessed with a good job but didn't see it her way or appreciate the opportunity they gave him. It was all too much for her and she decided it was time to depart.

By the time he came home, she was unable to have a decent conversation with him. She was asleep like most people would be at two in the morning when he came into the house falling all over himself. She could tell he was drunk, partly because he was leaning from wall to wall in the hallway but still holding his cup. The noise he made startled her as she gave his behavior her undivided attention. He hated to be lectured too because he was one of those type of people that knew everything. When she would ask about his day or how things were going, he would say she needed to stay out of his business. She grew unfamiliar with the man she was once in love with, no longer knowing who he was.

He made it to the toilet and began to vomit from the amount of liquor he consumed. She heard a loud noise, then things fell to the floor when she rushed in to see if he was alright. He had fallen next to the tub while holding the curtain and she heard him mumbling. She placed a cold towel on his neck and wiped his face as she tried to assist him through all her anger. Just then, he started to vomit again and told her he felt like he was being chased.

"It's like, I feel something! Baby, I'm battling with my own demons right now. I'm fighting demons. I need help." He managed to say in between his heavy breathing.

"Jordan, you are moving too fast. I don't know what you have going on but you are doing too much. Life is not rushing you, so take your time! Talk to God. You need to change the way you're living!" She stated.

Looking at him through tears in her eyes, she felt horrible that he was under what seemed like a spiritual attack. He was battling with himself or maybe the things he was doing had began to take a toll on him. Unsure of what to say next, she helped him from the floor to the sofa next to their bed. She wanted to believe that he wanted help but they had always tried to seek counseling through church or professionals. Nothing seemed to help them as he continued to wonder the streets and catch up on everything he missed while he was in jail. She told him time and time again that he can't chase the days he missed. The streets were not the same anymore and he had a wife with kids now.

Their discussions never seemed to change his ways because he was still doing what she had not exposed to him yet. One night he came home, she waited up for him because she had new information on him and the girl. They argued about it until the sun came up and once the sun was out, their marriage was over. She told him that she was willing to wait for him if he was at least trying to do the right thing but he wasn't. She was not going to sit around and patiently wait for a cheating man to come home everynight.

After hours of fussing, fighting and packing, they had finally come to a conclusion and went their separate ways. She allowed him to get some of his things to be gone before the girls woke up. However, that didn't stop him from going into their room and kneeling against their beds. Embracing them each with a hug and kiss, while tears freely fell from his eyes. She had never seen him cry like that, especially the way he seemed to be heartless at the time. Maybe he realized that after everything he put her through, enough was enough and things were way off track. It may had been bittersweet for him because he loved his family but he was not done loving the streets by far. He had his head in the right place for quite sometime when he first got out, then reality kicked in and flipped it all around.

When she returned from Miami, she continued to work the overtime hours so that her money would keep flowing. However, she still needed his help and he loved every minute of her asking for anything. A few months had passed since she put him out and he mentioned to her that he didn't want another man there since he was still paying bills. It seemed fine to her because she had no intensions on dating. Her mind was strictly on going back to Miami. It was so beautiful there and it was all she could think about once she landed back in Texas.

He began to sit outside her house during the weekends sometimes and just watch. She told him that it was a waste of time to continue lurking because she had already spotted his car. He would know her every move and even pass by her job to make sure she was at work. At first, she told him it was cute that he still seemed to care what she was involved in. He entertained his groupies but they weren't keeping him as happy now that he was separated.

It's crazy how the devil works because paths led her to encounter a guy named Black. He happened to be the boyfriend of the chic Ghost had been fooling around with from Facebook. There were a few rumors going around about the whole situation, so she had gotten his number to clear up the nonsense. Also, to find out what he had known about his girlfriend and her husband. In a weird way, Black didn't seem hurt that his girlfriend was cheating because he stated his cheating days were not over by far. Most women can't be trusted when their heart is broken, so his girlfriend did exactly what he expected, became vulnerable to another man.

They spent hours on the phone as their conversation drifted from one topic, then sailed into the next with a breeze. Even though she felt like a cheater, she had to admit that she enjoyed talking to him and having a real conversation about everything. After a few more laughs, they said their goodbyes and were just about to hang up until he changed his mind.

"Wait. What's up? You was just about to let me hang up so easy?" Black stated in laughter.

"What's so hard about it?" She asked. "It was nice talking too you but I have to go."

"Well, I wanna hear your voice again. Can I call you back?" He asked.

"No, that's not a good idea. Ghost still gets the girls during the week when I work and I'm not ready to confuse things even more." She replied.

"Y'all not together anymore, so you can do what you want. Look, I'll block my number when I call. If you're not busy and feel like talking, just pick up. Cool?" He suggested.

Hesitantly, she responded. "Cool."

One night, she was asleep when she heard loud banging on the door and Kali screaming for her to open up. She couldn't unlock the door fast enough, like she was in a scene from a horror movie when the killer is behind you with a knife. Once she stepped outside, Kali made her notice the commotion Ghost had created. He was standing in the middle of the yard with Kali's male friend in a head lock, yelling to her about not having any dudes at his house. She couldn't believe her eyes as she went outside to break it up and attempt to settle the misunderstanding. The smell of liquor reeked from his body as she pulled him inside and tried to talk about the situation. She told him the guy was dropping Kali off and was not coming inside. He wasn't trying to hear any of it as he kept accusing her of playing games. He felt if she was taking money from him, then she should still do as he said. To her, that sounded ridiculous because she had kids for him so his support should have been strictly because of the children. Not based on whether or not she obeyed his every command and live life under his terms. Since that is not what she did, he soon began helping her less and making up excuses about watching the girls when she had to work.

Word got around that Kash's grandmother had passed. It hit her hard because she had a tight bond with Kash's family, so the beef between them didn't matter at the moment. She never reached out to Kash but on the day of the funeral, she decided to attend. After the funeral, she stood outside with Kali and talked to a few cousins when she noticed Kash close by. Once Mrs. Brenda spotted her, she embraced her in a tight hug, then motioned for Kash to come over.

"Kash, come here. It's Loyalty!" She stated.

Awkward but full of relief, Kash walked closer and they all greeted each other with a two second smile. Mrs. Brenda invited them over to grandma's house for barbecue and a party. They accepted the offer and began to depart so they could follow the hearse towards the cemetary. Just as mentioned, they joined everyone back at grandma's house while they danced, ate and partied until night fell. After a few drinks, Kash and Loyalty sat in the loving room for hours. They talked about everything besides the issue that tore their friendship apart. She missed having a ride or die friend around like Kash. Even though betrayal sat on her heart for a long time, she genuinely enjoyed the conversation as they passed the blunt back and forth.

Later that night, Black heard she was in their hometown, so he called her phone nearly ten times before she picked up. Asleep on the couch at grandma's house, she snatched it from the coffee table and began to speak.

"What is it Black?" She asked.

"Come out with me. Where are you? I heard Kash grandmother's funeral was today. You must be staying with another dude, huh? You talk to somebody else? I called you over ten times. What are you doing?" He asked.

"Umm, Hello. What does it sound like? I was sleep and I'm not leaving out! I'm laying down at grandma's house man, we can chill tomorrow." She replied.

"You too beautiful not to have someone trying to get at you all day. So what's up? You messing with somebody else?" He waited.

"No and you're about to piss me off. Don't question me like I'm your girl, first of all. We only talk and it's about to get cut short." Rolling her eyes.

"Alright look, I'm about to pull up to Kash Grandma's house. Come outside right quick!" He hung up.

With doubt in her mind, she got up to look out of the window and noticed the headlights in the street. He was really outside and her heart dropped because she had never been out so late with him. Usually, she saw him in the day or during the evening but this time it was past midnight. She told Kash she was stepping outside then walked to his car. Talking to him for a second, he persuaded her to ride past the night clubs with him to hang out. Going against every bone in her body, she hopped in just to shut him up about her talking to someone else. They passed by a few spots before everything closed and it was time to head back in.

"Stay with me tonight?" He asked.

"Hell no! You tripping Black and you said you wouldn't ask me that. You acting drunk and I'm ready to go. Bring me back to my truck." She demanded.

Instead of doing as she asked, he jumped on the highway and drove to a hotel room. Her stomach was full of butterflies but she remained calm, telling him she was not staying.

"Why are you here? I can't believe you pulling up to a hotel. Black, I'm NOT staying with you!" She continued repeating.

"Look, I am kinda drunk. I can't drive myself back to the city so I'm gonna stay out here tonight. I promise I won't touch you. Stop treating me like we've never been on a date before. I'm no stranger! You acting like I'm some kind of weirdo." He stated.

Almost in tears, she sobbed. "You are a bitch for this. I told you I don't want to stay here."

"Come on Loyalty. Trust me! I put this on my dead grandmother's grave that I will not touch you." He reassured. "Soon as I sober up, we're gone." He got out of the car.

Walking slowly behind him, she wanted to run so badly and call Ghost to come get her. She kept telling herself that it was almost morning and as soon as the sun came up, they would be gone. Coaching herself on how to get through the night untouched, she uncomfortably stepped inside the hotel room. Slipping off her sandals, she hopped into the bed fully dressed with her shirt, pants and jacket zipped up. She sat on the bed and eased back on the pillow when she heard him already snoring. At least she thought he was, until he started talking.

"Why did you leave the light on? Why are you in the bed with filthy clothes on that you've been wearing all day? Weren't you at a barbecue?" He questioned.

"Yea but why does that matter? If you're so drunk, that little light shouldn't bother you. I'm not close to you, so I'm fine with sleeping in dirty clothes." She replied. Figuring that her being in dirty clothes would lessen his temptation, if there was any.

Right after her statement, he leaned up and cut off the lamp, then slipped out of his boxers. As soon as she saw him do that, she attempted to jump out of bed but he pulled her by the leg. The things that ran through her mind at that instant, killed every belief she had in him of just being a friend. He flipped her over, then placed his tall 250lb frame on her body, using his weight to pin her down. She tried to swing and fight him off but the strength he applied to her hands were to tight too break loose. The nerve that he was even trying to kiss her while he forced himself on her, made her try to push him away even harder. She felt her wind becoming shorter and the wrestle took forever before he finally got her pants off. When she felt her legs free, she could for once understand the struggle she had seen on TV with rape victims. She always wondered how a woman couldn't fight a man off her or allow him to yank her pants off. Yet now here she was, in the midst of her own scence, experiencing exactly what rape was.

"No, Black! No. Please. You said to trust you. You put that on your dead grandmother. Get off of me, Black! Let me go! You are hurting my arms. I'm not ready. Don't do this, please!" She begged.

"Chill out and stop fighting back! Just relax, damn!" He shouted.

After seconds of fighting back and forth, she felt the stiff skin of his man hood rub against her inner thigh and she shouted, NO, one last time. Within minutes, he was sleeping like a baby as she laid still thinking about what Ghost would do to her if he had found out.

The next morning, she got up to run a tub of hot water so she could soak before he woke up. She let her legs ease down because her thighs still ached from the way he handled her. Letting her arms drop into the water, they instantly started to sting as she focused her attention on the scratches around her wrist. She also noticed the cherry red passion mark that led from her neck to her chest. The reality hit her again of what happened last night as she quietly cried, placing her face into the hot towel.

She had already filed for divorce and decided to show him that she was serious about helping her look after the girls. Once he found out that she was trying to have him served with the divorce papers, he began to lose the last straw he had with her. When she got ready to leave one day, her truck made it to the stop sign a block away before it cut off and the battery killed. She made a few calls to make it back home while her truck was being checked out. Later on, she learned that it was water in her tank and she had to pay out of pocket to fix it. Her neighbor came over after noticing her sitting on the porch and informed her that she spotted Ghost pour a bottle of water into her fuel tank. She mentioned that she thought it was a prank, until she noticed Loyalty's truck had not been back in the driveway since. To hear such a spiteful thing Ghost had done, instantly made her call him to share a piece of her mind. He denied everything and stated that he would be more than happy to take care of the repairs if she took him back. Dismissing his request to come back home, she told him that she was beyond fed up and going to the court house immediately.

She made it downtown that following Monday and spoke with the clerk about finalizing her divorce due to the extra conflict they were having. She no longer wanted to be married to a man that done such awful things and she would have done anything to untie their knot. The clerk informed her of the document she needed to fill out and bring back with the original divorce packet to finalize it before they closed. That was great news! She headed to the parking lot, only to find that a boot had been placed on her car. Unfamiliar with downtown Houston, she had no idea the area was a no parking zone. She called the number from the yellow sticker that was stuck to her drivers side window. They told her it was $270 to have the boot removed and that she was parked in a tow zone.

No other option, she called Ghost and hoped he would understand. Once he heard that she was actually at the court house to make the divorce final, he hung up in her face and turned his phone off. She called her brother, who came almost an hour later, then they headed to her house for some money and the divorce papers. Her friend from work, Maurie, picked her up from home and headed back to the court house. When she noticed her truck, the boot was gone and the yellow sticker had been removed as well. Maurie looked at her in shock as if she made it all up, so she dialed the number in her call log to check the amount again.

"Hi, I'm calling about a boot that was just placed on my truck about two hours ago." She began to explain, reading the license plate to the operator.

"I'm sorry ma'am. We haven't spoke to you today and have no record of a restriction based on that plate number." The lady replied.

Laughing, she repeated. "The long, yellow, metal boot was just on my truck about two hours ago. I left to get the money and this document to finalize my divorce. Now that I make it back, you're telling me that I'm crazy, like I made all this up." She shouted in disbelief.

"I'm sorry ma'am but we have no records of this." She reassured.

Disconnecting the call, Loyalty gathered her things from Maurie's car and thanked her for the ride. Noticing that it was now past 5pm and the court house was closed, she had to wait for another off day to deal with it again. Everything had her emotional, as she walked to her car and Maurie pulled next to her with the window down.

"Don't look at everything as bad luck. Maybe there is some good in this too! I know one good thing about it so far is that you just saved $270. Go home and chill, better days are coming for you. You just have to trust the process, bro." She stated, then drove off.

CHAPTER 18

"The Cost of Trust"

WORKING SO MANY HOURS, THE opportunity never presented itself again, nor granted her time to make it downtown for the divorce to be final. During the days that passed, Ghost had been making so many excuses for him not being able to pick up the girls from school. Rushing from work on a lunch break, she would pick them up and bring them over to her family's house until she got off. Sometimes, he would surprise the girls and pop up at their school or just show up to the house. They each had become so attached to him during those short three years, so for her to watch their father-daughter bond was amazing. He knew how much they loved seeing him, so it bothered her that he would stop coming around because of the feud between them. If they had an argument that morning, it would affect whether or not he picked the girls up while she worked that evening. She grew tired of his games and blocked his numbers from her cell. Figuring that he would notice, she wasn't surprised when she started receiving calls from an unknown number.

"So, what's up? You acting real childish placing me on the block list." He calmly stated.

"Well, that explains why you dodging everybody around here. You don't like kids too much do you?" She argued.

"Say, stop playing with me and unblock my numbers. I love my children! I'm trying to win you back but looks like you moved on right? Why would you even mess around with a dude like Black? I'm saying though, I'm willing too accept that because I deserve it. Now you're taking things too far. How could you even do that to me? It's me!" He began to shout.

"It's you? How could you do all the stuff you've done, to me? Please don't play the victim here, Jordan. I wish I could tell you a lie, trust me, I wish none of it even happened. I'm not looking for a boyfriend because what I believe in doesn't exist in this generation. I only wanted you to be a good husband, not a perfect one. I loved you so much Jordan and you know I would've done anything for you. Yet, you destroyed everything we had." She cried, tears pouring down her face.

"I'm sorry. I love you, Loyalty. I hope one day you can forgive me." He hung up.

So many things had been happening, she couldn't believe how much chaos could stir within a few weeks. She was told that someone wanted to kill Ghost and Murder Mike over some beef that got out of hand. After hearing it about three times, she decided to give him a call to voice her opinion about the rumors. As expected, he went insane when he learned that the phone call was about some hearsay that came from the streets. He mentioned that he had already gotten an ear full of it and he wasn't bothered by it. She could tell that he was upset but his attitude was towards her and all she wanted to do was help. She offered him a place to stay, meaning that her cousin was moving out of a really nice condo that she could no longer afford and wanted someone to pick up the bill but he declined. She warned him that if he didn't lay low for awhile until the beef calmed down, then she was going to call his probation officer and have him arrested.

Hearing that, he hung up in her face and stated that she was wild for trying to get him locked up.

A few nights later, she woke up in a panic from having a bad dream and he was the first person that came to her mind. She called him and let it ring a few times before he picked up with music blaring in the background. She called out to him a few times before the music sounded further away and he spoke.

"What's up wife, why aren't you sleep?" He asked, blowing smoke from his nose.

"Jordan, what are you doing? No for real, what are you doing? Like, I have been so worried about you and I don't want you hurt out there. Can you please be careful and try not to trust so many of your so-called friends. Everybody is not riding for you just because they're riding with you." She stated.

"I'm not doing nothing baby! Just chilling, trying to live my life a little. I'm at the club right now but I walked out with my drink to come talk to you. You wanna get back together or what? I do." He replied.

"No Ghost, I don't." She rolled her eyes.

"Well, what you want? If you ain't talking about being together, then fuck you." He stated.

"You are so stupid. This is why I don't even call to be nice, I hate you." She laughed.

"Well, stop calling. I hate you too!" He shouted.

"You're the one that has been tryna make it harder for me! I wish you died!" She yelled back, before hanging up in his face.

She called his probation officer to have him arrested, in hopes that they would keep him for six months for violation. They collected his urine and told her that they could not arrest him for failing the drug test. He was only placed in a drug class that he had to attend once a week, which did her no justice. She returned back to his probation officer and told him that she feared for Jordan's safety and that if they didn't lock him up then the streets would kill him. The PO told her the types of things that could get him arrested and placed on a federal hold that would deny him a bond. That was all she needed to know, as she walked away thinking of her plot to have him arrested.

As crazy as it seemed, she forgave Black after the hotel incident. He woke up that morning apologizing for taking advantage of the situation and explained that he couldn't help himself. He admitted to forcing himself on her and that was what she wanted most, for him to own up to it. Seeing the scratches and marks, he laughed a little that he had gotten so carried away. At the time, she felt attached to him by default because he had already gotten what she wasn't ready to give. They saw a lot of each other and continued to talk on the phone for hours a day. What he had done didn't change the fact that she had enjoyed his conversation more than anything. She looked at him differently because overall, she realized he wasn't her type.

Sitting at work, the idea finally came to her mind about the charges to file against Ghost. She didn't want him to catch a case or anything that could cost years of his freedom. So she decided to make her own bruises by beating herself up like Brandi in the movie, "*A Thin Line Between Love and Hate*". All she needed was proof of injury to press charges on him for assault. She figured she could just drop the charges once he had served his six month violation. Either way, it was better than someone killing him.

Just like any news, she heard that he was becoming a more nonchalant person and developing a calm attitude about certain things. He had apologized to many of the girls he had bad blood with in the past and even resolved a few issues between a few of his friends. He called her one night from an unknown number since he was still on the block list. Answering the phone, she recognized the difference in his voice. She didn't know exactly what had come over him but the mood in his tone was something that made her pray for him that night. She got out of bed and leaned against the mattress on her knees, as she began a prayer.

On Friday morning, she was buckling the kids into their car seats when Ghost pulled in the driveway. The girls were so excited to see him as they began jumping and clapping with joy. Journei and Jream were old enough to hold a decent conversation, as if there toddler language was college level. He peeked his head in front of Klover's face so she could grab his ears and make spit bubbles through her giggles.

Kissing the girls before shutting the door, he waved at them through the window while making funny faces. Directing his attention towards Loyalty, he handed her a wrapped gift as an early Mother's Day present.

"I love you. Happy Mother's Day! You deserve the world Loyalty and I can't apologize enough for what I put you through. I have another gift for you but I'm only going to give it too you if you agree to have dinner with me Sunday. Let's try to start over. I promise, this time will be different. I'm a different man now! Before, I was the same man that was trying to be something I never thought I could be. Now, I'm ready! Just hear me out." Staring in her eyes.

"Jordan, I want to believe you but I can't. The lease is up next month. Maybe if you become a better person, we can try to build again. I'll think about the date. I'm heading to work, so I will call you when I have time." She replied.

He grabbed her hand and started to harmonize a *Tony Rich* classic, as he smiled.

"Nights are lonely and the days are so sad. I just keep thinking about the love that we had. I'm dying inside and nobody knows it but me. Like a clown, I been putting on a show but the pain is real, even if nobody knows." He continued to sing as he released her arms and backed away slowly to his car.

She was glad they were able to smile at each other and accept the peaceful vibe that graced their departure. She was more than positive that things were not right somehow, something felt strange but she couldn't put her finger on it. That Sunday, she did not attend the date as he had asked. It made him upset, so he did not pick the kids up on Monday, which made her reject any unknown number that called. She wanted to work on co-parenting and a friendship that would mold any piece of their relationship that could have been saved. He wanted to work on saving their marriage first, which seemed impossible because it had been destroyed so many times.

Journei was so excited to see him that morning, she couldn't wait till he showed up at daycare that evening. Instead, when she saw Loyalty at the entrance, the joy was gone and she was instantly filled with sadness.

"What's wrong Journei?" She asked, picking her up.

"I don't have no daddy. I don't have a daddy no more?" She stated, with every inch of seriousness, then dropped her face on Loyalty's shoulder.

"You do have a daddy! Why would you say that? I had to pick you up for him, that's it! You will see daddy in a few more days. It's okay!" She assured.

Walking to the car, she began receiving calls from unknown numbers and sent them all to the reject list. He usually liked to call her around pick up time to ask her how they got home. The night before, they argued for thirty minutes before hanging up on each other because she didn't meet him for dinner. Once she dropped the kids off to Kali, she headed back to work for overtime.

With only a hour left of her shift, she finally took her phone out to check the notifications. It had been ringing back to back with the same numbers that she repeatedly rejected earlier. Then she noticed a few missed calls from Mama Jewel. Figuring it was probably Ghost calling from his mother's phone, she was not in the mood to discuss the situation. She was just about to return her call when it started vibrating again. Seeing that it was Kali calling for the third time, she slid her work headset from her ear and began to whisper.

"What happened? This your thir…"She was cut off.

"Loyalty! Ghost is dead! What are you doi…" Kali shouted.

"WHAT?… My Jordan? What do you mean?" She jumped up with the headset still attached to her head as she ran to the conference room, dragging the cords with her.

"My baby daddy called and asked me how you were doing, so I asked him why. Then he said how he hated to hear about Ghost being shot. He was killed Loyalty! Somebody sh…" Kali yelled.

Loyalty hung up on her to look through her phone and gather her thoughts. With tears heavily flowing, it was hard to see the screen. She went through her messages and saw that a few people had already texted to give their sympathy. The lump in her throat was forming and at that moment she saw a new notification from her social media. Someone had tagged her in a picture and just from the view, she could tell it was Ghost. What she dreaded was the caption underneath it that read, *Rest In Peace*. She released the most painful scream she could find in her soul, as the reality hit her like a brick in the gut. She took a deep swallow and answered the incoming call from Mama Jewel.

"What's happening out there? What happened to Jordan?" She sobbed.

"One of these wanna be gangsters put a bullet in my son's chest and left him for dead. I'm watching these folks haul my baby off in a bag. Somebody led my son to this park because he would have never came here to meet someone he didn't trust." She stated, anger oozing from every word.

"Are you looking at him? Like, is this for real. Are they sure it's really him? Could he still be alive? Have they even tried to save him? We need him. I need him. My girls. Oh my.... I can't accept what y'all saying..." Loyalty cried.

"What? Are they sure? I made it up here while he still had breath in his body but he was barely hanging on. He heard me talking though! Then he gave in and died right in my arms!" She cried, disconnecting the call.

Loyalty sat on the floor crying for a few minutes when two of her supervisors walked in to find out what was wrong. She was very close with them, so they knew a little of what had been going on between her and Ghost. To learn of his death took them by total surprise, especially to know that he was murdered by someone he may have known. Her phone sounded off every minute and it was too much to explain or talk about at the time.

Their conversations replayed through her mind when they would discuss Jesus and Heaven. It instantly made her pray for his soul and wished him to be in the arms of angels instead of darkness. She said a prayer, forgiving him for everything he had done to her. Even asking for forgivness because she had said and done so many things she wanted to take back. She continued to cry more, thinking of the date he wanted to have just the night before. Maybe if she would have gone on that date, things would have gone differently? She regretted ever kicking him out of the house and blamed herself for his heavy presence in the streets. She sat on the floor crying uncontrollably as the short lived moments with her husband played in her mind. It was so bittersweet but it was all worth it because she wouldn't have changed a thing. She loved her kids even though her marriage wasn't a perfect picture. She would never forget the lesson in his death and never be too ashamed to share her story.

It made her think about Journei's words earlier that day. "I don't have a daddy". Did she feel that close to her father, where she had a feeling about his death? What would her children do without seeing their father? Everything she thought of took away layers of her heart and each tear she cried made her realize that she took so many things for granted. When she walked outside, Lucky and Kali were waiting by the exit where they embraced her at the same time. They all cried out as no one had anything to say that the tears didn't explain. Nothing ever seemed so permanent or unreal and it was by far the hardest pill she ever had to swallow. This was her new life now. It was real. Ghost was dead.

CHAPTER 19

"Living With Reality"

SHE NEVER WOULD'VE IMAGINED SHE'D plan a funeral and bury the man that she waited five long years for. Did she wait for nothing? She felt cheated but mostly for her children's sake. They adored him! She was two hours away from where he had been murdered and was unable to make it to the scene. She wanted to see him one more time, dead or alive. She had taken for granted the time he spent chasing her and now time was all she asked for. She only filed for divorce to prove to him how tired she was of his disrespectful ways. Only, she felt that in the midst of teaching him a lesson, she learned something her memory could not tolerate.

That night, she scrolled down her call log to view all the private calls she had received earlier that day. Her soul ached because she had been dodging calls trying to avoid the confrontation with him. The anger he had created inside of her made her deny every moment he tried to be a husband again. She figured that she had given him enough chances but now she would never get the chance to share another second with him. She called his phone at least twenty times and prayed that it wasn't true. She wanted to say that she forgave him for everything but it was too late. She could feel her sanity slipping away until her walk down memory lane was interrupted by her daughters. They came into the room with such concern on their small faces as if a gloomy vibe took over the house. Klover had just began to crawl, so she followed her every step with a cry that was adding to her heartbreak.

Everything required so much effort at a time when she felt like doing nothing and she needed help. She had switched numbers with Kash before she left town the weekend of grandma's funeral. So the next day, Lucky, Kali and Kash all sat on the couch and discussed Ghost's murder because the streets had already began talking. Once she made the funeral arrangements, they headed to Dillard's so she could buy his burial clothing and bring it to the funeral home. She was waiting on them to call back so she could make the payments, pick the flowers, casket and finally view his body. Everytime they mentioned *deceased,* she had to take a moment and regroup because she had yet to accept the truth.

Wanting to see the murder scene, they were on their way to the park when her phone rang. It was a friend of Ghost's who witnessed the shooting and was calling to tell her the story. Apparently, Ghost had become close with an old friend of his who had a hidden agenda. He was seen with the guy at several places, yet never knew he was affiliated with someone who wanted him dead. He had just rolled up a blunt when the dude called him to meet at a park on his end of town. In an unfamiliar area, he gave Ghost the directions and led him to believe that he was returning a gun of his.

"What's up Loyalty? I can't express to you how sorry I am for this happening. I watched my bestfriend get shot in the back and I have to live with this image forever. I feel that you should at least know what went down. Maybe it was meant for him to pick me up so we would know what happened to him. He was in love with you though and y'all separation was killing him too." His friend stated.

"I loved him too and I hate that so many ugly roads tore us apart. Now I feel like I should have never put him out and this would've never happened. I feel horrible like it's all my fault. That's all I been thinking about is who could've shot him. So yes, I want to know what happened." She replied.

"I can't tell you what made him drive to that park, knowing we had no gun of our own. I told him a few days ago that I didn't like the vibe or energy from that new cat he hung around. He told me that he knew the dude from back in the day and they bumped into each other a few weeks ago. He called me last night and said that he was about to meet him in the South. When he told me that, I knew in my mind it didn't sound right but I just rode with him anyway. It's crazy but with the rumors that had been going around, I just don't see why he would let a new face get so cool with him like that. So when we pull up to the park, ol' dude car was parked towards the street and he signaled for Ghost to come over. He told me to sit tight, then he got out and started walking towards the dude direction. He got about ten feet from the car when I heard the first shot. Damn!" He paused.

That enraged her to hear how he unknowingly walked into gunfire and neither of them had a firearm to shoot back. He probably thought about all the warnings he had gotten but it was too late by then. She could only pray that he spent his last breath talking to God.

"He turned around and tried running back to the car but I could tell he was already wounded. I heard more shots and he jumped the ditch like he was hit again. By the way he fell to the ground, I could tell he was dead. Then ol' dude started shooting at Ghost's car, so I hopped in the drivers seat and sped off. I drove straight to Mama Jewel's house so her and Dollar could know what happened. We went right back to the park but it took us a minute because I couldn't remember the damn directions. It wasn't our hood, ya' know. I feel like the dude caught us slipping and was able to kill him right in front of me." He finished.

"Wait. You left him? Why? He may have still been alive if you had waited 'till the shots were over. He must've felt alone knowing that you just drove off. He was left for dead! I can't believe this!" She cried.

As his friend continued to explain what happened, he mentioned that there was a calm spirit over Ghost that he had never seen before. He acted as if he wasn't afraid of anything set out to harm him. She was satisfied to know what really happened and even more pleased when the detective called to let them know they had arrested the guy. They caught him on a bus trying to leave town with the murder weapon.

Everything had fallen in place as they always seemed to do. She took her entire $1800 check and put it towards his homegoing celebration. Only thing was, it left her completely broke once she paid her own bills. A few good friends of his began reaching out to her to bring by wads of cash. Everyone crowded outside Mama Jewel's house for days at a time to attend the automatic gathering that takes place after a death in the family. She had just returned from seeing Ghost's body at the mortuary when they cleaned and dressed him up. She cried all she could for about twenty minutes while looking at every detail, touching his skin and feeling his chest. She couldn't help but question what was right before her eyes.

"Is he really dead? Are you SURE?" She calmy asked the staff who was standing at the foot of the casket.

"I'm so sorry, really! Denial is the first stage darling, you just have to trust the process and everything will work out." The elderly lady strongly stated.

Looking back at his cold and lifeless body, her weeping started over as Murder Mike walked in behind her. He took a step ahead of her and stood still for a very long time. He took a deep breath and began shaking his head in disbelief.

"Damn, I'm gonna miss you bro. Can't believe you got caught slipping!" In almost a whisper, he turned to walk away.

She had not answered for Black since the murder and saw no reason to continue entertaining the pointless situation between them. After things had taken the worse turn ever, she started to believe that the devil played a hand in things that were out of control. Black was placed in her path as a distraction to take her mind off Ghost and her failing marriage. Once she put Ghost out of the house for the last time, she knew for sure there was no way to work through their problems until he matured from running the streets. He always told her that she was abandoning him and leaving him in the streets with the wolves. That stuck with her the most, which is why she felt the need to tell Black once again, she was over it.

"What do you mean, we shouldn't talk? I was trying to see if you wanted to hang out and grab a bite to eat? Get your mind off of things and maybe catch this comedy show tonight." He stated.

"Does it look like I'm in the mood to sit around a bunch of strangers and laugh at some corny ass jokes? I don't think shit funny right now! As a matter of fact, everyone I've bumped into that showed Ghost love has offered some kind of something to pay their respect. Well, what about you? You were the one fake loving on me. Since you're so concerned about how I'm doing. How about you ask me if I need anything?!" She stated, with every bit of irritation.

"Why don't you just ask me for some money if you need it?" He laughed. "You're mad at me like I killed your dude. I didn't do you anything but I'm still here trying to be friends." He argued.

"No. You're still here to make sure you're the one around if I'm horny, which I'm not and I won't be. Need your money?" She laughed. "You can save your own coins! Even if, you're the devil in this situation who came to steal, kill and destroy. You stole my goodies at the hotel that night. Now Ghost is dead because I paid him no mind for months and for some reason, I feel you are apart of that destruction. Don't call me again!" She hung up and blocked his calls.

The image of Ghosts' lifeless body remained on her mind. He laid naked on a cold, steel table underneath a white sheet with specs of blood still on his face. The image was hard to erase and the words that she couldn't take back were beginning to peirce holes through her soul. An altercation at Mama Jewels house had occurred between a couple of females over Murder Mike. She told her mind to adjust to the pain but it was no use when her anger caught a whiff of the drama. A chic in the street was attempting to fight a female that was in the yard, when Loyalty decided to intervene.

"Obviously, the girl don't wanna fight you but I heard you have an issue with me. So what's up? Get out the car!" She stated, standing in fighting postion.

"Girl, you better get away from this car. Nobody worried about you but if you want to fight, let's meet at the park." The girl replied from the passengers seat.

The words *meet at the park* hit Loyalty like a train, knowing Ghost was just lured to a park nearby and killed. Without thinking, the emotions forced her right fist to connect with the girls jaw through the window. After throwing the first punch, she backed up to allow the chic a chance to get out of the car. However, she hopped out with a knife and Loyalty took off around the car as the crowd attempted to take the chics weapon. Once Murder Mike grabbed it, the fight started and it felt good for her to relieve a little stress. Her wind quickly grew short from the blunt she just smoked and her opponent locked up into a wrestling move. Mama Jewel separated them, which only built more anger until Loyalty ran up to the chic again. After the fight, the chic and her friends drove away but one thing remained the same. Ghost was still dead, no matter what she did to ease the anger. The pain found a new home in her heart.

She was exhausted the morning of the funeral because she stayed up all night folding obituaries with Kash and Kali. Everything came out nice but she wished there was more time to do the things her heart kept getting in the way with. Nevertheless, it was time to say goodbye as she looked at her daughters play around inside the limo. They had no idea what a funeral meant, all they were told was that their daddy was asleep forever. Once they saw his body laying inside the casket, their eyes wondered in confusion, soaking up the sadness that filled the atmosphere. When the men closed the casket, she could feel Jream's two year old arms grip around her waist even tighter. Loyalty stood before the church with hopes to say a few positive things that were on her mind. Once she faced the crowd, the only words she wanted to say was a list of inappropriate things that shouldn't be said in church. Instead, she thought of a shorter statement and took a seat before she broke down again. Ghost would always tell her to fix her face so that no one could see her crying, so that's exactly what she kept telling herself.

Once the crowd began leaving the cemetary, she sat under the tent and tried to hold on to the moment. Tears flowed down her eyes as she slowly got up and hugged the casket, then released a loud wail. There was no going back to anything in her past because life had changed whether she was ready or not. After minutes of leaving tears on his casket, Lucky pulled her away and walked her to the car where she just held on to her daughters in the backseat.

They proceeded to the repass, held at a wide park in the area where they set up a day full of celebration. Dollar and Mama Jewel had taken care of everything, so all Loyalty had to do was show up. Once the food was being served and everyone was comfortable, she walked down the sidewalk to her familiar crowd. Arielle, Kash, Kali and a few other friends already had blunts in the air, so she joined in and poured a cup as well. Right when she was feeling cool and laid back, there was an alteration that erupted out of nowhere between a few guys.

Slowly walking towards the dispute that was getting everyone's attention, she noticed that by the looks of things, it was about to get ugly. Just when she turned to look for her children, there was a gun shot that rang out. Before she could even scream, it was followed by more shots that disturbed the entire gathering as everyone began running from the scene. Once the gun fire ceased, she took a minute to look around and saw the park was in total chaos. A friend came up to her holding Klover while she spotted the oldest two standing across the street with Kali. She noticed that everyone's focus was still towards the park, when she noticed two bodies laying on the ground. She walked over to get her girls attention but could tell they were already mesmerized by what they just witnessed.

Once the police left and cleared the scene, everyone stood around for another hour or so discussing what took place. Apparently the guys came uninvited and it sparked up a heated conversation between Ghosts' homeboys. Both parties had prior history of conflict, so as a hunch that things were looking like another set up, the argument ended in gunfire. On top of her daughters never seeing their father again, they also had to wave good-bye to their uncle. Murder Mike was arrested for the shooting and charged with murder in broad daylight, on the same day of his little brother's funeral.

She went back home and stayed in bed for days, only giving her energy to things that required little effort. The kids were under their own supervision as she laid awake, suffering from a broken heart. Journei and Jream had so many questions about the shooting and wanted to know so much about Heaven. She was not emotionally strong enough to deal with the answers.

One morning, she received a notification from her social media that caught her eye by the profile picture. She couldn't believe that after eight years of not speaking to him, she was staring at an aged picture of Dylan. She responded, seeing that he was checking on her after hearing how her life had turned out. It was actually nice hearing from him, as he apologized for hurting her all those years ago. Seeing that it turned out to be a life full of pain so far, he only wanted to make sure she was still sane. They switched numbers and he immediately called to verbally express his sympathy. Talking to someone familiar who she once shared a thick history with, was exactlty what she needed. He told her he was married but also going through a separation that left them on non speaking terms as well. After she explained the situation between her and Ghost, he understood life was too short for cold shoulders. They talked nearly everyday and she called him anytime she woke up during the night so he could ease her thoughts.

"The tongue can speak life or death. We gotta control our words when we're upset, otherwise things are said out of hatred. You act like you don't see a point in living anymore, when you were actually created to live before you die. You think you're still alive by accident? Maybe this is everything being taken away from you, so God can provide what He wants for you. You will be blessed from what you thought would kill you. Trust His plan, Loyalty. Trust it." Dylan stated.

"I still have my mustard seed, don't worry!" She laughed. "Nah, on a serious note, you should give her a chance to talk things out. Even if you don't wanna hear it! One thing I wish I could get back is the times he wanted to just talk to me and I pushed him away. Now the tables have turned tremendously because all I want to do is talk to him." She stated.

"I got you! She hasn't called me again but I promise, I'll talk to her." He replied.

Things were the same, as far as her heart was concerned. Unable to explain life and death to someone so young was taking a toll on her that she couldn't fix on her own. Her duties of staying on top of things had flown out of the window. She barely had strength to comb her daughters hair, let alone her own. Mama Jewel would get the girls almost every weekend which gave her a chance to wallow in misery alone.

She had become so dependent on weed and alcohol to help her sleep at night, that she made it her meal plan. One night, she was about to take a bath when she caught a glimpse of her reflection in the mirror and watched the tears fall out of her own eyes. That particular night, she was drunk and the liquor had gotten the best of her. She popped a blade out from the razor in her medicine cabinet and was just about to pierce her skin on the neck. Journei walked in and disturbed her mild insanity, which probably saved her life.

"Mama… are you… making your own bobo?" She stared.

"Why are you in my bathroom? Didn't I tell you to knock on closed doors?" She replied, putting things away.

"Mama, I'm scared of my dreams. I miss my daddy! I had to tell him something and I hope he wake up tomorrow. Grandma Jewel said if we be good, then we will fall asleep one day and see Heaven too. I'm gonna climb the biggest tree and go get him from Jesus." She yawned.

Grabbing Journei by the arm, she walked her back down the hall to her own bedroom in silence. She laid down until Journei began snoring, then it was safe to let tears fall freely on the comforter, drifting off into a peaceful sleep of her own.

She was all set to move out of the house that constantly reminded them of Ghost, leaving everything behind but their clothes. She wanted to start over fresh and the only way to start a new life is to leave behind your old one. Once again, she was back at Lucky's apartment until the first of July. Her father helped her get everything approved, while Dylan offered to take care of the rest. He stated, in a way, that he was showing appreciation for all the years he didn't. One night, they talked on the phone for hours discussing their dreams. He told her about his producing that finally paid off from making beats. He was finally getting the recognition he wanted, while she stated that she began writing her own book. She was due to move in a couple days and even though he was planning to drive out and help, she hadn't met him for brunch yet. He previously tried to arrange for them to meet up and have dinner or something but she never had time. So she figured they would just catch a bite to eat once he drove to the city and helped her get situated. The next night, her text alert sounded at 2am. It proved that once again, she was not in control of her life and it could change just like that.

Incoming : Loyalty! You up? This Ceasar.
Outgoing : I am now. What's wrong?
Outgoing : I feel like this is about Dylan. Is it?
Outgoing : Cease??
Incoming : He just had a car accident.
Outgoing : Don't say what I think you're trying to say. Cease!!
Incoming : They said his wife called to discuss their problems. He was on his way to meet her and lost control of his car. I just talked to him yesterday, he told me y'all had gotten back cool. I'm sorry sis!
Outgoing : You lying!!

For confirmation, she called another best friend of Dylan's to get his reaction. Just by his tone when he answered, she could tell there was some truth to the shocking news.

"Darryl, what's up? Where is Dylan? What's wrong with you? Please don't tell me you're crying. Darryl? This is so unfair. Where is he?" She cried.

Sniffling, he stated. "We're just leaving the hospital. He's dead."

CHAPTER 20

"The Mustard Seed"

A RED LIGHT CAN REALLY be the longest two minutes of your life, especially when you've already lost patience before the signal even switched to yellow. One foot held down on the brake pedal and her head faced down on the horn with both arms hugging the steering wheel. Life suddenly became a movie replaying in her mind, as her imagination took a stroll down memory lane. Everything was all so bittersweet. It was like an invisible rain cloud followed above her head. Even if it seemed all good, she still carried the bad around like dead weights. For so many reasons, she pitied herself for everything unfolding the way it did. No matter what happened, all ten fingers pointed at the reflection of her very own, that she began to hate.

"What is the point?" She shouted. "I can't go through any more, I'm telling you… I've had it."

Her foot was starting to give in to the thoughts of releasing the brake and allowing her truck to roll into traffic. Thinking of dying is one thing but to actually take your own life is something most people are actually too coward to do. Yet, her tears began to roll faster while she was releasing such a silent cry, as her soul ached from the pain her heart kept enduring. Her body suddenly felt numb to any more emotion or feeling of being afraid to just do it.

"Here it goes." She thought.

She picked her head up to watch the movement of the busy intersection near Highway 145 in Houston, Texas. Assuming traffic was heavy enough to crash her car fatally, she prayed no one else would get hurt in what she hoped would be a successful attempt to take her life. She licked her lips out of habit and closed her eyes while she began to ease her foot off the brake. Just at the second her foot inched for the accelerator, her phone rang and an unfamiliar number grabbed her attention.

Startled, yet with hesitation, she softly answered. "Hello"

"Hi, sister Dawkins?"

"Yea, this is me. What is it?" Instantly annoyed from the approach, she knew it was related to church but the voice was so familiar.

"Well, sorry to bother you but I was just calling to see how you're doing, maybe pray for you and the family. Possibly invite you to church?" The male rambled off through the phone.

Loyalty couldn't believe it but she could then place his voice with the words, it was the Pastor. What made him call at this particular moment and interrupt her perfect date with death? The tears began to flow even harder as she tried to reply.

"Everything is just so messed up. I mean, if you don't mind, I do have so many questions… and I sure could use me some God right now."

Green Light.

Days went by a little easier after speaking with the Pastor. He answered so many questions about life and related most scenarios to scriptures from the Bible. She found it fascinating that many biblical stories could almost identically compare to real life situations. With more peace in her heart, it allowed her to pray for Ghosts' soul one last time in hopes that he was in a better place. She pushed her move-in date back a week until she figured things out.

After Dylan's funeral, they hung out at a gathering in his memory with old friends they hadn't seen in years. She found herself sitting in the car with Kash for almost thirty minutes in silence. They passed the blunt back and forth while she read through Dylan's old messages. He mentioned how he waited eight long years to apologize for their bad split and he missed her honesty most of all. With Ghost still fresh on her mind, the unexpected tragedy involving her first love was enough to drive her crazy. She was unable to view Dylan's body because they arrived late. It gave her an even deeper cut because she was hoping to say goodbye. Looking at the bright side, maybe it was best she kept the old memories of how she remembered him when they dated. Every so often, she would break down in tears but hated to continuously cry over the same thing that would solve nothing.

Something weird happened and she couldn't understand for the life of her why an elderly lady would make up a lie in church. However, she was approached by Dylan's mother and asked why she had slapped the usher who was assisting with the funeral. She was taken by surprise to learn the elderly usher had pointed her out, accusing her of physical harm before she entered the funeral. She denied the accusations, as they were false but laughed at how the devil just would not let up. It was after the funeral when she noticed the woman again, so she walked her direction to ask her why she would say such a thing. The lady noticed her coming and suddenly rushed away as quick as she could. Her actions made Loyalty laugh as she found humor in the lies people tell.

That night, she told Kash and Kali that she was about to take a shower then head for bed. Her unavoidable episode of tears in the shower began, as she thought about killing herself so many times. What was the lesson in everything that was going on around her? She definitely had never done anyone so wrong to deserve such karma. Was it bad luck or a curse? Could she spare another tear? She figured that dying was the easy way out but she had children to take care of. Instead, she decided to let go and let God, just like they said in church.

"I want to see you make a way, because I'm tired! Enough is enough and you better show me something real quick. I need help, Lord. I'm tired of going through it! When I wake up tomorrow, you need to make it happen for me. Do it for me! That's it. I've been doing it all, now you do the rest! I don't want to do nothing but wake up to the answers." She prayed while tears fell from her closed lids.

The next morning, she woke up with the sun peeking through the curtains. Before she could even look for her phone, the text alert sounded with a message from an unknown number.

Incoming : Good morning. Do you need me to do anything for you today?

Outgoing : What? Who is this and what do you mean?

Incoming : I tried to talk to you before but you said it was a bad time. Heard things got worse for you, my condolences. I'm making sure you're okay! Do you need me to do anything for you?

Looking from side to side, she was torn between feeling freaked out, blessed or it was either one heck of a coincidence.

Outgoing: Life happens, Thanks! If you mean financially, I need help with my rent and deposit so I can move.

Incoming : Send me your bank info. I got you!

Just like that, she sat up in the cover and began to look around the room as if she was being pranked. She could not believe a guy she had never met in person was willing to give her the rest of the money. It wasn't just a few dollars, so she called his bluff and sent her bank info to him a few hours later. She told her friends about the prayer she said the night before, then the sudden text she received that morning. It was like she made it all up. Kali mentioned that the guy was very sweet and she knew him from the dude she was dating. A few hours later, he texted her back.

Incoming : It's done. Call me tomorrow when you have time.
Outgoing : You are an angel. TRUST ME

She couldn't help but laugh in disbelief. Within a blink of an eye, it happened without her doing anything, just as she prayed. Everything worked out, so she moved into her new apartment with all their clothes and a few groceries. Mama Jewel and Dollar had purchased all the things to furnish the girls bedroom. She slept on the floor in her bedroom for awhile but she smiled knowing that her girls had brand new everything.

That weekend, she went out to meet up with the guy who had already proven his word was bond. He was definitely cute and by God sending him to her overnight, she was at least going to give him a fair shot. That night, she watched his moves and could tell that he was more of the quiet type than she had expected. He was playing with some real money and his behavior confirmed the activity she would over hear when they talked. She required too much attention and needed someone to talk too but he had zero time besides getting money. One night, he made it clear that he was a grown man with big things going on that left little time for play. She understood, yet explained to him that he didn't have time for what she needed. She wanted someone to listen and hang out with her or do things that considered moving on from that very hard chapter in her life. With not much to say besides they were not ready for the situation itself, she found herself back in bed wiping away her own tears.

It had been months since Ghost was killed and she had not returned to work because her depression was that overwhelming. She went back for the money once it got better but realized that working there was no longer her desire. Upon leaving, Maurie told her that the human resource lady had been looking for her to return to work. They did not want to bother her during her time of grief but had something she could use while she was away. Figuring it was a collection that the coworkers had gathered, she was surprised to know that the job itself had given her five thousand dollars for the loss of her husband. It was a blessing in disguise as she thanked them repeatedly for such a generous offering. She also learned that she was the beneficiary on his bank account, which gave her rights to the money he left behind. A letter from his last employer informed her that she was entitled to benefits. Then weeks later, she received a few more thousand that allowed her to live more comfortable and worry less about providing for her daughters.

She came across something while she was reading over some paper work from all the documents she had been receiving, signing and verifying. It stated that her proof of being legally married to him had granted her full benefits she had began to receive. One thing for certain, Ghost always promised to take care of his kids, even if he was not in their life. His ego wouldn't allow him to accept that she was fed up with his behavior. She realized that maybe the boot had miraculously been placed on her car that day, so that she was not able to finalize the divorce. In a sense, it was a blessing for her daughters because she had rights to being wifey. Their legal binding is what made it more than easy for her to take care of his funeral and survive afterwards.

For whatever reason, she felt her life was becoming more of a story. Like a weird fairy tale or a song that somehow turns up with the sweetest happy ending. At least she felt like she deserved the fairy tale every girl imagined. Thing is, was she the princess or the beast? How was she supposed to start a new life from scratch and forget what she had been through? There was no glass slipper or prince charming to save the day. Her therapist told her, that the only way to get over something is to go through it, completely. That was exactly what she had been doing; going through it.

CHAPTER 21

"Crazy Love"

THE MOST COMMON SYMPATHY LINE she heard all the time, was 'everything happens for a reason.' With that in mind, she forced herself to look forward to the brighter side of the trouble in her heart. She started to believe that maybe she had a greater purpose than her current situation and it was destined for her spirit to be broken. There was something forceful that kept taking blows at her, only to turn around and see things falling back into place. Was she too comfortable with her old life that God created a new one? One night, she cried the entire way home with Gospel music playing softly through the speakers. Making it safely, she woke the kids up to walk inside, while Jream walked slowly behind her and spoke very clearly.

" Mama, Jordan said him love you and he okay, mama. Him said that." She yawned.

"What! Who told you that?" She asked, a little spooked out.

" Jordan did, he okay too! Him said that to me. It's ok, mama." She replied, half asleep.

She couldn't believe her ears knowing that Jream would remember her father so well at only two years old. He had been dead for two months and for her to wake out of her sleep to mention such a thing, warmed Loyalty's heart. She couldn't complain, there were more bad days than good but she made it through. Whether she was sober or not! Crying for days at a time with her head to the sky, she was hoping the solution would just fall from the clouds.

A few days later, she was at the car wash just about finished washing her truck when her phone rang. At the gathering for Dylan, she bumped into Sade, who happened to be quite cool after they settled their high school beef. When her number showed on the screen, she knew it was going to be something crazy or funny.

"What's up girl? What you doing today? I'm on my way to the city for an outfit. Come meet me so we can grab a bite to eat and drinks." She stated.

"Girl, you're always getting into something! I wish but I don't feel like it!" Loyalty replied.

"You have too man, besides, I already told my homeboy that you coming. You need to get out of the house. Come on!" She laughed.

"Sade!! Why would you do that? Bruh, you crazy!" She yelled over the laughter.

"No, like for real, trust me with this one! He been liking you, plus he hella cute and you need someone to take your mind off things. Be ready to meet me when I call you back. We're already on our way! Bye." She hung up.

Loyalty sighed as she stared at her phone, then took a look at herself in the mirror. The girls were with her mother, so she decided to accept the invite. She didn't have much to do besides go home and cry, so she figured a few drinks wouldn't hurt before the tears came. She went home to change and flat iron her hair while she waited for Sade to call back. They were actually in the same area, so she pulled up to the mall in no time. Nervously, she walked around until she spotted them. When she saw Sade sitting on the bench, her attention zoomed in on a guy that was standing close by. All she needed was the side view to tell by his frame and muscles, it was Kokaine.

"How you doing gorgeous? She said you might not show up, so thank you for coming. Can I take you somewhere to eat? Is there something you would like from the mall?" He paused. "It's funny that you keep looking over there but I'm talking over here. What's wrong baby?" He asked.

"Nothing, it's just that I know who you are. I mean, you know who I am but what do you want?" She laughed. "Like really, why do you want to talk to me?" She asked.

"I want your time! All of it! I want you and I really always have. If you give me a chance, I know what it takes to keep a woman like you happy!" He cut her off.

"Oh yea and what will keep me happy?" She folded her arms.

"ME." He stared back.

She smiled as butterflies cluttered her stomach and her thoughts battled with her hormones. He was so cute and charming but the fact that he was Eve's baby daddy, plus the whole history behind the drama with Ghost gave her a headache. Yet, there was no need to deny his offer because he was decent to chat with at the time. After they went for food and drinks, she began to feel herself melt everytime he touched her. On the way to her car, she couldn't help but glance over at him side eyed as she tried not to let the alcohol take over the situation. Once they pulled next to her building, he leaned over to kiss her and it made every thing that said no, scream yes. Once he let her go, he dug into his pocket and handed her some cash, saying that he wanted to help her out. Shocked, she accepted his money and attempted to get out again when he told her to wait up. She figured he wanted another kiss or something but what he said took her by total surprise when he closed his eyes.

"Dear O' gracious Father, we come to you tonight…." He began to pray.

Instead of closing her eyes, she sat there and watched him speak peace and prosperity over her life. As each word left his mouth, she couldn't help but stare at his attractive lips, wanting to kiss him again in mid prayer.

"Amen." He opened his eyes. "Come on. Get out and I'll walk you to the door." He stated.

"Oh, NO you're not! I got it from here, thanks." She grabbed her things.

"Let me help you, ma! That's it." He stared from the sidewalk.

She burst into laughter. "Boy, that is not what's up right now."

"Boy?" He tilted his head in confusion. "Just keep walking to your door so we can say our good nights."

Walking playfully behind her until they reached the door, his charm turned back on. He grabbed her by the waist and hugged her tightly with a quick kiss to her neck. She pulled back and advised him that wasn't a good idea at the time.

"Don't do that, it's too much and I can see where this is going… we… don't…" She was silenced by his repeatedly slow kisses to her lips.

"You want me to leave?" He stepped her back and closed the door behind them. "Do you?" He smirked, kissing her again.

She thought her clothes were going to fall off by the way he was making her body melt in his arms. She gave in, letting him touch and kiss all over her because at that moment, she needed some physical love. He snatched her clothes away before they reached the bedroom and kneeled down between her legs. Looking at each other for a few seconds, he ripped his shirt and jeans away within seconds before he changed the level of realness. Everything about what he had done to her body and the way he made her feel was so much too take. Watching his reaction and movements, it seemed like he was in another world as he started to handle her like it was a workout session. She couldn't believe that after all the good sex she had in the past, he just swooped in and blessed her with the best love making of her life. The same man who had just showed her a good time and prayed for her, had instantly morphed into a beast.

The next morning, she woke up to get her day started and noticed she had a few missed calls from him. She was just about to reply to his text messages, when an incoming call from Kash came through with Kali on three way.

"Y'all, guess what? Why did I just sleep with Kokaine!! This dude just pop up out of nowhere, hands me a wad of money, pray for me and have the audacity to lay down the best sex of my life. Did I say, Kokaine, right? This shit is crazy!" She stated.

"No, his ass is crazy! Hella crazy! I didn't know he broke up with ol' girl he used to mess with. I forgot her name but oh well, because she doesn't matter to you if she doesn't matter to him. Y'all look better anyway!" Kash and Kali laughed.

"Wait. What girl? The same chic he was messing with when he first got out? I thought someone said before that they broke up or so the streets say. Dang, I can't even say I'm not disappointed because I had a good time with him. As long as he honest with me, I'm cool with it." She showered and fell back to sleep.

The next few days, he made it his business to stay with her every second. He was so thoughtful and showed so much concern towards her situation that nothing else he had going on mattered. Which indeed, a few days later he came out and mentioned that his recent girlfriend had just moved out of his house but they were still communicating. He assured that they were not in a committed relationship, so he was open to be whatever she needed. Accepting, she enjoyed having him around and was starting to feel her days fall back into a more normal routine. He allowed her to cry and talk about everything on her mind as he listened, then shared a few stories of his own. He swept into her life to ease her mind and satisfy her body every chance he got.

That following week, she was preparing to celebrate Klover's first birthday party, when she began to have an emotional breakdown. Knowing that Ghost would never get to hold her again, watch her walk or even attend a single birthday party. Kokaine comforted her when he saw the sadness in her facial expressions and body language. Kissing her cheek, he reassured that he was there to make everything a little easier. He instantly became attached to Klover and her heart loved him more for the bond he was forming with her daughters.

She was able to furnish her apartment and make it home sweet home for her and the girls to start fresh. He was always out spoken about his feelings, so it was no surprise when he came out and said *I love you*. She was not quite ready to fall in love again but his touch gave her goosebumps and his presence gave her security.

Like anything, there's always a test that comes along to try your loyalty and weakness. One night, she was sitting at Kash's house when she called Kokaine to have her food order picked up. Their morning sex usually gave her that 'lazy love' feeling during the day that drifted off into the night as well. Not in the mood to do much, she told him that she would chill over at Kash's crib until he was done handling his business. He arrived with the food, drinks, snacks and wine for her to be completely satisfied while she waited. He hated for her to ask anyone else for anything and she found it so awesome that he wanted to be her superman. Walking him out for kisses and hugs, he drove off and said that he would be right back. Within ten minutes, there was another knock but they expected his quick return. However, it was Kash's neighbor who began to explain that a car alarm was sounding off outside and he thought it belonged to them. Confused, they both stepped outside her apartment door to peek at the parking lot when someone grabbed her from the opposite side. She was shocked to see that it was Black, who seemed to be excited about his unexpected presence.

"What are you doing here? You had to fake a car alarm to knock on the door? What do you want Black?" She asked, as her eyes raced the parking lot for Kokaine's shiny black Chevy.

"What? I came to check up on you. How have you been? Stop being so mean Loyalty, damn. I just wanna be your friend this time, for real!" He stated.

"Look, if Kokaine walks up and catches this scene, he is gonna knock you both out. I don't want no parts of it!" Kash stated, rushing back inside.

"Get out of here! Like seriously, I'm not interested in being friends with you so don't ever do this again. Leave. Hurry!" She rushed.

"Wait." He laughed. "You really like him huh?" He burst into laughter. "Are you serious?"

"Love him! Now leave, because if he walks up, he'll kick our asses." She went inside without looking back.

She was completely satisified with the situation that was close enough to an official relationship between her and Kokaine. She saw no point in risking what they had for some pointless conversation or a waste of sex with someone else. If there was a hassle dealing with any other guy, she decided to deal with who had put up with her when she was at her lowest. He was there when she needed to talk. He saved her from the worst and forced her to shake it off while preparing for her best. There was no way to repay him financially but when it came to her loyalty, she was indebted to him.

Grateful for all the help from Mama Jewel, it was time for them to select the perfect headstone for Ghosts grave. She told her girls that every time they saw some pretty flowers, they would bring them to their daddy's garden to keep it beautiful. It began getting easier for them to understand but she could tell they were heart broken from his permanent absence. She knew his death would forever leave a scar on their hearts that no amount of time could heal. They would wake up and mention him first thing in the mornings, stating that they saw him in their dreams. She wondered if he was truly an angel watching over them, like a spirit that would visit them while they slept. Did he infact live up to his name and become a Ghost?

Months had gone by and she wanted to take a trip some place to forget about everything for just a moment. A few weeks later, they arrived in Atlanta and enjoyed a few laughs as she got caught up in her imagination. Only she was tired of imagining things and was so sick of dreaming that she was starting to plan the next level of her exsistence right at that minute. Staring at the buildings and lights in downtown ATL, she made a vow to herself that she would become exactly who she was destined to be. A person who was rising above all circumstances to share the greatness she had yet to find.

CHAPTER 22

"More Lessons"

FEELING LIKE SHE HAD TO reinvent her own way, she enrolled into college, which seemed like a smart thing to do. After giving it the attention she had to offer, it wasn't enough to pass her classes. She figured that taking a few courses and focus on furthering her education would be a great thing to dedicate her time too. However, she was not good at pretending, especially when it came to her feelings. There was no way possible she could continue to study and ignore the hurt that was eating her up everyday. Sadly, she dropped the classes and gave her all towards writing the book she had been working on. She didn't need college for that, so she kept a few tablets and continued to write down her thoughts as frequently as she could.

Things seemed to be on a steady level with Kokaine, which made her love it for what it was. There was no need to find a definition for their relationship. She was fine with the way he treated her, making sure she wanted for nothing while she tried to get a grip on her life. He intervened, telling her that health was the most important thing because he noticed how she barely took time to eat or rest properly. He told her to keep praying as much as she cried, then block out the bad to start enjoying the good. She found her strength somewhere in the pain and used everything that was meant to break her down, to help build herself back up. He wanted to see her survive and was willing to help her with whatever it took for a successful road to greatness.

His birthday came around and she wanted to get him something to show her appreciation. What do you get for a person who already has everything? She put some thought into how she really felt about him. Not only did he take care of her but he showed mad love for her daughters as well. By the way he made her feel, there wasn't a doubt in her mind that she was in love with the *Koko*.

The night before his birthday, she had just taken a bath when she walked into the bedroom and noticed him asleep. Saying nothing, she sat on top of him as he woke up and held on to her small naked frame. Burying his face in her neck while circling his tongue, her eyes began to roll and slowly close in pleasure. No one ever made intimacy feel that good.

"Money can buy you any gift but my gift was made for you." She kissed him, then took his hand and placed it between her legs.

"What is that? Is this real? For real?" He asked, turning on the lamp. "You tatted my name down there? I know that shit hurted, ma! Damn, you more crazy than me." He was smiling from ear to ear as he kept staring at his name marked with ink across her vagina.

"I don't know what made me get it but now that I did, it's cute huh?" She laughed.

"Yea, this means you're mine forever! I know what made you get it, let me remind you." He smirked, flipping her over.

Months later, he mentioned that there was a break in the case with Eve, so she would soon be out on bail. He explained that he was going to help her get situated once she was free, which was understandable. After five years of being in jail, she was finally blessed with freedom. It's almost unbelievable how miraculous God works and allows the most unexplainable things to happen. It was a blessing for her children that missed her, who were deprived of her presence when they needed a mother. Checking her phone the next morning, she was reminded that it was Ghost and Jream's birthday. She fixed breakfast for her and the kids, then sat around in her thoughts the entire day, brainstorming. He began calling the next day but she was not in the mood to hear any lies about where he had been. A man will say anything if he thinks you will believe him.

That Saturday, he showed up at Jream's birthday party and demanded that she stop the madness. His argument was that he had been there for her during her emotional melt down stages, so he wanted the same in return. He wanted her to be there for him while he still made mistakes and allow him to be comfortable enough to admit his wrongs if she caught him. Ultimately, he said he couldn't promise to be faithful and was afraid to lose her in the process. He didn't want to hurt her by hiding things, so he figured that telling her would justify his desire to be a hoe.

Looking on the bright side of things again, she had to weigh her options because she wasn't ready to just walk away from him. She wasn't mad, because she had no reason. Her heart was still mourning but he pleased her body just right and took her mind off things. She had not worked since Ghost was killed, so she was blessed to have someone who took care of all her needs. How could she complain when she was getting spoiled? Why would she sleep around if he met every sexual expectation? He would take her shopping, then she was his dessert or he would have them pray, then they would hit the gym. He was everything a woman could ask for in a man. Overall, she was satisfied with their unofficially official relationship.

Spring came around and things between them were the same but she was growing tired of his excuses. She was not the type of girl to sit around and accept disrespect, so she eventually had to let that be known. He was dealing with his ex-girlfriend, which was to be expected because their break up was so fresh. She knew the chic was not going to leave him alone, simply because she was there to secure the bag. She was an ordinary girl and Loyalty saw no need to compete with a basic competitor. It was always difficult to put a filter on her words when it came to being loyal, so she never bit her tongue when it came to their conversations. He was beginning to get comfortable with his ways and too relaxed in the double life he was living.

He showed up early that Thursday and made love to her all morning before they went out for brunch. After shopping the next day, he drove to the airport and told her that he was about to leave for the weekend. As if he spoke another language, she looked at him confused. He told her that his ex-girlfriend was in Miami for her birthday and he accepted her invite for the weekend. Handing her a wad of money, he told her to enjoy herself for a couple days but return to the airport Monday morning to pick him up. She drove away in his truck and laughed out loud in disbelief. She knew he had to be feeling like he had the *Juice*, because having his cake and eating it too was an understatement. Indeed, he had her mind wrapped up into the things he was doing and the way he made her feel. Per request, she returned that Monday when his flight landed and they carried on the rest of their week as usual.

He told her that since she was always talking about mountains, that he would take her to do the most passionate thing she dreamed of. The next few weeks, they landed in California to see some of the most beautiful scenery she ever laid eyes on. She had so much fun with him while making memories that would stick with her forever. They found an easy path up the mountain so they parked and decided to hike up. Making it to the top, she was determined to conquer each goal in her life the same way. Climbing!

Once they returned home, he was still on the same 'fooling around with different chics' routine. She told him that she was not going to sit around and play the fool while he played the *man* in another woman's household. He told her that eventually her mouth was going to make the monster in him lash out. Ignoring his warning, she told him that she was going to hang out with her friends that night and start living a more unpredictable life. He snatched her up by the shirt and she swung at him multiple times before he smacked her across the face. For the first time in her life, she had never been on the ground so long in a fight. She could then feel him trying to make her stand but her knees were weak. She couldn't believe that his force knocked her unconscious for a few seconds. Of course after most domestic disputes, the guy apologizes a million times and the girl forgives him.

Several weeks later, she almost fainted when he surprised her with a new black Chevy Tahoe. She needed the extra room for her kids and the gesture itself made her speechless because he upgraded her vehicle. His charm was captivating! She found it more and more difficult to put up the brick wall she should've built in their relationship months ago.

A year had gone by which marked the date Ghost was killed, so she allowed the girls to place new, beautiful blue flowers on what they knew as his garden. That night, she wanted to forget it all because Mother's Day weekend had left a bad taste in her mouth the year before. Thinking of her last conversations with Ghost, she drowned out all the images with her favorite liquors. Once they left the sports bar, she had just began to get comfortable when she saw the red and blue lights flash behind them. Instead of freaking out, they began to search around for the gun and weed that was in the vehicle. As soon as they pulled over, the officers quickly demanded Kokaine out of the truck. The inside lights came on once the door opened and she spotted the gun below the steering wheel. She grabbed the cash in the arm rest and had just enough time to stick the small Ziploc sack of weed inside her vagina. Once she placed her purse across her shoulder, an officer instructed her to get out and leave her bag inside. The color drained from her face as she tried to signal for Kokaine's attention to ask him how much money was inside the truck. Her heart dropped when the officer placed the gun and cash on the hood of the truck. She felt like running but knew that people of color already had less chances of surviving a traffic stop. She waited patiently for him to cuff her, as he started to ask questions about the hand gun along with the large amount of money. She told him she stayed out of town and only brought it along for protection because her late husband was murdered a year ago. Fearing for her life, she always carried it around, not knowing that it was illegal to do so. Unable to see Kokaine's face because they had him standing so far away, she had to take a guess for the amount of cash. Luckily she hit it right on the money, literally, because they let her keep every thousand of it. Turned out to be some very nice cops but she was still arrested for possession of a firearm, which booked her in on a felony charge.

Arrested so late that Friday, she was unable to make her arraignment that Saturday, which meant she was spending Mother's Day weekend in jail. Her alcohol was wearing off but she was still loaded from the weed, which reminded her that she had at least two grams of dro stuck inside her juice box. She was upset to know that she had to stay an entire two days with something so irritating up her vagina. Yet, she rathered it tucked from the police than risk taking it out and being unable to get rid of it properly. Wearing only a dress when she was arrested, they exchanged it for inmate attire that left her freezing naked underneath the red jumpsuit. She knew a few girls once she got assigned to her dorm, so she was thankful when they handed her a pair of socks and a big tshirt. Her munchies were at an all time high and nothing was appealing about the food on the jail trays, so she sat around having small talk. Kokaine bonded her out Sunday afternoon and brought her home to shower, grab a bite to eat and hit the mall for some shopping. After a long weekend of more lessons learned, she was thankful once again to lay under her own roof with her children.

CHAPTER 23

"Dream Chaser"

IT TOOK MONTHS OF REPETITIVE lies to show her that most men will bring you down the same road of deceit. It's up to you to determine who is worth waiting for and who has to be left behind. She wasn't wanting to be another wife so soon but she was not spending more years of her life playing games either. A loyal woman shouldn't have to spend a great amount of her life waiting for any man to act right. Most guys don't see any wrong in their actions anyhow. A real man would see the worth of his woman and mature in love instead of falling for flesh. There was no amount of money in the world that she would accept to allow a man to walk all over her. Was security from a man that serious? Is a woman's soul really for sale if she loves the man enough? Is it impossible to live without sex while you find yourself? How much do you accept before you realize that you deserve what you give in return? There was a difference in the way she wanted to be loved and she wasn't about to have her loyalty taken for granted AGAIN.

Enough about love because for as long as she could remember, love was bringing her through some of the toughest years of her life. Since her feelings changed, she figured that it was time to stop procrastinating because years fly faster than a bullet. Courage, strength and faith was the only thing she packed with her each day to find the person she needed to become. Her life wasn't meant to be mediocre and it was becoming more clear for her to see. Her vision was to help others like herself who needed a push to find their purpose. Maybe they could find new things together, because life is a never ending learning experience.

She began to start the publishing of her very own book and planned to throw an event launch party in celebration of her success. It was definitely an achievement for her to complete a memoir and start building a business that she could proudly say she earned. Putting in the work was one thing but to actually stay committed to something with so many distractions was another. The question she asked herself everyday seemed to get the same response. How bad do you want it? She wanted to share her story for a purpose she had not known yet but that was the beauty of it all.

She returned to work after almost eight months but barely reported to her shifts, so she had to speak with her supervisor about letting her go. She hated to leave so unexpectedly and was so grateful for everything they had done but it was time to move on. Not knowing what a better life meant at the time but she was more than sure that working there wasn't what it looked like. She hadn't paid a bill of her own since she met Kokaine and that was beginning to annoy her. It was routine that he expected her hand out for bills and although he seemed to feel that was his job, it was time for a change. She didn't want to become a millionaire but she wanted to fall back on her own fortunes if push came to shove.

Needing more room and a better look, she moved into a garaged townhome that made her feel more protected with her daughters. She began visiting the shooting range to relieve some tension and learn how to operate a weapon. She had a new membership with a gym, so she dedicated her mornings to a workout. Kokaine was the best thing to a trainer she had because he took his workouts just as serious. They motivated each other to get in the best shape of their life, living in their thirties.

He helped fix her credit and she soon had the highest scores she ever seen attached to her name. After getting her finances in order, she spiritually got back on track because she owed God everything. Even though Kokaine took care of her every need and made sure she depended on no one else for anything, it came with stipulations. At times she could deal with knowing he was with someone else but when her territorial side kicked in, she had no problem speaking up.

Learning more about him, she came to the conclusion that she was not depending on love anymore. She had to depend on the strength inside of her and have courage to keep riding the wave, even if she had to surf alone. As long as she survived the storm that was meant to destroy her, it didn't matter what washed away with it. If nothing lasted forever, why was she trying to hold every moment like she wouldn't be given another one? Why was she scared to lose anything again, when she had already lost everything before? With every doubt in her mind, holding that mustard seed of faith, she set out to conquer her dreams. Trying to break the emotional attachment she had with Kokaine was hard because he was so addicting and knew just what to do. She wanted more, whatever she was missing that she had never gotten before, LOYALTY.

He was quite successful with his trucking business and was only adding to his empire. Instead of working for him or with him, she wanted to start something of her own that would allow her to grow into her own person. Knowing that he was not going to take care of her forever and she was never filling out another job application, things were about to get real. Decisions that were affecting her future had started to interfere with her daily activities. It's never too late to start bettering yourself and being that she was thirty years old, there wasn't much more time she wanted to waste.

Focusing on the relationship with her daughters, she decided to enroll the oldest two into a dance academy and karate. They still asked so many questions about life, so she wanted to take their minds away from what they had been through. Klover had become so attached to Kokaine, she thought he was her biological father since that was all she remembered from crawling to walking. Their sweet bond reminded Loyalty that her baby girl would never know her real father but at least she skipped the painful memory of losing him. Yet, she couldn't ask for a better man to show her daughters any more love.

She had finally accomplished her main goal, which was all it took to get her started. Looking for a house to purchase, she felt herself finally able to accept and grow into her new reality. It felt good to see things as she had not seen before, which was that everything works itself out if you let it.

Mr. Ralph had invited them all to attend a church reunion in his hometown, Jasper, so they packed up and hit the road. When they first slid into the row to take their seats, she noticed there was a woman who kept staring at her. She mentioned it to her father that the woman was looking at them every two minutes with a grin. His reply was that he had never seen her before but she then slid over to tap Loyalty on the shoulder.

"You're Daphne's daughter aren't you? I know who you are, you are the youngest baby girl. You're grandma told me before she passed away that you were special. Just keep doing what you doing, baby girl. Just keep going." The elderly lady stated, patting her on the shoulder then slid back to her seat.

"Yes ma'am. Thank you." She nodded, leaning over to her dad to repeat what she was told.

"Baby, that lady does not know you. She tripping!" Mr. Ralph replied.

"Daddy, she said my mama name and she said I'm the youngest so..." She was cut off.

"That don't mean nothing." He began clapping at the speakers announcement.

Sure that the lady was not just some random crazy senior citizen, she took heed to the words as they had already became apart of her motto, *keep going*. It just seemed weird to her that the words had been spoken from the lips of a total stranger who knew nothing she had been through. It only seemed to place another answer before her eyes that she was headed in the right direction.

One day they went for dinner at their favorite place, Pappadeaux, who simply had the best drinks and great atmosphere. They sat down discussing their relationship status for a clear understanding that when it's time to put away childish things, the games must stop. He was tied up into too many situations that had him going in circles from one woman to the next. He had a big heart that sometimes means a gracious person no good. He wasn't the most faithful kind of man, nor the most polite when he was upset but she gave him credit for trying. He was the rock in her life that helped reposition her crown when she could barely sit straight in a chair. Her heart was forever grateful but she did not want to settle in his life being what he wanted and risk losing sight of who she needed to be. Without turning her back, she claimed to never give up on him as they sat around sipping their drinks in deep conversation.

"I don't try to be hard on you but I speak rough to you sometimes to see your strength. I want to see if you're actually what you proclaim to be. Nobody owes you anything Loyalty, especially not me! I'm here because I want to be. I wouldn't be wasting your time because I do have a vision too. Whatever you're passionate about, let me help you invest in it and still make sure you have everything you need to grow. Something that can feed you spiritually, mentally and definitely financially. Don't tell me shawty, show me! I'm like your drill sargent that forces you to do one out of two things, fight or give up. If you are a quitter, then you'll give up and make excuses for why you failed at something you stopped doing. If you're a fighter, then you will let nothing stand in your way to knock it out. I don't see a quitter, Loyalty, do YOU?" He stared, waiting for a response.

"There's something I'm meant to do. I have a purpose that's greater than the choices I've made. I'm not giving up because I don't know how to stop thinking about it. I want to fight." She said, looking in his eyes.

"My baby! Show me how hard you can hit then!" He smiled.

CHAPTER 24

"Life is but A Dream"

SHE WAS DRIVING DOWN I45 one day and a green SUV drove past with mud and dead bugs all over it. She was in deep thought about things that were beyond her control. She knew the answer was right in her face and was becoming harder to ignore. The filthy truck slammed on its brakes right in front of her due to a traffic jam. Aggravated with the sudden stop, her eyes focused on the words that were easy to read from a fingerprinted message on the rear window that read, *wake up*. She immediately took heed from the note on the passing vehicle. Sure it may not have been intentionally for her but it was intended for anyone who could relate. She was sleeping on her own life and desperately needed to *wake up*!

She still kept in touch with a few people from her old job. She connected with the right sources to get what she needed done. By changing her environment years ago, it allowed new doors to open that would have never presented itself had she remained in her hometown. She would always watch a friend of hers, Zoey, work on some sort of project and decided to ask her what she was up too. Either she was reading something, taking notes or browsing on her personal laptop. Whatever it was, Loyalty wanted to get on a business level and was willing to give it all the strength she had left.

Zoey shared with her that she had a faith based organization and was currently building the website for promotion. Hearing of her plan to work with a successful empowerment group for women made Loyaltys' dream seem more realistic and possible. She began to work harder and focus more on the things that were relevant to her goals. She indeed had been dreaming and talking about her plans for too long, so it was time to give them life. It seemed as if the death of Ghost had birthed a new person that shedded the soft skin she once wore. Now her scars had been seen and the courage inside of her was beginning to give her an unstoppable, radiant glow.

Once everything had fallen into place, she met a stylist and photographer for a photoshoot. Heading downtown, they made a right turn in the wrong direction when they noticed red and blue lights flashing behind them. Kokaine pulled over while they waited for the two officers to approach their car. It's always an uneasy situation when you're black, being pulled over by a cop who already appears to be nervous. They sat still and patient, calmly answering thousands of pointless questions from the uniform officers. They were asked to step out of the car while they searched inside, then lifted the trunk and hood. She began to explain that they were just about to pull into the studio next door to where they were stopped. The photographer's crew came outside to check out the scene once they noticed them being searched with their hands on the hood. Finding nothing, the officers allowed them to drive away and proceed with the photoshoot.

Everything was in motion for marketing her first book and it finally gave her time to focus more on her family. Liberty had her hand in a little bit of everything and had a business card for each profession she worked. She connected with her sister and Zoey to get a few ideas on her next task to tackle. If she remained focused and dedicated her time to success, then her game plan would rule as a win-win situation. She started searching for a house in the best school zones since her girls were starting elementary soon. Feeling more confident, she learned to become grounded with taking full responsibility for her new life. Did she dance with karma? Was she reaping what she had sown? Was it fate? How could things come together after years of falling apart? The visions that she had as a child and throughout her youth, were becoming her reality with each new milestone she tackled. With all the hurt, she managed to dust her self off and move on to the life that was already predestined for her. She believed that the seasons of her struggles were for a purpose. God positioned her! Regardless of her sins and flaws, she deserved happiness and was not willing to settle. Her destiny awaited. She felt it each time there was a new opportunity that allowed her to mature and increase her knowledge each day.

Shopping in the Galleria one evening with Kokaine, they stood at the jewelry counter while he looked for another watch. She took a seat on the stool next to the mirror and caught a glimpse of herself. Amazingly, she still looked the same! The invisible scars had not destroyed her at all. In fact, it helped her love the broken warrior she saw staring back at her. She noticed the little hands that were ticking on each watch and whispered to herself, *it's Time*.

CHAPTER 25

"Epilogue"

AT THIS POINT, THE GAMES come to an end. You should enjoy life with a purpose to fulfill everything, knowing that you have been blessed to do so. You remained standing after all odds were against you and the devil did everything he could to try and defeat you. An old supervisor of mine once said, 'that we search around for so many things trying to band aid our problems, when we have a direct connection with the source who heals.' Finding God and building a relationship with Him allowed me to find some peace and adapt to the life I own. I'm a sinner, yet I want to be a saint so bad and I'm giving it more effort than ever to become a better person. Once I began using what was provided to me, I worked with what I had. I wanted to give up so many times but quitting was not an option for me. I refuse to settle! Negativity may easily discourage you, so please be aware of dream killers. Be your own motivation!

Marriage is something that should mean more than a ring symbolizing fashion. It's a binding relationship that pairs two individuals who become ONE. Years pass and some things get lost along the way but love reinvents itself if you want it to work. There is little room for mistakes but forgiveness is key. How many mistakes can you make before they become a constant pattern of disrespect? Marriage is a committed friendship where love is present even when it isn't shown, it's always felt. Time will change a lot of what may not have been a factor before. If the fight is not as strong as the test, you will fail and so will your marriage. Marry only when you are ready to give up every selfish bone in your body and commit your heart to a union that you consider irreplaceable. Don't jeopardize what you can't rebuild because some things can be fixed but it will never be brand new again. There is nothing like giving yourself to a person who only has eyes for you and is committed to your exisitence. Just don't forget what they say, *love don't love nobody.*

    It's hard to define what a friend is because there are so many terms to describe the position. You could never put one finger on the word '*friend.*' I say, just choose the ones you know will have your back no matter what. There are too many people who claim to care about your best interest or concerned about your well being but will stab you in the back first chance they get. That's their job! They come along to show you that everyone who is smiling with you, are not smiling because of you. They have hidden agendas but will sale you a dream if they thought you were sleeping on them. Pay attention to those who talk the hottest gossip because you have to maneuver away from the circle of chaos. Don't let someone who is not a factor in your life, determine your attitude for a minute. Be positive around toxic people because they will try to feed you every doubt they have. When they assume you have the same life, they will approach you the same. Once they see you living differently, that will introduce your vibe. You can tell by the look or gesture if that person is genuinely in your corner for the fight or just standing behind you in hopes that you get knocked out.

    If someone is incarcerated that was of great value to your life when they were in the streets, then that obligates you to be there. If all they can be granted is a piece of mail, money, books, phone calls and visits, to keep in contact with their loved ones, then why not do it. I realized that turning your back on someone who has been there for you will cause some of the worst trust issues ever. You don't have to stop living your life to answer a few calls or return a few letters. You're either going to be there or not! Not everyone in a cell deserves to be behind bars. In contrast, not everyone on the streets deserves to have freedom. Don't let a judges sentence separate the contact between you and a person who would never lose contact with you.

Death is unavoidable. As scary as it seems, we are all going to die. It's not taken as serious as it should be because so many lives are taken for senseless crimes. The worry should not be 'how you are going to die', it should be 'where are you going when you die?' You must find something worth living for and have faith in God. When you or someone you love passes away, it is permanent and will change everything. Instead of letting the pain manifest and grow bitter, let the lesson in your pain make you better. It's a weird feeling knowing that there is nothing you can do to avoid it but you can make your time here on Earth more peaceful while you have the chance.

Find your purpose! Figure out whatever it is you're good at and become better at it. Work on it consistently and become the impossible thing you always thought was just a dream. Is it just a vision? I'm sure you have one. It's that one thing you always wanted to pursue or wanted to become but you think it's too late. You are wrong and the only way to fail is if you don't try. The only way to keep from losing, is to keep trying to win.

Don't settle for anything less than what you have to offer. Get what you derserve by letting that feeling in the pit of your stomach guide you when there is no lifeline. You will have to believe in yourself and trust your own instinct because the only value you have is the one you protect. It's yours! Your past does not define you, so don't let it stop you. Let everyone see how you managed to beat the odds by competing with the old you. You may begin to celebrate your birthdays differently and even hang out at upscale places that better suit you. All change is not good but as long as your life is elevating and the glow of your presence shows, then let nothing stop you. Not even YOU!

Forgive Me for A Day

I would like to sit and laugh with you,
just to watch your cheesy grin.
However, now that line between love & hate,
has trimmed so very thin.
I thought we'd share forever,
now it's like I'm a total stranger.
If you can forgive me for just one day,
I think that my life is in danger.
They think I've gone crazy since we don't speak,
I'm in circles without you like two left feet.
Believe me, I wish I could take it all back,
I've changed; I know I was completely off track.
If you could just hug me & say it's ok,
I need you to hear me.
Say everything is fine.
I'm begging for forgiveness, just one day,
come on… I'm running out of time.
It's hard to accept the paths we took,
led down this ugly road.
Your soul is so beautiful; don't let me change that,
stop being so mean, so cold.
Now that it's over, so much left unsaid,
my flesh is now gone, just know I did beg.
Grant someone forgiveness for just this one day,
tomorrow's not granted, I had something to say.

POST FACE

⁓

Everything that I have came at a cost. The cost of losing my husband and almost my sanity. I believe I'm just reaping my harvest. Nothing fell into my lap by mistake. I suffered and I persevered! I know now that not all storms end in rainbows. You have to dance like no one is watching and have faith that the sun will shine on a rainy day.

It's so easy to hate a person forever but we find it hard to forgive someone for one day. When you choose to lose the argument, you just might win the conversation. What if you lost something that you never even dreamed of sacrificing? We stay mad for days and stubborn for weeks. It's crazy how we can go without speaking to someone we once had one million words to say too. You have to know if someone is a blessing or a lesson. Will you learn from it or will you earn from it? There's no one person who wants to lose because winning just sounds more prosperous and powerful. Every win doesn't promise the best celebration or finest gifts. Losing doesn't always involve failure or doubt, especially when you walk away with your chin up and chest out. You will always appear stronger when you walk around like nothing is ripping you apart inside. Your heart can make you feel as if you cannot live without your desires and place fear where faith once was. The mind is your tool that's generated and fueling off the positive or negative energy it's taught. We are our best teacher. You can never forget a lesson learned from your own mistakes.

When you deserve more, you will know it because your heart won't be satisfied with the norm. Your mind could never accept a lie when you are a person of truth. I think nobody has the power to hurt you more, than the person who you thought was capable of loving you the most. Be mindful, the devil is real and bad things will happen but you can still have blessings through your curse. We must love, forgive and try to live more righteous while we have the chance. Tomorrow, life can be snatched from any of us and nothing will be left but memories. Death comes like a thief in the night! So many people are loyal to their job, friends or the streets. Yet, you should only be loyal to what grows you and lifts you to the strongest form of yourself that you didn't even know was reachable. Time really doesn't heal anything and it sure isn't pain. The time that passes only forces you to face reality. You are forced to walk into a future that you thought you couldn't face while you were damaged and broken hearted. So, you move forward with the mind frame of a survivor; someone who has tunnel vision and sees only the path winners take. When you realize opportunity is no longer an option but the only way, you will live differently. Doubt is no longer an excuse because you have nothing to lose. Life is a gamble anyway, you might as well bet on yourself.

To seek the kingdom of God first, was the most common thought during my trial period. The ways of the world will never allow you to be holier than thou. We must lose! We must give up things which are not pleasing to the Lord. The opinions of others only matter when you care. Take a look around you! Surround yourself with people who encourage you to reach higher. Facts of success are proven; they are demonstrated through the lives and careers of any person with a status that you admire. To be right and live righteous is your choice. Do you want peace? We battle with self-love and acceptance from others around us because it appears their opinion matters more than the obvious. With that being said, you truly know what you are capable or not capable of. It takes courage to step into an unknown place and walk with your head high, without acknowledging fear. Your past is only a rock. Once you start building with bricks, then no one can blow you down. I assure you that weakness is admitting to pity and I learned those pity parties went out of style a long time ago.

We act spiteful sometimes trying to teach others a lesson but God ends up teaching us. He will use your strength to make you tough enough to get there and your weakness to humble you; so that you're grateful when you arrive.

LOYALTY

www.ingramcontent.com/pod-product-compliance
Lightning Source LLC
Chambersburg PA
CBHW050856160426
43194CB00011B/2170